# ELIMINATING ONLINE CHILD SEXUAL ABUSE MATERIAL

This book uses a crime science approach to explore the ways in which child sexual abuse material (CSAM) can be tackled. It describes the CSAM ecosystem, focusing on the ways in which it is produced, distributed and consumed and explores different interventions that can be used to tackle each issue.

*Eliminating Online Child Sexual Abuse Material* provides a methodical approach to unpacking and understanding this growing problem, identifies approaches that have been shown to work and offers alternatives that might be tried. This analysis is set within a crime science context that draws on rational choice, routine activities, situation crime prevention and environmental criminology to better understand the nature of the problem and the potential ways in which it may be solved.

This book is intended for policymakers and practitioners working in child protection, online harms and related areas and for students studying sexual violence or internet-related crime. The book will also be of interest to crime scientists as it provides another example of how the approach can be used to understand and reduce crime.

**Rick Brown** is the Deputy Director of the Australian Institute of Criminology and lives in Canberra, Australia. He has been a criminologist for over 30 years and has worked extensively on issues associated with crime prevention, community safety and policing in Australia, the UK and the Republic of Ireland. Rick has published over 70 government reports, book chapters and journal articles on a wide range of crime issues and most recently has focused on online child sexual abuse. He holds a PhD from the London School of Economics and Political Science, a Master of Arts degree from the University of Westminster and a Bachelor of Arts (with Honours) degree from Hatfield Polytechnic in the UK. Rick is also a Visiting Fellow of Policing and Criminal Justice at the University of Derby and on the editorial boards of numerous journals.

# CRIME SCIENCE SERIES

Crime science is a new way of thinking about and responding to the problem of crime in society. The distinctive nature of crime science is captured in the name.

First, crime science is about crime. Instead of the usual focus in criminology on the characteristics of the criminal offender, crime science is concerned with the characteristics of the criminal event. The analysis shifts from the distant causes of criminality – biological make-up, upbringing, social disadvantage and the like – to the near causes of crime. Crime scientists are interested in why, where, when and how particular crimes occur. They examine trends and patterns in crime in order to devise immediate and practical strategies to disrupt these patterns.

Second, crime science is about science. Many traditional responses to crime control are unsystematic, reactive, and populist, too often based on untested assumptions about what works. In contrast crime science advocates an evidence-based, problem-solving approach to crime control. Adopting the scientific method, crime scientists collect data on crime, generate hypotheses about observed crime trends, devise interventions to respond to crime problems, and test the adequacy of those interventions.

Crime science is utilitarian in its orientation and multidisciplinary in its foundations. Crime scientists actively engage with front-line criminal justice practitioners to reduce crime by making it more difficult for individuals to offend, and making it more likely that they will be detected if they do offend. To achieve these objectives, crime science draws on disciplines from both the social and physical sciences, including criminology, sociology, psychology, geography, economics, architecture, industrial design, epidemiology, computer science, mathematics, engineering, and biology.

Edited by Richard Wortley, UCL

**Eliminating Online Child Sexual Abuse Material**
*Rick Brown*

For more information about this series, please visit: www.routledge.com/criminology/series/CSCIS

# ELIMINATING ONLINE CHILD SEXUAL ABUSE MATERIAL

*Rick Brown*

Routledge
Taylor & Francis Group

LONDON AND NEW YORK

Cover image: d3sign / Getty Images

First published 2023
by Routledge
4 Park Square, Milton Park, Abingdon, Oxon OX14 4RN

and by Routledge
605 Third Avenue, New York, NY 10158

*Routledge is an imprint of the Taylor & Francis Group, an informa business*

*British Library Cataloguing-in-Publication Data*
A catalogue record for this book is available from the British Library

ISBN: 978-1-032-35524-5 (hbk)
ISBN: 978-1-032-35523-8 (pbk)
ISBN: 978-1-003-32726-4 (ebk)

DOI: 10.4324/9781003327264

Typeset in Bembo
by Newgen Publishing UK

# CONTENTS

# FIGURES

# TABLES

# ABBREVIATIONS

| | |
|---|---|
| ASEAN | Association of Southeast Asian Nations |
| AUS | Australian |
| BBS | Bulletin Board System |
| CBT | Cognitive Behavioural Therapy |
| CEO | Chief Executive Officer |
| COPINE | Combating Paedophile Information Networks in Europe |
| CRC | Convention on the Rights of the Child |
| CSAM | Child Sexual Abuse Material |
| DNS | Domain Name System |
| ECPAT | End Child Prostitution and Trafficking |
| ESP | Electronic Service Provider |
| EU | European Union |
| FIU | Financial Intelligence Unit |
| HTML | Hypertext Markup Language |
| ICMEC | International Centre for Missing and Exploited Children |
| IoT | Internet of Things |
| IP | Internet Protocol |
| IRC | Internet Relay Chat |
| ISP | Internet Service Provider |
| MST | Multi-Systemic Therapy |
| NCMEC | National Centre form Missing and Exploited Children |
| NGO | Non-Governmental Organisation |
| OTR | Off the Record |
| RNR | Risk-Need-Responsivity |
| TCP / IP | Transmission Control Protocol / Internet Protocol |
| TOR | The Onion Router |

| UK | United Kingdom |
| UN | United Nations |
| URL | Uniform Resource Locator |
| USA | United States of America |
| VPN | Virtual Private Network |

# 1

# INTRODUCTION

## The problem

The proliferation of online child sexual abuse material (CSAM) has become a 21st century global crime problem. Despite increasing awareness and efforts by governments, non-government organisations (NGOs) and the private sector to address the presence of child sexual abuse images on the internet, it seemingly remains just a few mouse clicks away for those intent on finding it.

In 1998, the US National Centre for Missing and Exploited Children (NCMEC) introduced the CyberTipline to collate reports of child sexual abuse material, online enticement, child sex trafficking and child sexual molestation. The following year, 9,673 reports were received by the CyberTipline (Albanese, 2007). In 2021, that number increased to over 29 million reports, 99 per cent of which related to CSAM[1]. That represents a 3,000-fold increase in 22 years.

Other statistics also bear testament to the size of the problem. The Internet Watch Foundation, a UK-based not-for-profit organisation, identified over 153,000 new web pages containing child sexual abuse imagery in 2020 – a 16 per cent increase on 2019 (Internet Watch Foundation, 2021). INHOPE, a global network of 47 hotlines in 43 countries, dedicated to tackling CSAM, recorded over a million items of CSAM content in 2020 (INHOPE, 2021). In 2021, Google de-indexed over 1.1 million links from its search engine that it suspected of containing CSAM, and reported almost 6.7 million items of CSAM content to NCMEC[2].

This is, however, by no means solely a Western problem. The most common countries identified as the origin of the CSAM assessed by NCMEC in 2020 were India (2.7 million cases), Philippines (1.3 million cases), Pakistan (1.3 million) and Indonesia (0.98 million)[3], also noting that each has a GDP per capita that is below the world's median average[4]. Reanalysis of NCMEC data by the United Nations

DOI: 10.4324/9781003327264-1

Office on Drugs and Crime (2021b) showed that between 2015 and 2019 over 11 million reports of CSAM originated from ten ASEAN countries[5].

It is also important to recognise the impact of COVID-19. With people around the world spending more time at home, in lockdown isolation, or out of work, many spent more time surfing the internet. This also led to more viewing of CSAM. The United Nations Human Rights Council (2021) reported that COVID-19 had resulted in a 106 per cent increase in reports to the CyberTipline in March 2020 compared with the same month the year before, with warnings of increased online activity by CSAM perpetrators. We Protect Global Alliance presented a range of sources of information showing an increase in different parts of the world in the early stages of the pandemic[6]. Europol (2020) warned of an increase in online discussions by perpetrators about how to make contact with children who were expected to be more vulnerable due to increased isolation, reduced supervision and greater online exposure. These heightened risks were accompanied by increased workloads and increased stress for many of the professionals attempting to investigate CSAM during the pandemic (Salter & Wong, 2021).

Naturally, all of these statistics need to be treated with a degree of caution. On the one hand, they may well be an undercount of the true scale of the problem as, for example, only a fraction of CSAM is reported to NCMEC even when it is discovered (Krishna, 2021). On the other hand, it is currently unclear how many of the reports that are made relate to duplicate CSAM online, which inflates the true scale of the problem. Further, it is unclear whether these CSAM statistics represent an actual increase in sexual abuse, or increased public awareness and reporting and improved web-crawling technology to identify offensive material. Nevertheless, the sheer scale of reporting demands that more needs to be done to address the problem. This is now being addressed through a range of national and international measures, ranging from proposals for improved regulation in the UK, the USA and the European Union, through to a commitment by ASEAN countries to implement a range of reforms targeted at preventing the online sexual exploitation of children[7].

## But where's the harm?

We must deal from the outset with the question of whether child sexual abuse material is, in fact, harmful. If it is not, then one must question whether there is a need to eliminate it. This is a principle that can be traced back over 160 years to Mill's (1859) assertion that the prevention of harm to others is the only legitimate reason for a state to exercise power over its citizens. Some might argue that these are just images and simply viewing them does not necessarily corrupt the viewer if their intention is to view it (rather than innocently stumbling across it). Nor will viewing CSAM harm the Victim / Survivor because it has already been created and the act of viewing is separate in time and space (and therefore consequence) from the images' original creation. Some might argue further that, rather than being harmful, viewing CSAM could be beneficial if it prevents viewers from having the urge to sexually abuse children in real life. However, these arguments have limited validity when considered against the well-documented evidence associated with child sexual abuse and CSAM, which highlights the very real harm caused to others.

## Impact of child sexual abuse

There is already good evidence to show that child sexual abuse is associated with a range of negative outcomes that can be both severe and enduring for a Victim / Survivor. Although around a quarter may suffer no adverse life events from their victimisation (Smallbone et al., 2008), impacts for many others can be wide-ranging. Psychological impacts include increased likelihood of post-traumatic stress, anxiety, depression, low self-esteem, emotional problems, panic disorder, substance abuse and suicide ideation. Physical impacts can include increased risk of sexually transmitted disease, irritable bowel syndrome, pelvic pain, premenstrual stress and increased medical service contact for physical health problems. Behavioural impacts include earlier onset of sexual activity, binge-drinking, drink-driving and gambling. Child sexual abuse Victims / Survivors are also more likely to experience an array of adverse life events including lower educational attainment, unemployment and relationship break-up (Jonsson & Svedin, 2012; Kenny, 2018). They are also more likely to be re-victimised, experiencing both physical and sexual assault at higher than average levels (Fisher et al., 2017). These are the impacts of the initial offending involving the actual sexual abuse of the child.

## Impact of child sexual abuse material

In addition, we must consider the ongoing psychological trauma that results from Victims / Survivors knowing that their abuse is available for others to view in perpetuity online, with feelings of helplessness, powerlessness, shame and fear common experiences for Victims / Survivors (von Weiler et al., 2010). This can create a sense of constant vigilance and concern that people they know may find the material online and identify them in the images (Leonard, 2010; Paulino et al., 2020; Salter & Hanson, 2021).

There is also evidence that CSAM found on the internet involves more severe violence and younger children than was the case with CSAM in the pre-internet era, indicating that the internet has not only made CSAM more available but has also led to more serious harm than might otherwise have been the case without the internet (Salter & Whitten, 2021).

Given the scale of the problem, the harm it causes and the fact that it would appear to be growing, it would seem an understatement to suggest that more needs to be done to address online child sexual abuse material[8].

## Purpose of this book

The purpose of this book then, is to identify ways in which CSAM can be tackled. The starting point is that the creation, distribution, storage and viewing of CSAM can be eliminated if there is a will to do so. This is because the problem is human created. It is a by-product and indeed beneficiary of the internet. CSAM can be viewed at any time from practically any point on the globe thanks to an ecosystem of connected computers that makes it possible. As this ecosystem is a human feat of engineering, it should also be possible for humans to control how it operates. We should be able to change the ecosystem through technology, policy, regulation, legislation and enforcement in such a way that the creation, distribution, storage and viewing of CSAM becomes too difficult, too risky, or insufficiently rewarding for offenders to continue. In short, because the problem is human created, it can also be eliminated by us. Similar sentiments have been expressed by Hanson (2019), who has also noted that we have agency to make the internet hostile to sexual exploitation.

Libertarian critics may immediately jump on this admittedly naïve position and point out that the very nature and, indeed, benefit of the internet is that it should not be controlled for fear of limiting free speech; or that it cannot be controlled – that it would now be like trying to take the eggs out of a cake once it has been baked. Yet the purpose of this book is to explore how and, indeed, whether changes could be made to eliminate CSAM, if there was a will to do so.

## Defining child sexual abuse material

The term 'child sexual abuse material' is used here in favour of other similar terms, such as child exploitation material, online child sexual exploitation or child pornography. Jesrani et al. (2014) have noted that the term 'child sexual abuse' typically describes a situation in which a child is involved in sexual activity with an adult (or older / more mature child) who has responsibility, trust or power over the child. This highlights the power relationship of the adult over the child, with the abuse being beneficial to the adult, not the child. Jesrani et al. (2014) also note that the term 'exploitation' typically refers to a transaction in which a second party benefits through profit or through a quid pro quo. Under this terminology, exchanging images of child sexual abuse would be exploitation, while keeping images of abuse for a perpetrator's own viewing benefit may not. The term 'child sexual abuse material' is used here to encompass sexual abuse material that may be stored by the perpetrator for personal use or shared with others for personal gain[9].

While semantics matter, it is important to recognise that this is largely an argument about what lies on the periphery of a concept, noting there is a significant overlap in the behaviours associated with abuse and exploitation. At its most basic, child sexual abuse material refers to any representation of a child engaged in sexual acts or the representation (for sexual purposes) of a child's sexual parts (see ICMEC (2018) for a more detailed definition). More specifically, the concern here is with *online* child sexual abuse material and the way in which it is created, stored, shared and viewed. While such images may be created and stored offline, it is the widespread sharing of images through the internet which is of concern in this book.

## Defining 'child'

Although seemingly straight forward, the ICMEC definition disguises layers of complexity which can weigh down attempts to understand and address the problem. Let's start by what we mean by 'child'. A child is defined here as a person who has not reached the age of adulthood, as defined by the laws of a society. Under Article 1 of the United Nations Convention on the Rights of the Child, a child is defined as someone aged under 18 years, unless the legal age of majority (the age at which a person is considered an adult by society) in a country is lower (United Nations, 1989). While in many countries the age of majority is 18 years, in a few it is somewhat lower. For example, in Indonesia and Myanmar the age of majority is 15 years and in Cuba and Cambodia it is 16 years. A legal analysis of online child sexual exploitation in Sri Lanka found inconsistencies in the definition of a child, with different parts of the penal code defining a child variously as 14, 16 or 18 (ECPAT Sri Lanka, 2019).

These differences in the definition of a child create a problem when dealing with CSAM, which so often is multijurisdictional. Sovereign borders become irrelevant when images produced in one country can be shared with those in other countries at the click of a mouse. So images that are legally created in one country may in fact be illegal when viewed in another. This assumes that the viewer is aware of the age of the Victim / Survivor in the images (or indeed cares). It can be difficult to discern from an image whether a post-pubescent individual is a child or an adult. Indeed, some definitions, such as those offered by the Budapest Convention and European Directive 2011/93 include references to 'persons appearing to be a child' in their definitions of what constitutes an offence. There is also a market for 'barely legal' material that purposely straddles this grey area between what is adult and child-related (Prichard et al, 2021). We should also not confuse the age of majority with the age of consent for sexual intercourse and often the age of consent will be below the age of majority. These differences are not of concern here, as we will focus on the age of majority as the benchmark for determining childhood, which in most countries is 18 years.

It is also important to note that what is considered a sexual experience and what is sexual abuse is somewhat relative, depending on the time and place in which they occur and the context in which it takes place. What we define as sex and abuse are social constructs that become known and understood over time and through the situations in which they occur. This process of becoming known may explain why children sometimes do not become aware that they have been sexually abused until later in life (May-Chahal & Kelly, 2020). For the purposes of this book, a somewhat more normative approach to child sexual abuse is taken, although noting that this may be different in future years.

## Distinguishing CSAM from adult pornography

The question of age also draws attention to the intersection between adult pornography and CSAM. Pornography can be defined as sexually explicit imagery created with consenting adults, which is typically restricted to access by those above a certain age. CSAM involves children who by legal definition cannot consent to sexual activity and therefore sexually explicit images are considered abusive. In these terms, CSAM cannot be considered pornography. It is important to recognise that definitions are still rapidly evolving and contested. The term 'child pornography' has until recently been commonly used in academic literature, while the term also remains on the statute in many countries, as well as being the basis for international treaties[10].

But definitions are changing, with a gradual move away from child pornography terminology. This change in terminology was also identified in a 2019 draft resolution of the United Nations Economic and Social Council, which noted a shift by Member States to describing it as child sexual exploitation, or child sexual abuse material in recognition of the seriousness of the offence (United Nations Economic and Social Council, 2019). Similarly, the United Nations' Kyoto Declaration on Advancing Crime Prevention, Criminal Justice and the Rule of Law used the term 'child sexual exploitation and sexual abuse online', rather than child pornography (United Nations Office on Drugs and Crime, 2021a, p.16). So, by maintaining the distinction between pornography and CSAM, we are drawing a line between legitimate adult entertainment and illegitimate, abusive and exploitative material.

## Defining 'material'

Just as the definition of a child, age and sexual abuse raise complexities, so too there are questions over what we consider to be *material*. This can include photographs and videos[11], but may also include paintings, cartoons and computer images. It should also be noted that there are non-image-based types of material that could also be considered CSAM, such as audio files and stories. However, there are also other, physical forms of CSAM, such as sexually explicit, life-size dolls of children that can be purchased from Hong Kong, China and Japan. These have recently been the subject of restriction and prohibition, with attempts to legislate in Australia, Singapore, the United States and the United Kingdom (Brown & Shelling, 2019). These physical forms of CSAM are excluded from this discussion because, while they can be purchased via the internet, they cannot be stored or transmitted online, which are the primary interests here.

## The many facets of CSAM

There are multiple ways in which images may be created, distributed, stored and viewed. The creation of CSAM typically implies an adult creating an image of a child, but it could also involve the creation of sexual abuse imagery of a child by another child. If we consider how adults gain access to children, this can come through a variety of opportunities including, among others, parenthood or other close family connections (sibling, cousin, uncle etc.), being a family friend or trusted guardian (babysitter, teacher, sports coach, religious leader etc.). These are the types of roles that could offer the opportunity for an adult to be alone with a child, in circumstances conducive to the creation of sexually explicit material of the child by the adult. These roles differ from cases of abduction by strangers, which tend to be rarer and shaped by opportunities that are limited and transitory. However, there are opportunities in cyberspace for a stranger to groom or coerce a child to create and supply sexually explicit images of themselves without the Victim / Survivor or perpetrator physically meeting (Interpol, 2018). Such opportunities are increasing with the proliferation of social media and gaming platforms that allow anonymous users to communicate directly with each other.

Concerning the distribution of CSAM, it would not be an understatement to suggest that the most significant factor in explaining the proliferation of CSAM has been the advent of the internet. Prior to the invention of email and the World Wide Web, those intent on distributing CSAM were reliant on sending physical copies (such as photographic prints and DVDs) via the postal service, which introduced significant risks of detection by law enforcement authorities for the recipients, who were identifiable by their postal address (van der Bruggen & Blokland, 2020). The internet, with its multiple forms of communication (email, websites, social media platforms, file sharing platforms etc.) provides low-cost, low-risk instant access to CSAM. Similarly, storage of CSAM involves negligible costs. While some may store material on their own hard drives at no cost, others deposit their collections in cloud file storage services. Indeed, the Internet Watch Foundation (2021) found that 81 per cent of the CSAM URLs (Uniform Resource Locators – the specific locations online where the files are saved) they identified were in image hosting sites, which were generally free to use.

While complex and multifaceted, it is important to understand these issues of CSAM definition, as it highlights the potential opportunities for addressing the problem from a preventative perspective.

## Using crime science

In order to identify opportunities to reduce CSAM, the problem will be examined here from a crime science perspective. Crime science is concerned with the use of science to control crime (Laycock, 2008). As a discipline, it intersects with, but is separate to, criminology, in that it seeks to apply scientific methods to reduce crime through prevention, disruption and detection. This is not to be mistaken with forensic science, which applies methods from the natural sciences to criminal investigations and court proceedings, using an increasing array of techniques, from fingerprint and DNA analysis to shoeprint and ballistics matching. Rather, crime science is concerned with applying scientific methods of observation and experimentation to understand crime phenomena in the aggregate and to identify approaches that might be taken to reduce that class of crime[12]. This perhaps highlights the narrowly focused aims of crime science (crime reduction) and yet broad remit for achieving that aim by drawing on many disciplines (Wortley et al., 2019).

With its origins in situational crime prevention (Clarke, 1980), environmental criminology (Brantingham & Brantingham, 1981) and the rational choice perspective (Clarke & Cornish, 1985), crime science can be characterised by its focus on proximal causes of crime (especially those associated with the immediate environment which can be altered in the short term), rather than more distant causes (such as socio-economic disadvantage, political marginalisation etc. that can only be changed in the longer term). This means that, while the motivations for why perpetrators commit offences are important for identifying effective treatment options, they are secondary to understanding the circumstances and environment within which motivated offenders *decide* to offend. This draws on a rational choice perspective that sees offenders weigh up the benefits of committing crime against the risks (Clarke & Cornish, 1985; Cornish & Clarke, 1987), but which also takes account of situational precipitators that prompt criminal reactions, regardless of rationality (Wortley, 1997).

The approach taken here pays scant attention to the profile of CSAM offenders because the focus is primarily on the criminal event, although offenders are of interest insofar as their characteristics shape the creation, distribution, storage and viewing of CSAM. The general profile of offenders has also been addressed elsewhere (Babchishin et al., 2011; Brown & Bricknell, 2018; Henshaw et al., 2017).

Nor does this approach examine in detail the profile of the Victims / Survivors, or the harm caused to them. Understanding the impacts on Victims / Survivors of CSAM and giving them a voice is extremely important and has helped in shaping therapeutic responses to the trauma experienced. It is essential that further work be undertaken in this area. However, the concern here is with the event – the circumstances in which CSAM offences can be committed. By addressing the conditions which facilitate a CSAM event, the intention is to identify ways in which subsequent events could be prevented, thereby helping to reduce victimisation.

Crime science also seeks to be multidisciplinary, drawing on knowledge from areas seldom examined by traditional criminology, including engineering, computer science, physics and design. Viewing the world from different standpoints can bring new understanding and new tools that can be used to address criminological problems. In the case of CSAM, there could be benefit from drawing on computer science to understand the ways in which CSAM could be blocked from being created, distributed and stored, and for identifying new methods of detection. We may draw on mathematics and data science to understand the encryption technology that helps offenders to operate anonymously. And we may draw on designers to understand how potential viewers of CSAM could be prevented or dissuaded from accessing such material. This again highlights how the aims (crime reduction) may be narrow, but the means by which CSAM reduction is achieved can call on a broad range of disciplines in its execution.

An important stream of crime science examines the way in which systems operate to impede or facilitate criminal events. The systems we use can create opportunities for crime harvests, often because system designers fail to take account of the potential for their creations to be used for illegitimate use, or for loopholes to be exploited (Pease & Farrell, 2014). Sidebottom and Tilley (2017) described a range of ways in which systems could encourage crime and these are relevant for thinking of the internet as a criminogenic system. Systems can furnish rewards for crime, make crime easy, less risky, facilitate crime planning, disinhibit offenders / provoke crime, generate need, create crime networks and can teach how to commit crime. As we shall see in the following chapters, the internet as a system has the potential to facilitate CSAM through all these means.

Given the many CSAM risks posed by the internet, it may be possible to examine the system design from a crime prevention perspective. Ekblom (1997) suggested that system designers should identify how systems change crime opportunities, anticipate criminal countermoves, block as many countermoves as possible, anticipate design failure (allowing for system changes) and act on multiple fronts to prevent criminal attacks[13].

The focus here is therefore on using crime science to understand the internet as a system that facilitates CSAM. By understanding how the internet facilitates this problem, it should be possible to identify weaknesses that need to be addressed and strengths that can be utilised more fully.

## Structure of this book

This book is divided into two parts. Part 1 deals with how the internet operates as a constantly evolving ecosystem, responding to technology changes and user expectations change. Chapter 2 outlines the key features of the ecosystem that allow CSAM to flourish. Chapter 3 examines how CSAM is created and subsequently enters the ecosystem. Chapter 4 examines the internet infrastructure that allows CSAM to be distributed between those that collect or view such material. Chapter 5 explores the aspects of the system that allow material to be consumed. Chapter 6 summarises what we know about the problems associated with the CSAM ecosystem, identifying multiple issues that need to be addressed.

Part 2 examines the potential to address the problem of CSAM by changing the ecosystem. As identified in chapter 7, this part draws on some of the key concepts from crime science, including situational crime prevention, routine activity theory and environmental criminology. In particular, it draws on the idea of the '11 Ds' of crime prevention – an underutilised way of thinking about how offender decision-making can be influenced through intervention. Chapter 8 examines approaches to reducing the production of CSAM from a high-level crime script perspective, identifying interventions that might address target selection and offence preparation, perpetration and completion. Chapter 9 moves on to examining approaches that can be taken to prevent the distribution of CSAM, including the removal and blocking of content. Chapter 10 completes the analysis of responses by examining how the consumption of CSAM can be addressed. As well as identifying what is already being done to address the problem, chapters 8 to 10 also attempt to identify other approaches that might be taken to deal with these online harms. Finally, chapter 11 draws the various threads together and offers potential priorities for action that may help to make CSAM elimination a reality.

## Notes

1 Found at www.missingkids.org/gethelpnow/cybertipline/cybertiplinedata
2 Found at https://transparencyreport.google.com/child-sexual-abuse-material/report ing?hl=en&lu=urls_deindexed&urls_deindexed=period:2021H1
3 Found at www.comparitech.com/blog/vpn-privacy/child-abuse-online-statistics/
4 Found at https://worldpopulationreview.com/country-rankings/gdp-per-capita-by-country
5 These were Brunei (9,638 cases), Myanmar (595,218 cases), Cambodia (297,044 cases), Indonesia (3,802,150 cases), Lao PDR (58,764 cases), Malaysia (719,260 cases), Philippines (1,713,043 cases), Singapore (83,332 cases), Thailand (2,273,491 cases) and Vietnam (1,826,529 cases).
6 Found at www.weprotect.org/library/impact-of-covid-19-on-child-sexual-exploitat ion-online/
7 In 2019, ASEAN agreed to implement wide-ranging reforms that would improve child protection in Member States. Further details can be found at https://asean2019.go.th/ en/news/declaration-on-the-protection-of-children-from-all-forms-of-online-explo itation-and-abuse-in-asean/
8 Indeed, successive international treaties have called for more to be done to protect children from sexual abuse and CSAM-type victimisation, including Article 34 of the United Nations Convention on the Rights of the Child (CRC), the Council of Europe Convention on the Protection of Children against Sexual Exploitation and Sexual Abuse (the Lanzarote Convention) and the Council of Europe's Convention on Cybercrime (the Budapest Convention).
9 This is contested ground. The Luxembourg Guidelines, which set out the appropriate terminology to use in relation to the protection of children from sexual exploitation and sexual abuse, argued that sexual abuse was a subset of sexual exploitation. Sexual exploit- ation included all material related to the exploitation of children (including erotica and sexual posing), while sexual abuse mainly pertains to actual abuse, or a concentration on the genital and anal regions of a child (ECPAT International, 2016).
10 The Luxembourg Guidelines demonstrate that, at present, the term 'child pornography' is typically used in international, legally binding instruments. These include (among others) the UN Convention on the Rights of the Child (CRC), the UN Optional Protocol to the CRC on the Sale of Children, Child Prostitution and Child Pornography, the Council of Europe's Convention on Cybercrime (the Budapest Convention) and the European Union's Directive on Combating the Sexual Abuse and Sexual Exploitation of Children and Child Pornography (EU Directive 2011/93) (ECPAT International, 2016).
11 In 2019, reports of CSAM in videos to NCMEC exceeded reports of CSAM in photographs for the first time (Dance & Keller, 2020).
12 Just to confuse this distinction however, Morgan (2019) has described how forensic science can be employed as a crime science approach to reducing crime.
13 This approach has previously been used in reviewing the UK's vehicle licensing system, which resulted in a series of recommendations for improvements (Laycock & Web, 2005). In the Australian context, Brown (2015) has described how the vehicle registra- tion system includes a series of measures to help prevent vehicle theft and resale. Laycock and Webb (2005) also produced a series of design principles for thinking about how to

crime-proof systems. These included making changes that can be implemented quickly; with minimal need for legislation; that are cost-effective; future-proof; default to honesty; have clear lines of responsibility, from 'designer to shredder'; take account of privacy and data protection; and result in a system that is easy to use. These stand as principles that could be applied to addressing system design issues to tackle CSAM.

# References

Albanese, J. (2007). *Commercial Sexual Exploitation of Children: What Do We Know and What Do We Do About It?* Special Report. National Institute of Justice. www.ojp. gov/ncjrs/virtual-library/abstracts/commercial-sexual-exploitation-children-what-do-we-know-and-what-do

Babchishin, K.M., Hanson, K. & Hermann, C.A. (2011). The characteristics of online sex offenders: A meta-analysis. *Sexual Abuse: A Journal of Research and Treatment* 23(1), 92–123 https://doi.org/10.1177%2F1079063210370708

Brantingham, P.J. & Brantingham, P.L. (1981). *Environmental criminology.* Waveland Press.

Brown, R. (2015). Crime prevention design in a vehicle registration system: a case study from Australia. *Crime Science* 4(25). https://doi.org/10.1186/s40163-015-0038-1

Brown, R. & Bricknell, S. (2018). *What is the profile of child exploitation material offenders?* Trends & issues in crime and criminal justice 564. Australian Institute of Criminology. https://aic.gov.au/publications/tandi/tandi564

Brown, R. & Shelling, J. (2019). *Exploring the implications of child sex dolls.* Trends and issues in crime and criminal justice 570. Australian Institute of Criminology. https://aic.gov.au/publications/tandi/tandi570

Clarke, R.V. (1980). 'Situational' crime prevention: theory and practice. *British Journal of Criminology* 20(2), 136–147 https://doi.org/10.1093/oxfordjournals.bjc.a047153

Clarke, R.V. & Cornish, D. (1985). Modelling offenders' decisions: a framework for research and policy. In M. Tonry & N. Morris (Eds.), *Crime and justice: A review of research, Volume 6* (pp. 147–185). The University of Chicago Press.

Cornish, D.B. & Clarke, R.V. (1987). *The reasoning criminal: Rational choice perspectives on offending.* Springer-Verlag

Dance, G.J.X. & Keller, M.H. (2020, 7 February). Tech companies detect a surge in online videos of child sexual abuse. *The New York Times.* www.nytimes.com/2020/02/07/us/onl ine-child-sexual-abuse.html

ECPAT International (2016). *Terminology guidelines for the protection of children from sexual exploitation and sexual abuse.* Interagency Working Group. http://luxembourgguidelines. org/english-version/

ECPAT Sri Lanka (2019). *Sri Lanka: Online child sexual exploitation legal gap analysis.* www. ecpat.lk/wp-content/uploads/2015/12/Report-on-Online-Child-Sexual-Exploitat ion-Legal-Gap-Analysis_ECPAT-Sri-Lanka.pdf

Ekblom, P. (1997). Gearing up against crime: A dynamic framework to help designers keep up with the adaptive criminal in a changing world. *International Journal of Risk, Security and Crime Prevention* 2(4), 249–265. www.researchgate.net/profile/Paul-Ekblom/publ ication/291456106_Gearing_up_against_crime_A_dynamic_framework_to_help_ designers_keep_up_with_the_adaptive_criminal_in_a_changing_world/links/56b4b 1ab08ae83713174a339/Gearing-up-against-crime-A-dynamic-framework-to-help-designers-keep-up-with-the-adaptive-criminal-in-a-changing-world.pdf

Europol (2020, March). *Pandemic profiteering: how criminals exploit the COVID-19 crisis.* Europol. www.europol.europa.eu/cms/sites/default/files/documents/pandemic_profi teering-how_criminals_exploit_the_covid-19_crisis.pdf

Fisher, C., Goldsmith, A., Hurcombe, R. & Soares, C. (2017). *The impacts of child sexual abuse: A rapid evidence assessment.* Independent Inquiry into Child Sexual Abuse. www.iicsa.org.uk/document/iicsa-impacts-child-sexual-abuse-rapid-evidence-assessment-full-report-english

Hanson, E. (2019). 'Losing track of morality': understanding online forces and dynamics conducive to child sexual exploitation. In J Pearce (Ed.), *Child sexual exploitation: Why theory matters* (pp.87–117). Policy Press.

Henshaw, M., Ogloff, J.R.P. & Clough, J.A. (2017). Looking beyond the screen: A critical review of the literature on the online child pornography offender. *Sexual Abuse: A Journal of Research and Treatment* 29(5), 416–445. https://doi.org/10.1177/107906321 5603690

ICMEC (2018). *Child Sexual Abuse Material: Model Legislation & Global Review.* International Centre for Missing & Exploited Children. www.icmec.org/wp-content/uploads/2018/12/CSAM-Model-Law-9th-Ed-FINAL-12-3-18.pdf

INHOPE (2021). *Annual report 2020.* INHOPE. inhope.org/media/pages/the-facts/download-our-whitepapers/c16bc4d839-1620144551/inhope-annual-report-2020.pdf

Internet Watch Foundation (2021). *Face the facts: The annual report 2020.* Internet Watch Foundation. https://annualreport2020.iwf.org.uk/

Interpol (2018). *Towards a global indicator on unidentified victims in child sexual exploitation material: Summary Report.* Interpol. www.interpol.int/en/content/download/9363/file/Summary%20-%20Towards%20a%20Global%20Indicator%20on%20Unidentified%20Victims%20in%20Child%20Sexual%20Exploitation%20Material.%20February%202 018.pdf

Jesrani, T., Malby, S., Banuelos, T., Holterhof, A. & Hahn, M. (2014). *Study on the Effects of New Information Technology on the Abuse and Exploitation of Children.* United Nations Office on Drugs and Crime. www.unodc.org/documents/Cybercrime/Study_on_the_Effects.pdf

Jonsson, L. & Svedin, C.G. (2012). Children within images. In E. Quayle & K.M. Ribisl (Eds.), *Understanding and preventing online sexual exploitation of children* (pp. 23–43). Routledge.

Kenny, D.T. (2018). *Children, sexuality, and child sexual abuse.* Routledge.

Krishna, A. (2021). Internet.gov: Tech companies as government agents and the future of the fight against child sexual abuse. *California Law Review* 109, 1581–1635. https://doi.org/10.15779/Z38KW57J9B

Laycock, G. (2008). Special Edition on Crime Science: Editorial by Gloria Laycock – Guest Editor. *Policing: A Journal of Policy and Practice* 2(2), 149–153. https://doi.org/10.1093/police/pan028

Laycock, G. & Webb, B. (2005). Designing out crime from the UK vehicle licensing system. In R.V. Clarke & G.R. Newman (Eds.), *Designing out crime from products and systems* (pp.203–230). Criminal Justice Press.

Leonard, M.M. (2010). 'I did what I was directed to do but he didn't touch me': The impact of being a victim of internet offending. *Journal of Sexual Aggression* 16(2), 249–256. https://doi.org/10.1080/13552601003690526

May-Chahal, C. & Kelly, E. (2020). *Online child sexual victimisation.* Policy Press.

Mill, J.S. (1859). *On liberty.* John W. Parker and Son.

Morgan, R.M. (2019). Forensic science. In R. Wortley, A. Sidebottom, N. Tilley & G. Laycock (Eds.), *Routledge handbook of crime science* (pp. 190–203). Routledge.

Paulino, M., Gabriel, S., Alho, L. & Hipolito, J. (2020). Child pornography in the XXI century: Brief considerations about victims and offenders. *Journal of Forensic Sciences and*

*Criminal Investigations* 14(5), 555899. https://juniperpublishers.com/jfsci/pdf/JFSCI. MS.ID.555899.pdf

Pease, K. & Farrell, G. (2014). What have criminologists done for us lately? In M. Gill (Ed.), *The Handbook of Security* (pp.65–88). Palgrave Macmillan.

Prichard, J., Wortley, R., Watters, P., Spiranovic, C., Hunn, C. & Krone, T. (2021). Effects of automated messages on Internet users attempting to access 'barely legal' pornography. *Sexual Abuse* 34(1), 106–124. https://doi.org/10.1177/10790632211013809

Salter, M. & Hanson, E. (2021). 'I need you all to understand how pervasive this issue is': User efforts to regulate child sexual offending on social media. In J. Baily, A. Flynn & N. Henry (Eds.), *The Emerald International Handbook of Technology facilitated Violence and Abuse* (pp.729–748). Emerald Publishing.

Salter, M. & Whitten, T. (2021). A Comparative Content Analysis of Pre-Internet and Contemporary Child Sexual Abuse Material. *Deviant Behavior.* https://doi.org/10.1080/01639625.2021.1967707

Salter, M. & Wong, T. (2021). *The impact of COVID-19 on the risk of online child sexual exploitation and the implications for child protection and policing.* Research Report. University of New South Wales. www.arts.unsw.edu.au/sites/default/files/documents/eSafety-OCSE-pandemic-report-salter-and-wong.pdf

Sidebottom, A. & Tilley, N. (2017). Designing systems against crime: Introducing leaky systems. In N. Tilley & A. Sidebottom (Eds.), *Handbook of crime prevention and community safety* (pp.254–273). Second edition. Routledge.

Smallbone, S., Marshall, W.L. & Wortley, R. (2008). *Preventing child sexual abuse: Evidence, policy and practice.* Willan Publishing.

United Nations (1989). *Conventions on the Rights of the Child.* https://treaties.un.org/Pages/ViewDetails.aspx?src=IND&mtdsg_no=IV-11&chapter=4&lang=en

United Nations Economic and Social Council (2019). *Countering child sexual exploitation and sexual abuse online.* Commission on Crime Prevention and Criminal Justice. Revised draft resolution, 24 May 2019. file:///H:/CEM/CEM%20Book/Literature/ECN152019_L3REv1_e_V1903716.pdf

United Nations Human Rights Council (2021). *Impact of coronavirus disease on different manifestations of sale and sexual exploitation of children.* https://reliefweb.int/sites/reliefweb.int/files/resources/A_HRC_46_31_E.pdf

United Nations Office on Drugs and Crime (2021a). *Kyoto Declaration on Advancing Crime Prevention, Criminal Justice and the Rule of Law: Towards the Achievement of the 2030 Agenda for Sustainable Development.* United Nations Office on Drugs and Crime. www.unodc.org/documents/commissions/Congress/21-02815_Kyoto_Declaration_ebook_rev_cover.pdf

United Nations Office on Drugs and Crime (2021b). *UNODC Southeast Asia Pacific Written Submission to the Parliament of Australia Joint Committee on Law Enforcement.* Parliamentary Joint Committee on Law Enforcement Inquiry on Law enforcement capabilities in relation to child exploitation. Submission 7. www.aph.gov.au/DocumentStore.ashx?id=84dfa4c8-c020-4e07-8ccd-d09b153187a6&subId=712049

van der Bruggen, M. & Blokland, A. (2020). A crime script analysis of child sexual exploitation material fora on the darknet. *Sexual Abuse* 33(8), 950–974. https://doi.org/10.1177/1079063220981063

von Weiler, J., Haardt-Becker, A. & Schulte, S. (2010). Care and treatment of child victims of child pornography exploitation (CPE) in Germany. *Journal of Sexual Aggression* 16(2), 211–222. https://doi.org/10.1080/13552601003759990

Wortley, R. (1997). Reconsidering the Role of Opportunity in Situational Crime Prevention. In G. Newman, R.V. Clarke & S.G. Shohan (Eds.), *Rational Choice and Situational Crime Prevention* (pp. 173–188). Ashgate Publishing.

Wortley, R., Sidebottom, A., Tilley, N. & Laycock, G. (2019). What is crime science? In R. Wortley, A. Sidebottom, N. Tilley & G. Laycock (Eds.), *Routledge handbook of crime science* (pp. 1–30). Routledge.

# PART I
# The ecosystem

# 2

# THE CSAM ECOSYSTEM

## What is an ecosystem?

The internet provides the perfect conditions for creating an ecosystem that supports the production and proliferation of CSAM. To proceed, we need to understand in greater detail what we mean by an 'ecosystem' and explore how this might be useful in our quest to address CSAM.

An ecosystem can be defined simply as a group (or community) of organisms that interact with each other and also interact with their environment (Yallop et al., 2005). This simple definition is the starting point for our exploration of the CSAM ecosystem. Yet even this definition raises a number of important questions regarding what constitutes the environment, what constitutes an organism in the ecosystem, how a community is formed, how members of the community are able to interact with one another and how they interact with the environment. When applied to understanding CSAM, these questions provide an alternative way of understanding how the internet is used to create, share, store and view such material.

Before proceeding, it is important to note that this is not the first time that CSAM has been considered in the context of an ecosystem. Drawing on the foundational work of Bronfenbrenner (1979), Martin and Alaggia (2013) described CSAM within a cyber-system that exists simultaneously and, indeed intersects, with other dimensions of a child's social ecosystem. In contrast to Martin and Alaggia's cyber-system approach, the key to understanding the CSAM ecosystem described in this book is to explore how it operates at the structural, instrumental level rather than within a social system. Much less effort is devoted here to understanding how an individual interacts and develops within the ecosystem and more to exploring how CSAM is fostered by the ecosystem itself.

DOI: 10.4324/9781003327264-3

## What constitutes the environment in the CSAM ecosystem?

Of all the questions asked in this chapter, understanding what constitutes the environment is, perhaps, the most complex to answer. In the context of the CSAM ecosystem, the environment relates to the internet and how it operates. At its simplest, this environment consists of the internet infrastructure and the applications that operate within it.

### *The internet*

The internet consists of both hardware and software dimensions. The hardware dimension relates to the physical electronic devices that can be connected to the internet and, through their connectivity, become part of the internet itself. This includes information and communication technology (ICT) devices such as desktops, laptops, tablets and mobile phones that most of us use daily. As well as these tools with which we constantly interact, there is an increasing array of internet-connected devices that make up the Internet of Things (IoT). A few examples of the devices that belong to the IoT include interactive home hubs, such as the Amazon Alexa and Google Assistant, e-readers, home CCTV / alarm systems, doorbells, televisions, light bulbs, baby monitors, children's dolls, toothbrushes, smartwatches and even sex toys, each allowing created data to be stored and shared. As a side note, it is worth mentioning that there have been concerns that internet-connected dolls could be used by offenders to attempt to engage with children. In 2016, concerns were raised about interactive toys such as i-QUE and My Friend Cayla, which, with no in-built security, could allow strangers to connect via Bluetooth (although noting that Bluetooth connectivity is not the same as being internet connected) and speak to a child user through the toys (Deutsche Welle, 2016; Tait, 2016).

These devices all represent the hardware used by the end user, or consumer. To enable them to connect with each other, *servers* sit at nodes in the network, playing an essential role in storing data created by consumers. These servers will typically sit in *data centres*, or *server farms*, containing racks of computers with software that allows files to be stored and retrieved remotely. These can, in some instances, consist of thousands of servers, each storing and managing data created by consumers. Just to confuse matters a little, computers used by end users can also act as local servers, creating their own mini-network. These allow files to be shared by those within that network. However, for now, we are only concerned with remote servers located in data centres.

Between the end user's device and the server in the data centre, there is a network of routers that direct information in the most efficient means possible through the network. For most of us, the only connection with the network of routers is the box sent to us by our Internet Service Provider (ISP) that connects to the phone line in our homes. This home router connects each device on the local network (most commonly by connecting wirelessly) to the internet.

## Signposting information – IP addresses and the Domain Name System

Information is passed through the internet by moving packets of data from one address to another until it reaches its destination. Each computer in a network is assigned an Internet Protocol (IP) address, which consists of a logically structured set of numbers, separated by decimal places. This IP address locates the computer within the network. When information is sent, both the destination IP address and the source IP address are included. In a home network, the router will provide the IP address that is publicly accessible and enables information sent from that location to be traced back to that router. Within the local network, the router will assign IP addresses to each individual piece of hardware connected to the network, including computers, printers etc., although these IP addresses are private and cannot (usually) be viewed from outside of the local network. Information moving through the internet uses the Transmission Control Protocol / Internet Protocol (TCP / IP), which simply provides the framework for how data passing through the network should be structured and therefore allows information produced on different computer systems to be recognised.

Although probably as technical as we will get, understanding this principle is important from a law enforcement perspective, as it can enable information to be traced back to an individual user via their IP address.

As it would be difficult to remember the configuration of numbers that make up the IP address each time we wanted to access a website, the IP address system is overlayed with a Domain Name System (DNS), which uses alphanumeric characters, rather than purely numbers. The DNS defines the website names and the pages within websites – such as www.google.com or www.aic.gov.au. Each time a page is searched for, the DNS servers are interrogated to identify the corresponding IP address, which will identify the location on the internet where that file can be found.

## The World Wide Web

The World Wide Web is probably what comes to mind when we think of the internet. This is a system of 'web' servers that contains all websites. Web servers are computers that maintain software that allow websites to be securely uploaded and then accessed by anyone on the internet. Depending on its size, a website may be held on one web server, or across many web servers. Each page in a website has a Uniform Resource Locator (URL) which provides the address on the internet where the file containing that information can be found. Note that underlying that URL is the IP address for that page, as described above. Within any given website, files are typically structured in a hierarchical form, with the home page at the top of the hierarchy, cascading down to subdomains within the website. The files that make up the pages within a website are produced in a common computer language (Hypertext Markup Language – known as HTML) that are read by an internet browser, such as Internet Explorer, Firefox or Chrome.

## Internet Service Providers

Internet Service Providers (ISPs) are organisations that provide access to the internet, typically by connecting a router to the telephone system. Mobile phone companies provide a similar function when they provide access to the internet. ISPs also often provide an email account and access to limited space on a web server to allow one to upload a website. An ISP may also host websites with names that have been purchased by customers and registered with the Domain Name System. As will be discussed later, ISPs play an essential role in the CSAM ecosystem and have become important allies for tackling the problem.

## Online applications

Internet browsers, such as Safari and Chrome, are applications that make the internet work in the way we know. Browsers are computer programs (applications) that are stored on the devices we use and are intended to read the HTML code on a web page and to present that information as it was intended by the designer.

Each file that makes up a web page is produced using specific website development software. This may be written by the developer in HTML, or translated into HTML by the software application before it is published. It is then uploaded to the specific location on a web server, where it is made available for anyone with access to the internet to find. That location will have its own IP address, overlayed by a URL, with the two being matched by the DNS. However, from the end user perspective, much of this can be taken for granted. The user need not know how HTML is created, or really what it does, other than it creates web pages that can be viewed on the World Wide Web by a browser.

Browsers find the information by typing the URL into the address box. This is fine if we know the URL we are looking for, but in practice we rarely remember URLs beyond the top-level domain name. To find information on the World Wide Web, we typically use a search engine to identify the most likely results, in hierarchical order of relevance, for any given search term. These search engines, such as Google and Bing, are themselves websites accessed through a browser. These websites create an index of all URLs on the internet and order them according to proprietary algorithms that aim to return the most relevant URLs, thereby providing an effortless means by which an end user can retrieve the information they are seeking – even when they do not know the name of the website they are looking for.

From this perspective, online applications provide the means by which we engage with the internet. They allow us to create files that are stored in a particular location on the internet, which can subsequently be found and used when needed. However, online applications also include the programs that operate on the internet. These programs come with a seemingly infinite array of uses, although from the perspective of the CSAM ecosystem, there are certain types of application that are particularly relevant and which have made such material easier to create, store, share and access. These include social media sites, discussion forums and file storage sites to name just a few. Each of these are discussed in more detail in later chapters. These applications will generally have been created with legitimate uses in mind, but subsequently adopted for illegitimate use by those in the CSAM ecosystem. In fact, that is one of the defining features that allows CSAM to flourish, with it often being hidden in plain sight by the much larger supply of legitimate material available online. Indeed, one of the key considerations for those working to eradicate CSAM is how such abhorrent material can be identified among all the legitimate material and then removed automatically, rather than requiring manual searching.

## *The financial system*

The financial system also plays an important role in the CSAM ecosystem, providing a means by which material is monetised, allowing for perpetrators to profit from such activity. It is important to note that most CSAM is exchanged without financial payment, with the Internet Watch Foundation (2021) estimating that only about 8 per cent of this material is traded for commercial gain.

Payments are sometimes made to access a website that sits behind a paywall. For example, Wortley and Smallbone (2012) reported a case from the early 2000s of Landslide Productions, a company that specialised in distributing CSAM, which customers accessed through credit card payments. In other cases, payments are made for time-limited access. This is the case in relation to the livestreaming of child sexual abuse (discussed further later in this chapter). Livestreaming of CSAM typically involves offenders in affluent countries and child Victims / Survivors in much poorer countries and the sums paid are typically small by Western standards, but can be significant for the recipients in, for example, Southeast Asia, where many of these cases of abuse are occurring. An analysis of over 2,000 financial transactions made by Australians to individuals in the Philippines known to arrange livestreamed child sexual abuse found that the median value of a transaction was AUS $78 (Brown et al., 2020). In some cases, livestreaming is organised by crime groups who encourage families to provide child victims in return for payment. However, the ubiquity of the video-streaming technology means that parents will sometimes organise the sexual abuse of their own children in return for payment (Terre des Hommes, 2014).

Financial payments have often been made by perpetrators using their everyday credit and debit cards, or through online banking transactions. This underlines the low perceived risk of detection among those making the payments, in the expectation that the payment details will be held securely by websites selling CSAM. Indeed, one might expect that this business model relies on payment security and anonymity of the client for CSAM vendors to maintain the confidence of their clients. However, in recent years, a collaboration between Visa Europe and financial investigators from the UK's National Crime Agency was reported to have significantly reduced the use of cards issued by mainstream providers for purchasing CSAM (Independent Inquiry into Child Sexual Abuse, 2020).

Money remittance services may be used in cases where there is contact between the Consumer and the vendor of the CSAM. These operate by paying money to a remittance service, which then agrees to deposit the funds in an overseas bank account, or make it available for the vendor to collect from the office of the money remittance service in the destination location. These services facilitate financial transactions without the need for bank accounts, although the customer will usually need to provide personal identification to make the transaction.

In cases where anonymity is needed, the Consumer may choose to use one of the many cryptocurrencies that employ blockchain technology[1]. These allow transactions to be made from an encrypted wallet on the Consumer's computer, or through a wallet held on an online exchange, to an account held by the vendor without the transaction being recorded by the regulated financial sector.

This discussion demonstrates that, while financial transactions will often rely on online applications (as would be the case in cryptocurrency transactions and standard debit / credit card purchases), this need not necessarily be the case. Indeed, financial transactions through remittance services can be wholly completed offline – at least from an end user perspective. However, CSAM transactions undertaken for profit (although noting this is not the primary motivation for sharing) invariably rely on an online application at the point of purchase.

## A climate that is conducive to growth

As it currently stands, this interdependent ecosystem has a climate that is perfectly balanced to support its growth. For almost 30 years, the internet has been able to expand, thanks in part to a cyber-libertarian climate that has promoted the rights of all internet users to free speech, unfettered by government intervention through legislation or regulation (Salter & Hanson, 2021). This climate emerged as a radical alternative counterculture to a world marred by international conflict, failed political economy ideologies and the perception that the state was creeping into every aspect of day-to-day life. Set against this backdrop, the early Silicon Valley architects of the internet turned to neoliberalist doctrines espousing the importance of individual choice, free markets and the small state.

This cyber-libertarian climate was further advanced by legal developments in the USA that would help it to foster the growth of corporations operating online. In the early years of developments in ISP services, US courts determined that corporations that chose to remove obscene content were making judgements on what could be uploaded and were therefore deemed to be publishers of content and so were civilly liable for the content they carried. Perversely, ISPs that chose not to remove obscene content were not considered publishers and so were not civilly liable for their content. Section 230 of the Communications Decency Act (1996) attempted to clarify and provide redress for this perverse situation by stating that interactive computer Service Providers would not be considered the publisher of information provided by another content provider. This simple clause changed the future of the internet. It essentially gave immunity to ISPs and other Electronic Service Providers (ESPs) for the content carried on their servers. They were not deemed to be the publishers of the content uploaded by users and so could not be held liable (either civilly or criminally) for that content. Section 230 also provided ESPs with immunity from civil action for action taken in good faith to remove objectionable material. This meant they *could* remove obscene content posted by users, but were not *obliged* to do so. With the law clarified in this way, the internet and the services it provided grew rapidly in a climate of self-regulation in which government intervention was openly hands-off.

The unregulated nature of the internet has only recently been challenged by the US government. A Department of Justice review of Section 230 in 2020 recommended that immunity from prosecution for ESPs should be removed in a limited number of situations including those involving child exploitation and sexual abuse. At the time of writing, these recommendations are still subject to further debate, but they reflect an appetite to place limits on the activities of the internet in a way that could at least begin to curb its pro-cyber-libertarian approach.

While climate change in the CSAM ecosystem may be on the distant horizon, the current environment provides near-perfect conditions for CSAM to flourish. Hanson (2019) has noted that this climate has created ethical drift in technology companies with values such as 'freedom', 'connection' and 'creativity' being encouraged over others such as 'equality' and 'protection from exploitation'. This has led to software developers being blind to the way in which their creations may draw in young people to use their applications (thereby creating revenue) and at the same time fail to protect the vulnerable from being preyed upon by sexual predators. This has occurred in a global political environment that has largely seen a hands-off governmental approach, allowing the internet to flourish unabated and without censure – at least until recently.

## What constitutes an organism in the CSAM ecosystem?

The 'organisms' within the CSAM ecosystem consist of groups of individuals that play different roles in ensuring its continued operation. Each group is in some way connected to the others in the ecosystem. In some cases, these connections are mutually beneficial, while in others they are exploitative. The groups discussed here include Consumers, Content Producers, Content Distributors, Service Providers and Victims / Survivors.

### Consumers

Consumers are those who view CSAM material. Consumers are problematic 'organisms' in the ecosystem because they create the demand for new material. Without this demand, it is questionable whether CSAM would exist to the degree that it does online. Some Content Producers might continue to share their images as a way of legitimising, or affirming their offending behaviour, or as a means of enhancing the power imbalance between Victim / Survivor and offender, but it would seem implausible to conclude that CSAM would continue to feature to the extent that it does online if it were not demanded by Consumers. This assumes the increase in CSAM availability is demand-led. While this is partially true, one cannot ignore the supply side of the equation. More people are also viewing CSAM because it is more available than ever before. Wortley (2012) has called this supply-led demand. The demand for CSAM has grown in recent years because the infrastructure that supports the supply has also grown. It is much easier to distribute CSAM through a variety of channels and this has helped to further fuel demand. This points to the importance of both increases in supply and demand in explaining the increase in CSAM in recent years. However, in the context of the Consumer, there is clearly a demand for more content of this nature. Yet, Consumers are probably the most difficult organism in the ecosystem to target from a preventative intervention perspective, because of their ubiquity, wide distribution and significant potential for being replaced by other Consumers.

As noted above, Consumer demand creates a market for CSAM that in some cases can be monetised. More often, it is freely exchanged in support of an insatiable appetite for fresh content. In those cases, the Consumers may also be Producers of content.

There is also a significant cohort of Consumers who surf the web for free CSAM content. Some of these may be casually curious, looking for something different, or as an escalation from adult pornography. Indeed, adult pornography sites abound with CSAM. A search for 'girlsunder18' on Pornhub, an adult pornography site with over 3.5 billion visits per month, was reported to return over 100,000 videos (Kristof, 2020). Some Consumers may be regular viewers of freely available CSAM, who may be on a pathway to more serious consumption of this material. Krone (2004) identified five types of Consumer. These included the 'Browser', who may stumble across CSAM while browsing the internet, but then decide to keep it; the 'Private Fantasy' in which the Consumer fantasises about sex with a child and then records those thoughts (either in text or recording) on a digital device; the 'Trawler', who actively collects CSAM from open sources, often along with other types of sexually explicit material; the 'Non-Secure Collector' who actively seeks CSAM both by trawling the internet, exchanging through peer-to-peer networks and engaging with online communities in chatrooms and forums, typically employing low levels of security; and the 'Secure Collector' who engages in closed forums and uses encryption to secure the material that is stored (Krone, 2004).

Unlike many other forms of crime, there are low barriers of entry to being a CSAM Consumer (at least at the outset). It does not require much in terms of background knowledge, skill, access or social connections to commence offending as a Consumer. Simply access to a computer or smartphone, time and a little persistence is probably all that is needed. All else that is required, such as contacts with other CSAM Consumers, can follow as an offender becomes more proficient. However, that does not mean that the likelihood of being a CSAM Consumer is evenly spread across society. Indeed, such offenders are by no means a heterogeneous group. A review of existing literature on CSAM offenders by Brown and Bricknell (2018) found that they were most likely to be male, white and aged between 35 and 45. They also found that between 1 per cent and 11 per cent typically had a previous criminal record for a contact sexual offence.

## Content Producers

Content Producers are those that produce CSAM images, or cause such images to be produced. In some cases, the Content Producer will be the person who perpetrates the physical sexual abuse of the child. A study of US offenders who were involved in internet-facilitated commercial sexual exploitation of children, which included CSAM offenders, identified a sample of ten individuals who were selling CSAM they had created (Mitchell et al., 2011). These accounted for half of the cases they found in which offenders were profiteering from the sexual exploitation of children – the other half involved selling sex with a child.

Where the demographic profile is concerned, an analysis of over one million records held on Interpol's International Child Sexual Exploitation (ICSE) database, containing CSAM from 53 countries, found that an offender could be identified in only around a quarter of cases. Analysis of ethnicity revealed 79 per cent as being white, with a further 12 per cent being Hispanic / Latin American (Interpol, 2018). Mitchell et al. (2005) examined internet-related sex crimes against minors and found that those cases involving a family or acquaintance member (43% of which involved CSAM production) were likely to involve an offender who was male (99%), non-Hispanic white (95%), in full-time employment (78%) and aged 40 or older (44%).

## Content Distributors

Content Distributors are those that provide access to CSAM that they may or may not have produced themselves. This may be for profit, or in exchange for other CSAM. Presented here as a unique group, they have a significant overlap with Consumers, Content Producers and Service Providers, each of whom may also be Content Distributors. But they also exist as a discrete group, acting as retailers, profiting from the sale of CSAM produced by others. Across 66 cases involving some form of CSAM possession, Mitchell et al. (2011) found that six (9%) were selling CSAM that had been produced by others. They highlighted the example of one 32-year-old male offender who had established a for-profit CSAM website on which he was supplying images produced by others, with police finding over 6,000 images on his computers.

## Service Providers

Sandwiched between the Content Producers and the Consumers are the Service Providers who provide the technical wizardry that allows the content to reach those that view it. These come in many forms, including, at the most basic level, public websites that host CSAM content. Such websites are often hosted by ISPs who are unaware that such content is being housed on their servers, although in other cases dedicated servers may be used to host CSAM with the full knowledge of those managing the infrastructure.

Service Providers provide access to a wide range of web applications for legitimate purposes, often at no cost to the Consumer. Their focus is often on creating demand for their services through constant innovation, typically designed to facilitate communication – whether that be through sharing messages, images, other types of files, geolocation information etc. This is intended to drive internet traffic to their sites, which is then analysed to produce tailored advertising. Indeed, there are now numerous social media platforms with well over a billion active users, including Facebook, Instagram, YouTube, WhatsApp and WeChat[2]. While most of their content will be for legitimate use, within the terms and conditions of use, a small proportion will include CSAM, as well as other abhorrent material[3].

Both Content Producers, Content Distributors and Consumers are reliant on Service Providers to make the necessary infrastructure available that allows CSAM to be efficiently distributed. However, Service Providers may also be reliant on Content Producers and Consumers when they are also Content Distributors, with business models that rely (at least in part) on the distribution of CSAM. This is particularly the case when these illicit Service Providers operate on the darknet, operating infrastructure that allows CSAM to be sold for profit (whether that be through websites with paywalls or premium hosting sites that charge customers to access stored content). These rely on a steady stream of new content from Content Producers to keep Consumers returning to their sites. This may or (more often) may not be for profit, with darknet transactions made on the basis of mutual exchange, using closed, invitation-only user groups and forums, or peer-to-peer networks. Regardless of the method of sharing, Service Providers remain essential to creating the environment in which Content Producers and Consumers come together.

One of the key features of illicit Service Providers who knowingly operate in the CSAM infrastructure market (as distinguished from legitimate Service Providers who unwittingly provide the infrastructure) is their ability to constantly innovate to avoid detection by law enforcement agencies and web crawlers that seek to identify and block their content. In its 2019 annual report, the Internet Watch Foundation reported identifying a type of website that was publicly available on the open-net that displayed legitimate content to the casual user. However, if a Consumer followed a series of URL links in a sequential order (collecting cookies in the correct order along the way), the website would reveal CSAM (Internet Watch Foundation, 2019). This is intended to foil web crawlers searching for CSAM that would subsequently be removed and to avoid detection by law enforcement agencies.

This innovation demonstrates a process of offending co-evolution, in which offenders respond to changing environmental circumstances by altering their modi operandi for offending (Ekblom, 1997; 2012a; 2012b). In turn, changes will be made in the environment by legitimate Service Providers, NGOs or law enforcement to address the evolving nature of the offence risks. And so, the co-evolution process continues. Where CSAM is concerned, there have been various innovations by offenders to circumvent attempts to block / remove images. For example, the requirement for offenders to share new CSAM before they are given access to private, password-protected image-sharing forums is a response to concerns that the group could be infiltrated by law enforcement (Awais et al., 2012). Similarly, the move of some CSAM content from the open-net to the darknet, with its greater anonymity, is another Service Provider countermove designed to avoid detection by law enforcement authorities. It is therefore reasonable to assume that any attempt to reduce access to CSAM will be met by Service Provider countermoves to make it available.

## Victims / Survivors

Victims / Survivors in the CSAM ecosystem consist of children and young people who are either subject to physical sexual abuse by a perpetrator that is filmed / photographed, or who are coerced into self-producing CSAM by a Content Producer. In either case, intimate images of the Victim / Survivor, often depicting them being abused, are made available for others to consume. On creation, the images are no longer in the control of the Victim / Survivor.

There are multiple points of victimisation in CSAM offences. The point at which the images are created marks the point of the physical crime scene, but each time an image is shared, stored or viewed it creates a virtual crime scene, with its own unique circumstances, marked by the confluence in time of a Consumer, with images of the Victim / Survivor, who exists in both virtual and physical space simultaneously. Therefore, once created, images can generate victimisation regardless of any action taken by the Victim / Survivor. Every time those images are viewed they violate the rights of the children depicted (Royal Commission into Institutional Responses to Child Sexual Abuse, 2017a). Indeed, the Victim / Survivor may age into adulthood and yet remain as a child in the CSAM ecosystem. In this sense, child Victims / Survivors are essential for the creation of CSAM but not necessary for its maintenance. Once the maximum quantity of images has been extracted from a Victim / Survivor, they can be physically discarded from the ecosystem and yet remain virtually in perpetuity to be victimised through the consumption by an unlimited number of unknown perpetrators. In a sense, the physical Victims / Survivors then become surplus by-products of CSAM creation.

The exception to this general proposition is found in the livestreaming of CSAM, where images are seldom saved for later use. There is an increasing trend towards the use of livestreaming services in which off-the-shelf encrypted video-streaming services are used to make contact between a perpetrator and victim, with sexually explicit acts being performed, often directed by the viewer. The live nature of this CSAM can mean that no trace of the activity is stored once the video-streaming session ends (Acar, 2017).

Livestreaming of CSAM can involve multiple paying clients tuning in simultaneously to watch the abuse of a child. It can also involve private sessions with one client, who may direct the child to perform sexual acts or instruct a third-party offender to sexually abuse the child. In this sense, livestreaming of CSAM represents electronic child sexual slavery that relies on the contemporaneous availability of child Victims / Survivors, with the generated CSAM lasting only as long as the current session. It represents a unique corner of the ecosystem in which the Content Producer, Consumer and Victim / Survivor interact to generate temporary CSAM which is not able to be shared later with other Consumers, or to be watched again by the original Consumer. That is, unless they choose to record the session, in which case they create evidence of the livestreaming event which could be used by law enforcement authorities.

As such, the proliferation of livestreaming as a means of satisfying demand for CSAM is dependent on the availability of sufficient children at any given time, which places a natural limit on the extent to which this method can be applied. That is assuming the child sexual abuse is in fact broadcast live. There are reported to be instances where facilitators have placed a webcam in front of a screen showing a previous recording of a livestreamed CSAM event, thereby extracting additional value from the original victimisation[4].

Where the profile of CSAM Victims / Survivors is concerned, ECPAT International (2018) noted that, while significant effort has been devoted to understanding offenders, relatively little attention has been paid to Victims / Survivors. However, from that which is available, it is possible to piece together a general demographic profile. Across all images assessed by the Internet Watch Foundation (2021), 64 per cent of children were assessed as being 11–13 years old, 32 per cent were 10 years or younger and 3 per cent were assessed as 14–15 years old. One per cent were aged 2 years or younger. The Canadian Centre for Child Protection (2016) found that almost 50 per cent of the 46,859 children in images and videos it analysed were estimated to be under 8 years old. A further 29 per cent were aged between 8 and 11 years. Analysis of the International Child Sexual Exploitation Image Database found the mean age of Victims / Survivors was 11 years (Quayle et al., 2018).

However, there is evidence to suggest that the age profile varies according to the way in which material is created (content creation is discussed in more detail in the next chapter). Self-produced CSAM would appear to have an older age profile. Analysis of over 66,000 self-produced CSAM images by the Internet Watch Foundation (2021) found that 84 per cent were produced by 11–13 year olds. Quayle et al. (2018) found that the mean age of children in self-produced coercively created images was 14 years. They also found that self-produced images created since 2010 accounted for more than 40 per cent of the images they examined in each year (from 2006 to 2015) and that they were increasingly likely to be created in coercive circumstances. A report on online sexual coercion and extortion by Europol's (2017) European Cybercrime Centre suggested that there may be an increase in self-produced material being coerced from young people during teen years due to increased unsupervised access to the internet, combined with a failure to perceive risk, given their developmental stage. Indeed, a study of Dutch adolescents found that receiving an online sexual request was more likely to be considered bothersome when the young person was female and when they demonstrated a high level of online disinhibition, low self-control and had low psychological well-being (Kerstens & Stol, 2014).

The severity of the abuse experienced by children would appear to vary by age, with the youngest children likely to experience the most severe abuse. The Canadian Centre for Child Protection (2016) found that 60 per cent of toddlers in their sample were subject to explicit sexual activity / assaults and extreme sexual assaults, compared with 44 per cent of 12–17 year olds. Similarly, the Internet Watch Foundation (2021) found that 81 per cent of imagery showing children aged 0–2 years were classified in the most serious category (showing sexual abuse activity between adults and children, including rape or sexual torture). By contrast, the proportion of imagery falling into this category for 11–13-year-olds, 14–15-year-olds and 16–17-year-olds was 10 per cent, 15 per cent and 24 per cent respectively.

There is general agreement that images of females are more common than males (Canadian Centre for Child Protection, 2016; May-Chahal et al., 2018; Quayle et al., 2018; Seto et al., 2018). Estimates of the proportion that are female range from 62 per cent (Seto et al., 2018) to 80 per cent (Canadian Centre for Child Protection, 2016). In relation to self-produced images, a review of 1,428 reports of sextortion of children made to NCMEC (n.d.) in 2013–2016, through the CyberTipline, found that 78 per cent of cases involved females. The Internet Watch Foundation (2021) found that 95 per cent of self-produced CSAM involved females.

There would also appear to be a preference for White / Caucasian children over other ethnic backgrounds, although this could be a function of where resources are available to report cases, rather than indicative of global demand. Estimates of the proportion that are White / Caucasian can range from 79 per cent to 93 per cent (We Protect Global Alliance, 2019; Quayle et al., 2018). Examining a UK database of CSAM, Quayle and Jones (2011) estimated that the odds of the abuse image being of White versus non-White were about 10 to 1. They also found that images of White and Asian males were more likely to be of children who were prepubescent and very young, compared with images of females (Quayle & Jones, 2011).

## Other 'organisms' operating in the CSAM ecosystem

Consumers, Content Producers, Content Distributors, Service Providers and Victims / Survivors are not the only organisms operating in the CSAM ecosystem, because the ecosystem is not sealed off from other parts of the internet. For example, members of the public browsing the internet may inadvertently come across CSAM, although, as described later, significant effort is being devoted to prevent this from happening. As noted, there are also NGOs and law enforcement agencies that are devoted to seeking out CSAM and removing it from the internet. In addition, there are legitimate businesses and organisations that make up the internet (e.g. ISPs, ESPs, software developers and financial services companies) who invest time and resources to eliminate CSAM. From a societal perspective, these particular 'organisms' play a hygiene role, by seeking out and removing CSAM. From a CSAM ecosystem perspective, they play a negative, predator role within the system by removing new material as it is identified. From the CSAM organisms' (Consumers, Content Producers, Content Distributors and Service Providers) perspective, this is not a risk-free environment, with what they may consider as multiple predators seeking to remove them from the ecosystem.

## How are communities formed in the CSAM ecosystem and how do their members interact with one another?

The internet allows communities to be formed in the CSAM ecosystem in a variety of ways. Davidson and Gottschalk (2011) identified 17 internet characteristics that support CSAM production and distribution. Among the most salient for this discussion include the internet's *universality* (its widespread availability and ability to shrink geographic distance); *network externalities* (the more users that participate online, the more powerful the internet becomes); and its dynamic social network (the ability for more and more people to meet online but also to be replaced by other new people).

Online communities of interest allow Content Producers, Content Distributors and Consumers to share information on where to find CSAM content and to share content with each other. Krone and Smith (2017) explored the role of networks in CSAM and contact offending, finding a significant relationship between involvement in a CSAM network and contact offending. Contact offending was significantly associated with passive participation in a network, providing images to others and producing CSAM images. An analysis of discussions in forums on the darknet found that the most frequent topics were associated with identifying the best social media sites on which to engage with children (33%). Other frequent topics were associated with technical discussions of the best tools and applications to use, including secure tooling (15%) and content storage and exchange (13%) (We Protect Global Alliance, 2021).

This online networking not only serves an instrumental function in providing information on where to find CSAM and how to operate securely, it also plays an important psychological role in helping paedophiles and other perpetrators operating in the CSAM ecosystem. For some, online engagement establishes a sense of community with other like-minded individuals (O'Halloran & Quayle, 2010). Treated as taboo in the real world, online forums and groups provide perpetrators with an opportunity to develop an online persona where justifications for child sexual exploitation are created, shared and adopted. Typical justifications have included condemning those who condemn, by transferring the sense of wrongdoing on to those that oppose CSAM; denial of injury to the Victim / Survivor; claiming a benefit to the Victim / Survivor as a result of an adult having sex with a child;

denial of victim, with the child conceived as deliberately attracting sexual attention from an adult; appealing to higher loyalties, in which those with pro-paedophile views consider that they are supporting a higher cause, such as the sexual rights of children; and basking in reflected glory, in which links are made with positive historical figures who engaged in child sex (O'Halloran & Quayle, 2010).

Beyond providing a means of sharing justifications, these online networks can help CSAM perpetrators to grow in status, with those that are able to post new material sometimes being provided with special rights to enter subforums that are only intended for those with a certain level of recognition (van der Bruggen & Blokland, 2020).

Forums can also help in the enculturation of norms that support a deviant subculture, separate and different to the mainstream culture. These norms help to shape the way in which their members view CSAM and sexual activity with children more broadly (Holt et al., 2010). This deviant subculture not only shares common interests, but also a common language to describe CSAM activity. They also share knowledge of how to find CSAM and how to avoid detection (Jenkins, 2001). As such, forums and groups help to sustain and support organisms in the CSAM ecosystem by creating communities that cannot exist so easily in the real world.

## Summing up the CSAM ecosystem

At the beginning of this chapter, an ecosystem was defined as *'a group (or community) of organisms that interact with each other and also interact with their environment'*. In the context of CSAM, the 'organisms' that interact are the Consumers of CSAM, the Content Producers, Content Distributors and the Service Providers. Victims / Survivors are necessary for the CSAM ecosystem to function, yet at the same time are largely disposable, once their abuse yields no further new material. Others interact with these key groups, typically attempting to impede the operation of the CSAM ecosystem.

The CSAM ecosystem that functions on the open-net is largely parasitical in nature in that it functions within an existing legitimate internet infrastructure. Arguably, it is the proliferation of easy-to-use software applications that helps to explain the apparent increase in CSAM. Unlike earlier generations of the internet that relied on a modicum of knowledge and skill to create CSAM websites, these applications typically require no technical ability to store, share and view CSAM. The financial system is also important in the CSAM ecosystem for those cases involving the sale of CSAM. However, this is only relevant in a minority of cases and, even then, there are sometimes alternatives to making transactions through the regulated financial system, such as through stored value cards, or by using virtual currencies.

The next chapter examines how images are created and find their way into the CSAM ecosystem. Indeed, the intention is to unpack how the ecosystem operates from start to finish to begin to identify particular points of intervention.

## Notes

1 Blockchains are just one form of distributed ledger technology that can be used for cryptocurrency purposes. Other, more flexible versions of distributed ledger technology are being developed and will no doubt pose their own challenges in future. For a description of the difference between blockchain technology and distributed ledger technology see https://medium.com/brandlitic/difference-between-distributed-ledger-and-blockch ain-vs-dlt-7969f3837ded

2 According to a report by Smart Insights – www.smartinsights.com/social-media-market ing/social-media-strategy/new-global-social-media-research/

3 Following the shootings at two Christchurch mosques in March 2019 by an Australian man, Brenton Tarrant, which were livestreamed on Facebook, there were concerns that social media companies were not doing enough to remove abhorrent material from their sites in a timely manner. This led to a voluntary code being introduced by social media companies, requiring them to rapidly remove material considered to be offensive to society as soon as they became aware of the material. In Australia, the Criminal Code Amendment (Sharing of Abhorrent Violent Material) Act 2019 received Royal Assent in April 2019, allowing fines to be imposed on a social media company if it failed to act quickly to remove abhorrent material (including images of rape, which, by definition, would include CSAM).

4 This information was received from a police officer who had worked on child protection operations in the Philippines, where livestreaming is a common method of CSAM.

## References

Acar, K.V. (2017). Webcam child prostitution: An exploration of current and futuristic methods of detection. *International Journal of Cyber Criminology* 11(1), 98–109. http:// dx.doi.org/10.5281/zenodo.802941

Awais, R., Greenwood, P., Walkerdine, J., Baron, A. & Rayson, P. (2012). Technological solutions to offending. In E. Quayle & K.M. Ribisl (Eds) *Understanding and preventing online sexual exploitation of children* (pp.228–243). Routledge.

Bronfenbrenner, U. (1979). *Ecology of human development: Experiments by nature and design.* Harvard University Press.

Brown, R. & Bricknell, S. (2018). *What is the profile of child exploitation material offenders?* Trends & issues in crime and criminal justice 564. Australian Institute of Criminology. https://aic.gov.au/publications/tandi/tandi564

Brown, R., Napier, S. & Smith, R.G. (2020). *Australians who view livestreaming of child sexual abuse: An analysis of financial transactions.* Trends and issues in crime and criminal justice 589. Australian Institute of Criminology. www.aic.gov.au/publications/tandi/tandi589

Canadian Centre for Child Protection (2016). *Child sexual abuse images on the internet: A Cybertip.ca Analysis.* Canadian Centre for Child Protection. www.protectchildren.ca/en/ resources-research/child-sexual-abuse-images-report/

Davidson, J. & Gottschalk, P. (2011). Characteristics of the Internet for criminal child sexual abuse by online groomers. *Criminal Justice Studies* 24(1), 23–36. https://doi.org/10.1080/ 1478601X.2011.544188

Deutsche Welle (2016, 7 December) Internet capable 'spy' toys put data protection and child safety at risk. *Deutsche Welle.* www.dw.com/en/internet-capable-spy-toys-put-data-pro tection-and-child-safety-at-risk/a-36674091

ECPAT International (2018). *Trends in online child sexual abuse material*. ECPAT International. www.ecpat.org/wp-content/uploads/2018/07/ECPAT-International-Report-Trends-in-Online-Child-Sexual-Abuse-Material-2018.pdf

Ekblom, P. (1997). Gearing up against crime: A dynamic framework to help designers keep up with the adaptive criminal in a changing world. *International Journal of Risk, Security and Crime Prevention* 2(4), 249–265. www.researchgate.net/profile/Paul-Ekblom/publication/291456106_Gearing_up_against_crime_A_dynamic_framework_to_help_designers_keep_up_with_the_adaptive_criminal_in_a_changing_world/links/56b4b1ab08ae83713174a339/Gearing-up-against-crime-A-dynamic-framework-to-help-designers-keep-up-with-the-adaptive-criminal-in-a-changing-world.pdf

Ekblom, P. (2012a). The private sector and designing products against crime. In B.C. Welsh & D.P. Farrington (Eds.), *The Oxford handbook of crime prevention* (pp.384–403). Oxford University Press.

Ekblom, P. (2012b). Happy returns: ideas brought back from situational crime prevention's exploration of design against crime. In G. Farrell & N. Tilley (Eds.), *The reasoning criminologist: Essays in honour of Ronald V. Clarke* (pp.52–63). Crime Science Series. Willan Publishing.

Europol (2017). *Online sexual coercion and extortion as a form of crime affecting children: Law enforcement perspective*. Europol. www.europol.europa.eu/publications-documents/online-sexual-coercion-and-extortion-form-of-crime-affecting-children-law-enforcement-perspective

Hanson, E. (2019). 'Losing track of morality': understanding online forces and dynamics conducive to child sexual exploitation. In J Pearce (Ed.), *Child sexual exploitation: Why theory matters* (pp.87–117). Policy Press.

Holt, T.J., Blevins, K.R. & Burkert, N. (2010). Considering the Pedophile Subculture Online. *Sexual Abuse: A Journal of Research and Treatment* 22(1), 3–24. https://doi.org/10.1177/1079063209344979

Independent Inquiry into Child Sexual Abuse (2020). *The internet: Investigation report*. www.iicsa.org.uk/publications/investigation/internet

Internet Watch Foundation (2019). *Once upon a year: The Internet Watch Foundation annual report 2018*. Internet Watch Foundation. www.iwf.org.uk/sites/default/files/reports/2019-04/Once%20upon%20a%20year%20-%20IWF%20Annual%20Report%202018.pdf

Internet Watch Foundation (2021). *Face the facts: The annual report 2020*. Internet Watch Foundation. https://annualreport2020.iwf.org.uk/

Interpol (2018). *Towards a global indicator on unidentified victims in child sexual exploitation material: Summary Report*. Interpol. www.interpol.int/en/content/download/9363/file/Summary%20-%20Towards%20a%20Global%20Indicator%20on%20Unidentified%20Victims%20in%20Child%20Sexual%20Exploitation%20Material.%20February%202018.pdf

Jenkins, P. (2001). *Beyond tolerance: Child pornography on the internet*. New York University Press.

Kerstens, J. & Stol, W. (2014). Receiving online sexual requests and producing online sexual images: The multifaceted and dialogic nature of adolescents' online sexual interactions. *Journal of Psychosocial Research on Cyberspace* 8(1), article 8. http://dx.doi.org/10.5817/CP2014-1-8

Kristof, N. (2020, 4 December). The children of Pornhub: Why does Canada allow this company to profit off videos of exploitation and assault? *New York Times*. www.nytimes.com/2020/12/04/opinion/sunday/pornhub-rape-trafficking.html

Krone, T. (2004). *A Typology of Online Child Pornography Offending.* Trends and issues in crime and criminal justice 279. Australian Institute of Criminology. www.aic.gov.au/publicati ons/tandi/tandi279

Krone, T. & Smith, R. G. (2017). *Trajectories in online child sexual exploitation offending in Australia.* Trends and issues in crime and criminal justice 524. Australian Institute of Criminology. www.aic.gov.au/publications/tandi/tandi524

Martin, J. & Alaggia, R. (2013). Sexual abuse images in cyberspace: Expanding the ecology of the child. *Journal of Child Sexual Abuse* 22, 398–415. https://doi.org/10.1080/10538 712.2013.781091

May-Chahal, C., Palmer, E., Dodds, S. & Milan, S. (2018). *Rapid Evidence Assessment: Characteristics and vulnerabilities of victims of online-facilitated child sexual abuse and exploitation.* Independent Inquiry into Child Sexual Abuse. file://aicfs/downloads/rick.brown/Downloads/rapid-evidence-assessment-characteristics-vulnerabilities-victims-online-facilitated-child-sexual-abuse-exploitation-%20(2).pdf

Mitchell, K.J., Finkelhor, D. & Wolak, J. (2005). The internet and family and acquaintance sexual abuse. *Child Maltreatment* 10(1), 49–60.

Mitchell K.J., Jones, L.M., Finkelhor, D. & Wolak, J. (2011). Internet-facilitated commercial sexual exploitation of children: Findings from a nationally representative sample of law enforcement agencies in the United States. *Sexual Abuse*, 23(1), 43–71.

National Centre for Missing and Exploited Children (NCMEC) (n.d.). *The issues of Sextortion.* www.missingkids.com/theissues/sextortion

O'Halloran, E. & Quayle, E. (2010). A content analysis of a 'boy love' support forum: Revisiting Durkin and Bryant. *Journal of Sexual Aggression* 6(1), 71–85. https://doi.org/10.1080/13552600903395319

Quayle, E. & Jones, T. (2011). Sexualised imaged of children on the internet. *Sexual Abuse* 23(1), 7–21. https://doi.org/10.1177/1079063210392596

Quayle, E., Jonsson, L.S., Cooper, K., Traynor, J. & Svedin, C.G. (2018). Children in identified sexual images – Who are they? Self and non-self-taken images in the International Child Sexual Exploitation Image Database 2006-2015. *Child Abuse Review* 27, 223–238. https://doi.org/10.1002/car.2507

Royal Commission into Institutional Responses to Child Sexual Abuse (2017a). *Final Report: Volume 2, Nature and cause.* Commonwealth of Australia. www.childabuseroyalcom mission.gov.au/sites/default/files/final_report_-_volume_2_nature_and_cause.pdf

Salter, M. & Hanson, E. (2021). 'I need you all to understand how pervasive this issue is': User efforts to regulate child sexual offending on social media. In J. Baily, A. Flynn & N. Henry (Eds.), *The Emerald International Handbook of Technology facilitated Violence and Abuse* (pp.729–748). Emerald Publishing.

Seto, M.C., Buckman, C., Dwyer, R.G. & Quayle, E. (2018). *Production and Active Trading of Child Sexual Exploitation Images Depicting Identified Victims.* National Centre for Missing and Exploited Children. www.missingkids.com/content/dam/missingkids/pdfs/ncmec-analysis/Production%20and%20Active%20Trading%20of%20CSAM_ExecutiveSumm ary.pdf

Tait, A. (2016, 6 December). Are smart toys spying on children? *New Statesman.* www.newst atesman.com/science-tech/privacy/2016/12/are-smart-toys-spying-children-0

Terre des Hommes (2014). *Webcam child sex tourism: Becoming Sweetie: A novel approach to stopping the global rise of webcam child sex tourism.* Terre des Hommes. www.terredeshom mes.org/wp-content/uploads/2013/11/Webcam-child-sex-tourism-terre-des-hom mes-NL-nov-2013.pdf van der Bruggen, M. & Blokland, A. (2020). A crime script analysis of child sexual exploitation material fora on the darknet. *Sexual Abuse* 33(8), 950–974. https://doi.org/10.1177/1079063220981063

We Protect Global Alliance (2019). *Global threat assessment 2019: Working together to end the sexual exploitation of children online.* We Protect Global Alliance. www.weprotect.org/s/FINAL-Global-Threat-Assessment.pdf

We Protect Global Alliance (2021). *Global threat assessment 2021: Working together to end the sexual exploitation of children online.* We Protect Global Alliance. www.weprotect.org/global-threat-assessment-21/#report

Wortley, R. (2012). Situational prevention of child abuse in the new technologies. In E. Quayle & K.M. Ribisl (Eds.), *Understanding and preventing online sexual exploitation of children* (pp. 188–213). Routledge.

Wortley, R. & Smallbone, S. (2012). *Internet Child Pornography: Causes, Investigation and Prevention.* Praeger.

Yallop, C., Bernard, J.R.L., Blair, D., Butler, S., Delbridge, A., Peters, P. & Witton, N. (2005). *Macquarie Dictionary.* Fourth Edition. The Macquarie Library, Macquarie University.

# 3

# HOW IS CSAM PRODUCED?

## Introduction

A CSAM ecosystem can only exist if it has material to share in the first instance. This chapter explores the ways in which CSAM is created and enters the ecosystem at the outset. Here, we examine four different ways in which CSAM is created. First, we consider what we most commonly conceive of as CSAM creation – that involving perpetrators creating images of children. Next, we examine the growing problem of self-produced material, which will often (although not exclusively) involve perpetrators grooming[1] children to provide the material. A third type of material creation is through livestreaming of CSAM, whose creation is different from perpetrator and self-produced material in that it can be interactive with the viewer, transitory (not automatically saved) and either perpetrator or self-produced (although in the latter case it may involve a third-party facilitator who arranges the transaction). The fourth method of creation is through animation – often computer generated – which does not involve a direct physical victim. Importantly, these are not ideal types. They represent the most common methods by which CSAM is created and are sufficiently distinct to warrant separate descriptions. But they do overlap. For example, self-produced material may be created at the instigation of a perpetrator in the first instance. And perpetrators may pay for access to children online, involving livestreaming technology. These overlaps serve to demonstrate the multifaceted nature of the offence.

## Perpetrator-created CSAM

Chapter 2 introduced Content Producers – the perpetrators that create CSAM in the first instance. The material generated by Content Producers still probably accounts for the clear majority of CSAM. Understanding how Content Producers

DOI: 10.4324/9781003327264-4

are responsible for 'perpetrator-created CSAM' is best achieved by describing the known range of circumstances in which the material is created, focusing on the actions taken by the perpetrator to produce CSAM.

## Perpetrator exploits child in their care

This is a common means by which perpetrator created CSAM is generated and will depend on the opportunities that are available to the Content Producer. Typical scenarios involve family members, or others with access to children in their daily lives. Mitchell et al. (2005) found that approximately half of the internet-related sex crimes against minors they examined, using a national survey of law enforcement agencies in the USA, involved family members or close acquaintances. CSAM production was involved in 61 per cent of the cases that had a family-related victim and 49 per cent of the cases with an acquaintance-related victim.

Parents have consistently been shown to account for high proportions of CSAM production (Salter, 2013; Canadian Centre for Child Protection, 2017; Gewirtz-Meydan et al., 2018; Salter et al., 2021). Parental figures involved in CSAM production can often include biological fathers, stepfathers, foster fathers, partners of the child's mother and biological mothers. When biological mothers are involved in CSAM production, it is frequently with a male co-offender (Salter et al., 2021). A rapid review of the evidence associated with online child sexual victimisation found that in a quarter of reported cases and a third of CSAM scraped from online, the perpetrator was a family member (May-Chahal & Kelly, 2020).

Other perpetrators in this group can include a non-parent family member, or other caregiver, but may also include casual, infrequent caregiving, such as when a child is sexually abused by a parent of a friend, when having a sleepover at the friend's home (Canadian Centre for Child Protection, 2017). In other cases, the perpetrator may be an employee of an institution (school, out-of-home care facility etc.) that has been given responsibility for the care of a child (Royal Commission into Institutional Responses to Child Sexual Abuse, 2017a). Regardless of who the caregiver is, the CSAM generation will involve being in a situation where it becomes possible to create such material.

## Perpetrator exploits child with whom they are in a relationship

A child may create material of another child with whom they are in a relationship. This could be consensual, with the child Content Producer creating sexual images while engaging in intimate behaviour with another child (Lim et al., 2016; SWGFL / UK Safer Internet Centre et al., 2017). Images may also be produced as a result of coercive or threatening behaviour by the perpetrator, which forces the child victim to participate. Alternatively, non-consensual images may be created during sexual encounters, by for example, using hidden mobile phones or laptop webcams.

### Perpetrator predates on children not in their care

There are a variety of means by which a stranger may be able to create CSAM of a child that is not in their care. For example, this might involve the abduction of a child, who is subsequently sexually abused, with CSAM being created in the process. In these cases, the abducted child may be released, trafficked to others or murdered. Rose Kalemba represents just one example of such cases. In 2009, when aged 14, Rose was seized by a man on a street in a small town in Ohio, USA and bundled into a car driven by a second offender. She was taken to a house and raped repeatedly over the course of a night, parts of which were filmed by a third offender. The videos found their way on to the popular porn site, Pornhub, with titles such as *'teen crying and getting slapped around'* and *'teen getting destroyed'*. In time, these videos were found by boys from her school, resulting in her not only being retraumatised, but humiliated and shunned by her friends (Mohan, 2020).

CSAM may also be created as part of an organised crime ring, who arrange for the supply of children for sexual abuse (Salter, 2013; Canadian Centre for Child Protection, 2017). Children may be recruited through a variety of means (e.g. school friends, agents targeting homeless children on the street, gang members) into sexual exploitation including prostitution and CSAM production in return for financial gain for themselves or their families (Estes & Weiner, 2002). The CSAM that is produced is then sold to others.

There may also be other circumstances in which a Content Producer takes an opportunity to create CSAM by taking photos of children in public areas – perhaps at swimming pools, or at the beach. These images may also involve physical sexual abuse if the perpetrator has the opportunity to be alone with the child – perhaps in public toilets.

Hidden cameras may also be used to create images without the knowledge of Victims. For example, this might include the placement of cameras in a school's sports changing rooms. 'Upskirting' (Powell, 2010), in which cameras are placed in such a way as to capture images of a child's underwear as they pass over the camera may also be used to create CSAM. This form of CSAM may also be created by the perpetrator holding a camera at an angle that will capture the desired image – perhaps while sitting opposite a child on public transport.

### Perpetrator pays for access to a child

In some cases, a perpetrator will be willing to pay for access to a child in physical space. This may involve paying a third-party facilitator for access to a child who has been abducted. The facilitator may also provide access to a child who has been paid to meet with the Content Producer. Ramiro et al. (2019) provide examples in which Filipino children, in conditions of poverty and parental neglect, agree to meet a stranger (often a foreigner) to create CSAM in return for payment.

## Self-produced CSAM

Self-produced CSAM needs to be distinguished from other forms of sexting. Sexting is the sending and / or receiving of nude or sexual images or text messages (Henry et al., 2019)[2]. Often consensual between two individuals in a relationship, sexting can provide a safe way to explore sexuality, with nude images sent voluntarily. Young people are increasingly engaging in sexting, often at an early stage in a relationship. However, in some jurisdictions, this can result in them being prosecuted for using a carriage service to share or possess an indecent image, with almost 1,500 young people being prosecuted over the decade to June 2016 in Queensland, Australia alone (Hunt, 2017). Sexting can also lead to negative unintended consequences when images meant for the private consumption by another are shared more widely and subsequently find their way on to the internet. When such images involve a young person aged under 18 years, they are, by definition, classed as CSAM.

Beyond consensual sexting, self-produced CSAM can involve perpetrators obtaining sexual images of children that have been created by the Victims / Survivors themselves. A survey of Victims / Survivors of sextortion found that 67 per cent felt pressured, tricked, threatened or forced to provide the images, even though in more than two-thirds of cases the Victim / Survivor was in a relationship with the perpetrator. Threats made by the perpetrators included posting the sexual image of the Victim / Survivor online (65%), sending or showing the image to a friend or acquaintance (64%), sending the sexual image to the Victim's / Survivor's family (47%), tagging or including the Victim's / Survivor's name with a posted image (41%), creating fake accounts of sexual images of the Victim / Survivor (26%) or posting other personal information about the Victim / Survivor along with the image (14%) (Wolak et al., 2018). However, overt persuasion on the part of the perpetrator (such as making direct demands) may be more common than extortion as a method for gaining victim compliance (Chiang & Grant, 2018).

In some cases, the Victim / Survivor will know the person to whom they provide the image in the physical world. Indeed, a survey of self-reported victimisation involving coerced self-produced imagery found that 70 per cent of child Victims were in a romantic relationship with the perpetrator when they first gave the sexual image to the perpetrator (Wolak et al., 2018). In other cases, the relationship may only exist online. Images may also be provided on the understanding they are being shared with another young person of a similar age, when in fact they have been tricked by an adult posing online as a young person (Jonsson & Svedin, 2012). In a process that has become known as 'capping' Content Producers encourage children to self-produce CSAM which is recorded and then shared with others through online sites (often on the darknet). In some cases this has become competitive, with Content Producers vying to share the most (voluminous or extreme) capping videos (We Protect Global Alliance, 2021).

Social media sites now offer significant opportunities for Content Producers to contact children. For example, a police operation (Operation Arkstone) in Australia in 2020 identified a large group involved in production and sharing of CSAM, some of which was produced through social media forums (Australian Federal Police, 2020). One notable case in the UK related to a male offender who was sentenced in February 2021 to 25 years in jail after pleading guilty to 96 sexual offences against 52 child Victims / Survivors aged 4 to 14 years. These offences, which took place over several years, involved grooming children online to send sexually explicit images and to perform sexual acts via livestreaming applications. Originally identified and reported by Facebook for grooming teenage boys to provide sexually explicit images to him, the police investigation revealed multiple prepaid mobile phone SIM cards found to be associated with different Facebook accounts, each of which revealed new lists of Victims / Survivors.

Two experiments serve to demonstrate how Content Producers search for children online. The first involved a test of four social networking sites in which researchers set up accounts posing as children (Broadhurst & Jayawardena, 2011). The intent was to test a range of conditions to see what factors would entice perpetrators to contact children for sexual purposes. They found that across four profiles set up on three separate social networking platforms, those with public profiles and photographs were more likely to attract attention from perpetrators than those without those features. The researchers noted how one perpetrator used the presence of the photo to flatter the child about their looks. One interesting indirect finding from this study was that one site, whose community members self-policed the site, quickly reported one profile to a moderator when it was discovered one of the fake users set up by the researchers was underage. This perhaps points to an effective approach to guardianship.

The second experiment in 2013 involved Dutch researchers from Terre des Hommes, who posed as a 10-year-old Filipino girl on 19 online chat rooms, using a computer program with a realistic looking 3D avatar. This avatar was codenamed 'Sweetie'. Over a ten-week period, they were contacted by over 20,000 offenders from 71 countries who solicited for livestreamed sex performances (Terre des Hommes, 2014). The Terre des Hommes team subsequently developed an artificial intelligence driven version of Sweetie (2.0) that, unlike the original version, did not require a human operator to interact with CSAM perpetrators and could instead chat directly (Henseler & de Wolf, 2019). This significantly increased the number of perpetrators that could be identified by the program. Analysis of 200 randomly selected cases identified two ways in which children were engaged by perpetrators. One involved an active, goal-directed approach in which sexually explicit questions were asked of children very quickly following first contact. A second approach involved more small talk to build rapport with the child, before moving to sexually explicit requests (Kleijn & Bogaerts, 2019).

Online contact with children by Content Producers is not limited to social media. There have been reports that gaming platforms are becoming increasingly popular as a means of grooming children to self-produce CSAM (We Protect Global Alliance, 2021). In 2017, the Canadian Centre for Child Protection reported that a multiplayer gaming site, Roblox, was being used to target young people, with sexually explicit approaches being made through the site's chat feature (CBC News, 2017). There have been reports that the computer game Fortnite, popular with children, had been used by an offender to contact children, threatening them if they did not comply with their instructions (Jolly, 2019). Bowles and Keller (2019) have reported cases in which other popular online games, including Clash of Clans, Minecraft and League of Legends have been used to groom children to provide self-produced CSAM. Vedelago (2020) also reported police concerns about Fortnite and Minecraft being used to groom children and noted the inherent risks of consoles like Xbox and PlayStation that incorporate text and audio chat functions.

There is evidence that self-produced CSAM is a growing problem. More than a decade ago, Mitchell et al. (2007) reported that 4 per cent of internet-using youth in the USA had received a request to send a sexual picture of themselves in the previous year. A more recent survey of 5,000 young people aged 18–20 years by We Protect Global Alliance (2021) found that, during childhood, 34 per cent had been asked to do something sexually explicit online they were uncomfortable doing. As an indication of the scale of incidents, the Internet Watch Foundation reported that it dealt with 68,000 cases of 'self-generated' child sexual abuse in 2020. This represented a 77 per cent increase on the previous year (Tidy, 2021). Similarly, the NSPCC reported that cases of online grooming in the UK had increased by almost 70 per cent in three years (Freeman-Powell, 2021).

### The role of adult pornography in the CSAM ecosystem and how it facilitates self-creation

There have been concerns about the normalisation of sexting, with young girls and women often asked early in a relationship for nude or sexually explicit photos of themselves. Bluett-Boyd et al. (2013) noted that this can happen within a matter of minutes of meeting someone on a social media / dating site, with conversations quickly moving on to messaging services. They also noted that the ease with which adult pornography is accessed – particularly by boys – creates an environment in which the production of sexualised images becomes normalised and expected in new relationships. Similarly, a report by the UK's Independent Inquiry into Child Sexual Abuse (2020) described how online interactions by young people can quickly result in requests for self-produced nude images.

This highlights another branch of the CSAM ecosystem that should not be overlooked. Young people may be self-producing CSAM because they think that is what is expected of them in an early 21st century relationship – mimicking acts and images found in adult pornography. As Layden (2021) has noted, pornography can be a particularly effective teacher, showing young viewers what they should expect from a sexual encounter. As a result, girls may become accustomed to being expected to perform sexual acts seen in adult pornography (Hilton, 2021). In support of this pattern, a European survey of young people aged 14 to 17 years (involving samples from Bulgaria, Cyprus, England, Italy and Norway) found that watching adult pornography and sending or receiving sexualised images were associated with an increased likelihood of sexual coercion in boys (Stanley et al., 2018). In this sense, CSAM may be encouraged by that aspect of the internet that creates and distributes adult pornography.

## Livestreaming of CSAM

Livestreaming cuts across all other forms of CSAM creation already discussed, in the sense that the methods of creating perpetrator-created CSAM and self-produced CSAM also apply here. While the technology is different, the motivations remain the same. This can involve livestream Consumers paying to watch a live performance in which a child is sexually abused by one or more third parties. These performances may be open to the public, with multiple viewers watching simultaneously. They may also be interactive, with viewers able to curate the performance by requesting sexual acts to be inflicting on the child. In each of these situations, the livestream performances can be considered perpetrator created, in the sense that, while a third party may be performing or overseeing the actual abuse, they will be guided directly by someone viewing the performance, or guided by the kind of activity that those facilitating the performance believe is demanded by Consumers. In addition to public (multi-viewer) performances, similar activities can occur during private performances in which a Consumer pays for exclusive access, which typically involves them directing the performance. Terre des Hommes (2014) has noted that child Victims / Survivors often experience severe psychological trauma and distress as a result of engaging in livestreaming performances.

As well as these perpetrator-created performances, that will involve third party facilitators, livestreaming performances can be self-generated. As far back as 2005, teenagers in the USA were self-generating CSAM, using webcams to perform in front of viewers for payment. One such example was the case of Justin Berry, an underage teenager in the USA who, over a five-year period, built up his own business by performing a range of sexually explicit acts to up to 1,500 subscribers who paid to watch (Huang et al., 2009; Westlake, 2018). More recently, Ramiro et al. (2019) described how, driven by poverty and an environment in which engaging in livestreaming is normalised among peers, children (particularly young girls) from poor neighbourhoods in the Philippines may trawl common dating and social media sites to engage with men willing to send money in return for a livestreaming performance. That may involve the child undressing or revealing parts of their body, through to masturbation. While described here as self-produced, it is still in response to a demand for sexual content from the viewer. Ramiro et al. (2019) note that some girls feel they have some control over this form of CSAM in the sense that the images are ephemeral, not saved for others to view later, and that they involve performances to strangers – foreigners at that. This means they feel the risk of friends and family becoming aware of, or seeing, this CSAM is considered low by the girls and so the financial rewards outweigh the risk of shame and stigma. Added to this, engaging in this form of paid sexual encounter may be considered by the girls to be less harmful (in terms of risk of sexual violence and disease) than meeting a foreigner in person, which is also common in the Philippines (Ramiro et al., 2019).

Livestreaming chatrooms, such as Chatroulette and Omegle, in which users are randomly connected, typically have no login requirements or age verification and seemingly minimal moderation. There have been reports of such sites being used by Content Producers to target children and groom them to provide self-produced CSAM, which is subsequently recorded by the groomer (Tidy, 2021).

## CSAM in computer-generated images, animation and computer games

CSAM need not only involve real participants but can also include imagery that is generated from computer images, animation and computer games. It can also include cartoons, drawings and paintings. While involving no direct child Victim, such material is still considered detrimental as it can desensitise Consumers (and indeed society at large) to what is considered acceptable norms and can lead to real children being sexually abused. The Explanatory Report to the Budapest Convention notes that images that are realistic, but not actually involving a child, are included in the Convention because such images might encourage child abuse (Council of Europe, 2001). Similarly, in Australia, the explanatory memorandum to the Crimes Legislation Amendment (Telecommunications Offences and Other Measures) Bill 2004 (Cth) (Parliament of the Commonwealth of Australia, 2004) raised concerns that representations of children in cartoons and animation may create demand for similar material and ultimately lead to greater abuse of children. There have subsequently been prosecutions for possession of CSAM animations. In 2007, a man was convicted for attempting to import DVDs from Japan that contained animations depicting children under the age of 14 involved in sexual violence (Westlake, 2020).

Al-Alosi (2018) has characterised the arguments for and against the production of CSAM animations. The arguments against such images are that they may reinforce negative views towards children; desensitise viewers towards the seriousness of child sexual abuse; be used to groom children; place a burden on prosecutors to prove whether the depiction was real or created; and incite child sexual abuse. In favour of their production is the argument that they may be used as a substitute for offending against real children; that items should not be criminalised because of the potential for them to be used by child molesters to groom children; and the argument that liberal democracies should not criminalise speech or conduct without empirical proof that they would cause direct harm (Al-Alosi, 2018).

### Computer-generated images

CSAM can also be generated from existing non-CSAM images. This has included the creation of morphed images in which a child's head is copied on to an adult's body, or where an image of an adult is aged-down so that it appears to be a child (Eneman, 2005; Gallagher, 2019). Other examples might include a photograph of a child in a swimsuit, where the clothing is digitally removed, or where the separate images are combined – for example superimposing a child's hand on to an adult's penis (Krone, 2004). Photorealistic images that are wholly computer generated have also been used to produce CSAM (Al-Alosi, 2018). Computer-generated CSAM was reported to account for 2 per cent of all CSAM seized by the Irish Gardaí in 2018 and was considered to be a growing problem (Gallagher, 2019).

## Computer games

Computer games are not only used to groom children to self-produce CSAM but can also be designed to include depictions of child sexual abuse as part of the game play. In 2011, the Nintendo-created game, Dead or Alive Dimensions, a manga cartoon-style combat game, was removed from sale in Sweden when it was discovered that three of its characters (described as being under 18 years) could be depicted in pornographic poses (White, 2011). The virtual reality world, Second Life, has previously been investigated for sharing both virtual and actual CSAM (BBC, 2007). Acting out CSAM in Second Life has also previously been reported as common, with users participating in 'age-play' in which adults choose child avatars and subsequently have sex with adult avatars (Meek-Prieto, 2007).

## Cartoons and animation

Depictions in manga (comic books and graphic novels) and anime (cartoon animations), both originating from Japan, can include sexualised images of children (Al-Alosi, 2018). This has led to calls for tighter control on the availability of such material (MacLennan, 2020).

## Summing up the ways in which CSAM is created

This discussion highlights the complexities associated with CSAM creation, which begin to explain why it may be difficult to address. Rather than viewing CSAM as a single problem, it needs to be understood as a series of separate, if related, problems that each describe methods by which CSAM may enter the ecosystem. These problems result from perpetrators predating on children they know (who may be in their care, or with whom they are in a relationship), or finding ways to access children (whether that be by procuring access to a child from a third party, abducting a child or taking opportunities to attack children in vulnerable locations). Perpetrators are also finding ways to extract sexually explicit imagery from children they engage with online and whom they may never physically meet. This may initially be through encouragement or cajoling, but can later lead to bribery and extortion. Two additional variants to the scenarios noted above, each of which relate to the creation of sexual imagery involving child Victims / Survivors that is subsequently shared online, includes livestreaming where no recordings are kept and cartoons, animation and computer-generated material, where images can be created without the need for child Victims / Survivors.

Each of these means of creation (apart from livestreaming) potentially have a similar end – CSAM created in one place and time that is subsequently made available anywhere in cyberspace for anyone to view at any point in the future. So, while the CSAM ecosystem relies on material being available and indeed arguably requires a constant flow of *new* material to keep viewers excited, it can flow into the ecosystem from many different sources. Tackling the inflow of CSAM will therefore require strategies that prevent material from reaching the ecosystem from multiple sources. This highlights one of the reasons why the CSAM ecosystem is resilient to change, with intervention being required on multiple fronts to prevent new material accessing the system.

### Understanding how the ecosystem facilitates the creation of CSAM

Now that the range of ways in which CSAM can be created has been examined, we can begin to explore how the CSAM ecosystem facilitates the creation of such material.

The focus of attention here is on how online applications facilitate the creation of CSAM. Perhaps the most important role relates to the provision of file storage applications that allow users to store their documents, photographs and videos for free on the cloud. These applications can be beneficial to both perpetrator-produced and self-produced CSAM. While one could argue that CSAM would still be created, regardless of whether cloud storage was available, it provides a means by which such material might be saved with a semblance of security from the perpetrator's perspective. Storing CSAM on a local hard drive runs the risk of detection in possession of the material if the device is seized by law enforcement authorities. By contrast, storing all material online (without a link to a locally stored copy) may provide a basic level of protection from casual discovery, especially if passwords are not automatically stored on a device. This also has the added benefit of allowing the perpetrator to access the material and upload new material from other devices in any location. This, of course, raises the risk that the ESP responsible for the file storage application could detect the CSAM, remove it from its site and report the individual in possession (or rather their account details) to the authorities. As noted earlier, a significant number of reports of CSAM derive from just such a source. However, not all ESPs routinely scan their sites for the presence of CSAM. Commenting on reports of CSAM made to NCMEC in 2019, the *New York Times* noted that some cloud storage sites owned by Amazon, Apple and Microsoft did not routinely scan for such material (Dance & Keller, 2020). The UK's Independent Inquiry into Child Sexual Abuse (2020) also reported an unwillingness among media companies (including Google, Microsoft, Apple and Facebook) to prescreen for CSAM at the point of upload, with a preference to screen at the point of sharing instead.

Online applications also facilitate CSAM creation because of the role played by social media sites in allowing strangers to contact each other. This facility is relevant for scenarios in which a perpetrator predates on children not in their care, by abducting a victim and when a perpetrator successfully encourages a victim to provide self-produced imagery. In such cases, a perpetrator will use social media applications to make the initial contact, although further discussions may quickly move to private messaging applications (often those provided by social media platforms) (Awais et al., 2012). Without these social media applications, it would be much more difficult for perpetrators to identify and contact potential victims. Indeed, the ease with which contact can be made allows perpetrators to target many prospective victims simultaneously, with the expectation that CSAM may be extracted from at least some of those contacted.

An extreme example of how social media sites can be used by perpetrators to contact children can be seen in the case of an Australian academic who in 2017 was charged with over 900 offences of allegedly contacting children online by pretending to be a well-known popstar, with the intent of extracting sexually explicit images, which could then be used to extort them for further imagery. He would typically make contact through social media and then move to livestreaming applications, where videos of the children would be created (NBC News, 2017). This was not an isolated case however. Dalton (2017) described the case of an international network of web developers who built their own social media platform, supported by sophisticated data analytics to identify potential child victims. Lists of potential targets would then be circulated within the network, who then attempted to contact the children on social media with a view to grooming them for CSAM. Dalton reported that, in the USA alone, 1,800 children were Victims / Survivors of this network. In each of these cases, victimisation was possible because of children being present on social media applications that were also accessed by offenders, intent on grooming them for sexually intimate images of the children. In France, Operation Horus investigated the grooming of children aged between 12 and 13 years, through the use of social media, which resulted in the sharing of sexual images and videos. Eight potential Victims / Survivors were identified and over 1,000 images were recovered (Europol, 2021b).

The livestreaming of sexual abuse is also only possible thanks to the availability of online applications that makes it possible to abuse children from anywhere in the world with an internet connection. Unlike other forms of CSAM, livestreaming of child sexual abuse is shared with the Consumer at the time of creation. Creation and sharing are therefore simultaneous, although wider distribution of the event through subsequent sharing by the Consumer is much rarer.

## Notes

1 Grooming is defined as the process by which an adult establishes a relationship with a child with the intention of sexual contact. Both the way in which the relationship is established and the intended sexual contact can occur either online or offline. See ECPAT International (2020) for further details on definitions.

2 While sexting was originally defined in relation to the sending of text messages with sexual images, sexting will also involve other commonly used forms of communication, such as instant messaging applications.

# References

Al-Alosi, H. (2018). *The criminalisation of fantasy material: Law and sexually explicit representations of fictional children*. Routledge.

Australian Federal Police (2020, 11 November). *Operation Arkstone results in 828 charges laid with 46 child victims identified*. [Media release]. www.afp.gov.au/news-media/media-relea ses/operation-arkstone-results-828-charges-laid-46-child-victims-identified

Awais, R., Greenwood, P., Walkerdine, J., Baron, A. & Rayson, P. (2012). Technological solutions to offending. In E. Quayle & K.M. Ribisl (Eds.), *Understanding and preventing online sexual exploitation of children* (pp. 228–243). Routledge.

BBC (2007, 9 May). Second Life 'child abuse' claim. *BBC News*. http://news.bbc.co.uk/2/ hi/technology/6638331.stm

Bluett-Boyd, N., Fileborn, N., Quadara, A. & Moore, S. (2013). *The role of emerging communication technologies in experiences of sexual violence*. Research Report 23. Australian Institute of Family Studies. https://aifs.gov.au/publications/role-emerging-communication-techn ologies-experiences-sexual-violenc

Bowles, N. & Keller, M.H. (2019, 7 December). Video Games and Online Chats Are 'Hunting Grounds' for Sexual Predators. *The New York Times*. www.nytimes.com/interactive/2019/ 12/07/us/video-games-child-sex-abuse.html

Broadhurst, R. & Jayawardena, K. (2011). Online social networking and pedophilia: An experimental research 'Sting'. In K. Jaishankar (Ed.), *Cyber Criminology: Exploring internet crime and criminal behaviour* (pp.79–102). CRC Press.

Canadian Centre for Child Protection (2017). *Survivors survey: Full report*. Canadian Centre for Child Protection. https://protectchildren.ca/pdfs/C3P_SurvivorsSurveyFullReport2 017.pdf

CBC News (2017, 24 February). Child protection group warns parents about luring, explicit chat on game site Roblox. *CBC News*. www.cbc.ca/news/canada/manitoba/winnipeg-roblox-luring-warning-1.3997258

Chiang, E. & Grant, T. (2018). Deceptive identity performance: Offender moves and multiple identities in online child abuse conversations. *Applied Linguistics* 2018, 1–25. https://doi. org/10.1093/applin/amy007

Council of Europe (2001). *Explanatory report to the Convention on Cybercrime*. European Treaty Series 185. Council of Europe. https://rm.coe.int/CoERMPublicCommonSearchServi ces/DisplayDCTMContent?documentId=09000016800cce5b

Dance, G.J.X. & Keller, M.H. (2020, 7 February). Tech companies detect a surge in online videos of child sexual abuse. *The New York Times*. www.nytimes.com/2020/02/07/us/onl ine-child-sexual-abuse.html

Dalton, T. (2017, 27-28 May). The Bieber trap: Paedophiles don't need to hide behind bushes. They just create a 'Justin Bieber' profile and wait. *The Weekend Australian Magazine*. www. theaustralian.com.au/life/weekend-australian-magazine/bieber-trap-gordon-chalmers-paedophiles-and-grooming/news-story/9498f6d09c6f33f3ed785d4213ee5bd2

ECPAT International (2020). *Summary paper on online child sexual exploitation*. ECPAT International. www.ecpat.org/wp-content/uploads/2020/12/ECPAT-Summary-paper-on-Online-Child-Sexual-Exploitation-2020.pdf

Eneman, M. (2005). The New Face of Child Pornography. In M. Klang & A. Murray (Eds.), *Human Rights in the Digital Age*. Cavendish Publishing.

Estes, R.J. & Weiner, N.A. (2002). *The commercial sexual exploitation of children in the U.S., Canada and Mexico: Full report (of the US National Study)*. https://abolitionistmom.org/wp-content/uploads/2014/05/Complete_CSEC_0estes-weiner.pdf

Europol (2021b, 20 January). *France arrests 14 suspects in sweep against child sexual abuse online*. [Press release]. Europol. www.europol.europa.eu/newsroom/news/france-arrests-14-suspects-in-sweep-against-child-sexual-abuse-online

Freeman-Powell, S. (2021, 24 August). Children groomed online reach record numbers as offenders exploit 'risky design features' to communicate. *Sky News*. https://news.sky.com/story/children-groomed-online-reach-record-numbers-as-offenders-exploit-risky-design-features-to-communicate-12389102

Gallagher, C. (2019, 25 February). 'Virtual' child abuse imagery a headache for gardaí: Sophisticated tech used to simulate child sex and 'age down' adult pornography. *The Irish Times*. www.irishtimes.com/news/crime-and-law/virtual-child-abuse-imagery-a-headache-for-garda%C3%AD-1.3803910

Gewirtz-Meydan, A., Walsh, W., Wolak, J. & Finkelhor, D. (2018). The complex experience of child pornography survivors. *Child Abuse & Neglect* 80, 238–248. https://doi.org/10.1016/j.chiabu.2018.03.031

Henry, N., Flynn, A. & Powell, A. (2019). *Image-based sexual abuse: Victims and perpetrators*. Trends and issues in crime and criminal justice 572. Australian Institute of Criminology. www.aic.gov.au/publications/tandi/tandi572

Henseler, H. & de Wolf, R. (2019). Sweetie 2.0 technology: Technical challenges to making the Sweetie 2.0 chatbot. In S. van der Hof, I. Georgieva, B. Scherner & B.J. Koops (Eds.), *Sweetie 2.0: Using articifical intelligence to fight webcam child sex tourism* (pp.113–134). TMC Asser Press.

Hilton, D.L. (2021). Pornography and the developing brain: Protecting the children. In E. Caffo (Ed.), *Online child sexual exploitation: treatment and prevention of abuse in a digital world* (pp.49–56). Springer Nature.

Huang, W., Leopard, M.E. & Brockman, A. (2009). Internet child sexual exploitation: offenses, offenders, and victims. In F. Schmalleger & M. Pittaro (Eds.), *Crimes of the Internet* (43–65). Pearson Education.

Hunt, E. (2017, 9 May). Sexting to blame for nearly 1,500 children convicted for child exploitation. *The Guardian, Australia Edition*. www.theguardian.com/australia-news/2017/may/09/sexting-guidelines-created-by-queensland-police-as-child-convictions-soar

Independent Inquiry into Child Sexual Abuse (2020). *The internet: Investigation report*. www.iicsa.org.uk/publications/investigation/internet

Jolly, B. (2019, 16 January). Fortnite warning as kids told to perform 'inappropriate acts' by online predators. *Daily Mirror*. www.mirror.co.uk/news/uk-news/fortnite-warning-kids-told-perform-13867477

Jonsson, L. & Svedin, C.G. (2012). Children within images. In E. Quayle & K.M. Ribisl (Eds.), *Understanding and preventing online sexual exploitation of children* (pp. 23–43). Routledge.

Kleijn, M. & Bogaerts, S. (2019). Sexual-oriented online chat conversations-Characteristics and testing pathways of online perpetrators. In S. van der Hof, I. Georgieva, B. Scherner & B.J. Koops (Eds.), *Sweetie 2.0: Using articifical intelligence to fight webcam child sex tourism* (pp.95–133). TMC Asser Press.

Krone, T. (2004). *A Typology of Online Child Pornography Offending*. Trends and issues in crime and criminal justice 279. Australian Institute of Criminology. www.aic.gov.au/publications/tandi/tandi279

Layden, M.A. (2021). Pornified: Pornography's connection to long-term damage and violence. In E. Caffo (Ed.), *Online child sexual exploitation: treatment and prevention of abuse in a digital world* (pp.57–74). Springer Nature.

Lim, M.S.C.,Vella, A.M., Horyniak, D.R. & Hellard, M.E. (2016). Exploring attitudes towards sexting of young people: a cross-sectional study. *Sex Health* 13(6), 530–535. https://doi. org/10.1071/SH16029.

MacLennan, L. (2020, 29 February). Anime and manga depicting sexual images of children spark calls for review of classification laws. *ABC News*. www.abc.net.au/ news/2020-02-29/mps-wants-review-of-classification-laws-for-manga-and-anime/ 12012522

May-Chahal, C. & Kelly, E. (2020). *Online child sexual victimisation*. Policy Press.

Meek-Prieto, C. (2007). Just age playing around? How Second Life aids and abets child pornography. *North Carolina Journal of Law & Technology* 9(3), 88–110. https://ncjolt. org/articles/just-age-playing-around-how-second-life-aids-and-abets-child-porn ography/

Mitchell, K.J., Finkelhor, D. & Wolak, J. (2005). The internet and family and acquaintance sexual abuse. *Child Maltreatment* 10(1), 49–60.

Mitchell, K.J., Finkelhor, D. & Wolak, J. (2007). Online requests for sexual pictures from youth: Risk factors and incident characteristics. *Journal of Adolescent Health* 41, 196–203.

Mohan, M. (2020, 10 February). I was raped at 14, and the video ended up on a porn site. *BBC News*. www.bbc.com/news/stories-51391981

NBC News (2017, 9 March). Justin Bieber Impersonator Accused of 900 Child Sex Crimes. *NBC News*. www.nbcnews.com/news/world/justin-bieber-impersonator-accused-900- child-sex-crimes-n731061

Parliament of the Commonwealth of Australia (2004). *Crimes Legislation Amendment (Telecommunications Offences and Other Measures) Bill 2004* (Cth) (Austl). https://parlinfo. aph.gov.au/parlInfo/download/legislation/bills/r2131_first-reps/toc_word/04149b01. doc;fileType=application%2Fmsword

Powell, A. (2010). Configuring Consent: Emerging Technologies, Unauthorized Sexual Images and Sexual Assault. *Australian & New Zealand Journal of Criminology* 43(1), 76–90. https://doi.org/10.1375/acri.43.1.76

Ramiro, L.S., Martinez, A.B., Tan, J.R.D., Mariano, K., Miranda, G.M.J. & Bautista, G. (2019). Online child sexual exploitation and abuse: A community diagnosis using the social norms theory. *Child Abuse and Neglect* 96, 104080. https://doi.org/10.1016/j.chi abu.2019.104080

Royal Commission into Institutional Responses to Child Sexual Abuse (2017a). *Final Report: Volume 2, Nature and cause*. Commonwealth of Australia. www.childabuseroyalcom mission.gov.au/sites/default/files/final_report_-_volume_2_nature_and_cause.pdf

Salter, M. (2013). *Organised sexual abuse*. Glasshouse / Routledge.

Salter, M., Wong, W.K.T., Breckenridge, J., Scott, S., Cooper, S. & Peleg, N. (2021). *Production and distribution of child sexual abuse material by parental figures*. Trends & issues in crime and criminal justice 616. Australian Institute of Criminology. www.aic.gov.au/publications/ tandi/tandi616

Stanley, N., Barter, C., Wood, M., Aghtaie, N., Larkins, C., Lanau, A. & Överlien, C. (2018). Pornography, Sexual Coercion and Abuse and Sexting in Young People's Intimate Relationships: A European Study. *Journal of Interpersonal Violence* 33(19), 2919–2944. https://doi.org/10.1177/0886260516633204

SWGFL / UK Safer Internet Centre, University of Plymouth, Netsafe & Office of the eSafety Commissioner (2017). *Young people and sexting – attitudes and behaviours: Research findings from the United Kingdom, New Zealand and Australia*. www.esafety.gov.au/sites/defa ult/files/2019-07/Young%20people%20and%20sexting-netsafe-UK%20Safer%20Inter net%20Centre-Plymoth%20University-eSafety%20Commissioner.pdf

Terre des Hommes (2014). *Webcam child sex tourism: Becoming Sweetie: A novel approach to stopping the global rise of webcam child sex tourism.* Terre des Hommes. www.terredeshom mes.org/wp-content/uploads/2013/11/Webcam-child-sex-tourism-terre-des-hom mes-NL-nov-2013.pdf

Tidy, J. (2021, 18 February). Omegle: Children expose themselves on video chat site. *BBC News.* www.bbc.com/news/technology-56085499

Vedelago, C. (2020, 19 June). More than 7.4 million images of child abuse circulating in Victoria. *The Age.* www.theage.com.au/national/victoria/more-than-7-4-million-ima ges-of-child-abuse-circulating-in-victoria-20200619-p554dy.html

We Protect Global Alliance (2021). *Global threat assessment 2021: Working together to end the sexual exploitation of children online.* We Protect Global Alliance. www.weprotect.org/glo bal-threat-assessment-21/#report

Westlake, B.G. (2018). Delineating victims from perpetrators: Prosecuting self-produced child pornography in youth criminal justice systems. *International Journal of Cyber Criminology* 12(1), 255–268. https://doi.org/10.5281/zenodo.1467907

Westlake, B.G. (2020). The past, present, and future of online child sexual exploitation: Summarizing the evolution of production, distribution, and detection. In T. Holt & A. Bossler (Eds.), *The Palgrave Handbook of International Cybercrime and Cyberdeviance* (pp. 1225–1253). Palgrave Macmillan. https://doi.org/10.1007/978-3-319-78440-3_52

White, C. (2011, 1 June). 'Child porn' Nintendo game gets PG rating. *ABC News.* www.abc. net.au/news/2011-06-01/child-porn-nintendo-game-gets-pg-rating/2741104

Wolak, J.D., Finkelhor, D., Walsh, W. & Tritman, L. (2018). Sextortion of minors: Characteristics and dynamics. *Journal of Adolescent Health* 62(1), 72–79. https://doi.org/10.1016/j.jad ohealth.2017.08.014

# 4

# HOW IS CSAM DISTRIBUTED?

## Introduction

So far, we have focused only on how CSAM is created. That material might just be kept in private collections, for personal consumption only, stored on laptops, phones, hard drives or in cloud storage. However, what really makes CSAM insidious is the way in which it is so often shared with others online. By distributing images on the internet, the CSAM ecosystem is strengthened in the sense that, once shared, attempts to remove images may take down some copies of those images, but other copies may remain. Indeed, just one copy of an image is all that is needed for it to be (re)propagated across the internet.

There are multiple ways in which images may be shared, from the very simple, to the highly sophisticated. These methods of sharing might include posting on websites, on forums, use of social media, direct messaging or file storage / file sharing. There is a distinction to be made here between the open-net and the darknet, with the latter providing an anonymous, more secure way of sharing CSAM. The darknet is treated in a separate section of this chapter, although recognising that the methods of sharing will be similar to some of those found on the open-net.

## Email

Email provides the most rudimentary form of CSAM distribution, with images sometimes being attached to messages, or lists of links to websites that contain CSAM being provided via email. This approach may be used by amateur CSAM collectors to share their images (Wortley & Smallbone, 2012). However, using email in this way comes with inherent risks, including the CSAM being stored in sent / received messages, the lack of anonymity with email and the potential for messages to be intercepted and subsequently reported by an ISP (Wortley & Smallbone,

DOI: 10.4324/9781003327264-5

2012). A degree of anonymity is possible by using remailers that strip the identi-fying features of the email before sending it on to its destination (Steel et al., 2020), although their use would appear to be limited in practice. A study of offenders arrested for CSAM possession in the USA in 2006 found that just 1 per cent had used a remailer to share material (Wolak et al., 2011).

According to Bursztein et al. (2019) the use of email as a means of sharing CSAM peaked in the early 2000s and declined in use after that time. Examining the frequency distribution by year associated with 86,601 reports of CSAM in emails made to NCMEC between 1998 and 2017, they found that reports peaked in 2004, when 18 per cent of reports were made. This declined in more recent times, with 2017 accounting for just 2 per cent of reports of CSAM in emails.

## Websites

Websites continue to be a common way in which CSAM is shared. Indeed, one of the key functions of organisations such as INHOPE, as well as the Internet Watch Foundation in the UK, the Canadian Centre for Child Protection, NCMEC in the USA and the e-Safety Commissioner in Australia, is to identify website URLs hosting CSAM and to arrange for the ISPs operating within their respective jurisdictions to remove the content. As an indication of the scale to which websites continue to be used, the Internet Watch Foundation (2022) reported that in 2021, 2,746 URLs in websites were identified as containing CSAM. INHOPE (2022) found that websites accounted for 31 per cent of the CSAM reported to its members in 2021 – more than any other distribution method.

Banner sites (which are websites that contain lists of URLs that provide links to sites providing access to other websites containing CSAM) are commonly used to share CSAM. They provide a kind of contents page for the CSAM viewer to find the material they are seeking. The Internet Watch Foundation (2022) identi-fied 8,086 banner sites in 2021. There is evidence to suggest that the prevalence of such sites is associated with the age of the Victim / Survivor, with the number of sites increasing as Victims / Survivors become younger. An analysis of victim age by type of site provided in the Internet Watch Foundation's (2020) annual report showed that there were 421 banner sites associated with victims aged 0–2 years, accounting for 26 per cent of reports associated with Victims / Survivors of that age. Banner sites peaked among reports of Victims / Survivors aged 3–6 years, with 2,381 banner sites being reported, accounting for 16 per cent of reports for that Victim / Survivor age. This declined to 1,880 (4%) reports of Victims / Survivors aged 7–10 years; 445 (0.7%) reports of Victims / Survivors aged 11–13 years; three (0.01%) reports of Victims / Survivors aged 14–15 years; and one (0.2%) report of a Victim / Survivor aged 16–17 years.

As noted in chapter 2, new approaches to sharing CSAM on websites have emerged since 2011 that attempt to disguise the content of websites, thereby making it difficult for existing web crawlers and law enforcement analysts to detect CSAM. Directly accessing the site will only display legal content. However, if a user visits a predefined sequence of other websites first (thereby collecting a series of cookies), the disguised website will reveal CSAM. In 2021, the Internet Watch Foundation (2022) discovered 26,272 websites using this method, representing a 541 per cent increase on the previous year.

## Peer-to-peer networks

Peer-to-peer networks offer a decentralised means of sharing information. By installing an application on one's computer that allows peer-to-peer networking, other computers in the network can access files on one's device (held within specified directories), thereby avoiding the need for routing via central servers that may monitor for certain types of file. Once a file has been obtained from another user in the network, it then becomes available for use by others. This means that the more times it is shared, the more it becomes available within the network, so that, if for example, the original source of the file is removed from the network (perhaps due to law enforcement activity) it remains available from others in the network that have previously received that file. Peer-to-peer networks have therefore been popular with CSAM users because they provide public access to files on demand and for free (Wolak et al., 2014; Lee et al., 2020). They are also robust to changes in network infrastructure (users being removed), avoid connection with the authorities and are relatively anonymous. Files can be obtained without first knowing or having contact with another CSAM user, as the network acts as an intermediary, providing the file on demand (Lee et al., 2020). Depending on the design of the peer-to-peer network, anonymity can be given to both the user requesting the resource and the provider that supplies it (Saboori & Mohammadi, 2012). However, the latter aspect has been undermined by the development of applications that are used by law enforcement to reveal the identities of users, which subsequently lead to arrests and convictions. Indeed, these new applications allow police to track peer-to-peer network users in near real time and even identify local areas in which users were operating (Steel et al., 2020). The fact that files are stored and shared from the user's device also makes the user vulnerable to law enforcement action if the device is seized and scanned for CSAM. Al Mutawa et al. (2015) noted that CSAM may be identified on the devices of peer-to-peer network users, even when steps had been taken to delete the material in question.

Steel (2009) noted that the top search terms using peer-to-peer networks were CSAM related, compared with them being ranked 198th highest on the web, providing an indication of how such networks were being used to share CSAM. However, according to analysis by Bursztein et al. (2019), CSAM that appears on peer-to-peer networks is seldom reported to NCMEC (probably due to the lack of moderators in such networks). Indeed, just 8,900 reports were received by NCMEC between 1998 and 2017, accounting for less than 0.04 per cent of CSAM reported. They also found that reports to NCMEC peaked around 2006–2007, which may have coincided with the peak use of peer-to-peer networks for distributing CSAM (Bursztein et al., 2019).

It would also appear that CSAM is not evenly distributed across peer-to-peer networks, but is typically concentrated in a relatively small proportion of computers in a network. Examining a year of traffic associated with one particular peer-to-peer network, Gnutella, Wolak et al. (2014) found that 91 per cent of computers that shared CSAM shared only one file during the year – typically material that was highly duplicated across the network. In contrast, less than 1 per cent of computers that shared CSAM during the year had distributed more than 100 different files, with a median contribution of 471 files. They estimated that removing these high-sharing computers from the network would reduce the overall availability of CSAM (unique material) by 30 per cent (Wolak et al. 2014).

Bissias et al. (2016) found that 161,000 known (previously identified by law enforcement) unique CSAM images were available worldwide across five peer-to-peer networks (Ares, BitTorrent, eDonkey, Gnutella and Gnutella2) in December 2014. This number had increased from approximately 59,000 in September 2012. While the number of unique images available on these five networks had increased, the number of users of the networks had declined from approximately 1.3 million in 2012 to 840,000 in December 2014. This disparity between the increasing number of unique CSAM images on the network and the decreasing number of users was explained by significant improvements in the number of images known to law enforcement as a result of investigations and an increase in the number of images shared by users. The latter point was supported by the observation that, once shared on a peer-to-peer network, CSAM is hard to remove. Indeed, Bissias et al. (2016) found that survival rates (the proportion of content observed in September 2012 that was still available in December 2014) ranged from 80 per cent or above for three networks (Ares, BitTorrent and eDonkey) to 12 per cent and 49 per cent for Gnutella and Gnutella2 respectively. However, even though the survival rates were relatively low in these cases, the authors found that 60 per cent of the CSAM available at the start of the study period on those two networks was available on at least one of five networks examined at the end of the study.

These findings suggest that peer-to-peer networks may not be as popular as they once were among CSAM Consumers and Content Distributors, but they remain a significant means of distribution. Once shared, material on such networks would appear to be difficult to eliminate.

## Forums

Forums are virtual meeting spaces where users can share information and hold online discussions. There is (by internet timeframes) a long history of forums being used to share CSAM. Bulletin Board Systems (BBSs) were an early type of forum, dating back to the 1980s, that allowed messages to be posted by users to a message board on a centrally located server that could subsequently be retrieved by other users. In the early days of microcomputers, acoustic modems and dial-up connections, BBSs provided a low-cost and efficient means of sharing information. As early as 1982, there were reports of BBSs being used to share CSAM (Jenkins,

2001). In the pre-World Wide Web era, they were one of the main ways by which CSAM would be shared, with links to CSAM websites being posted on message boards along with site ratings and discussions about those sites (Steel et al., 2020).

During the 1990s, there was a series of successful police operations that targeted offenders sharing CSAM on bulletin boards. One such notable example was Operation Long Arm involving law enforcement agencies in the USA and Denmark targeting a bulletin board operating out of the latter's jurisdiction. The operation resulted in over 900 leads associated with offenders sharing CSAM (Krone, 2005; Akdeniz, 2008). Despite these law enforcement successes, bulletin boards were still seen as a source of CSAM into the 2000s. For example, Jenkins (2001) estimated that there were 50,000 to 100,000 users of bulletin boards globally in 2001. An analysis of CSAM search terms on three commonly used search engines found that the search term 'BBS' was often associated with an additional search term that related to CSAM (Steel, 2009). Indeed, the top ten search terms involving 'BBS' all involved searches for CSAM. However, most reputable ISPs now block such bulletin boards and subsequent technological developments have rendered BBSs largely obsolete – both for legitimate and CSAM purposes (Wortley & Smallbone, 2012; Steel et al., 2020).

Although more technologically advanced, Usenet newsgroups emerged at a similar time and fall into a similar category as BBSs. Unlike a BBS, Usenet newsgroups were hosted on multiple servers, which would synchronise with each other so that each held the same information. Like BBSs, they provided a means by which users could post text-based information, although coding developments allowed binary images to be transferred in ASCII text format (Steel et al., 2020). Wortley and Smallbone (2012) noted that some Usenet newsgroups (such as the alternative binaries pictures erotica pre-teen (abpep-t) group) were notorious for sharing CSAM. This was further supported by the introduction of the alt.* hierarchy of newsgroups that covered *alternative* topics, with alt.binaries.* and alt.sex.* being popular for sharing CSAM (Steel et al., 2020). Such newsgroups not only provided a means of sharing CSAM, but were also found to perform an important social function for their participants. Their online posts helped them to justify their behaviour, influence their attitudes towards sex with children and ultimately helped to shape their identity (Durkin & Bryant, 1999; O'Halloran & Quayle, 2010; Quayle & Taylor, 2011). These are attributes shared with subsequent generations of forums.

While BBSs and Usenet newsgroups have been superseded by new technologies that provide forum functions, there are still some newsgroups that share CSAM material. In 2010, O'Halloran and Quayle found that a 'boy love' forum on a Usenet newsgroup (that had been studied by Durkin and Bryant (1999) more than a decade before), continued to function, with 1,570 subscribed members (although noting that these included both those with pro- and anti-CSAM views). In 2019, the Internet Watch Foundation (2020) issued 51 takedown notices on newsgroups found to be sharing CSAM and recommended to its members not to carry 260 newsgroups containing or advertising CSAM. In 2021, just five newsgroups were identified containing CSAM (Internet Watch Foundation, 2022).

Image boards (also known as chan) represent a newer generation of forum. These provide users with the ability to upload photographs and videos to bulletin board-style websites that are shared by others viewing the content on the site. These sites typically do not require usernames or login details, which means that information can be posted with a semblance of anonymity, although like other types of website, IP address details will typically be left behind (Gonzales, 2019). Some image boards, such as 4chan and 8chan, have garnered a degree of notoriety for some of the material hosted and the political views expressed, including by white supremacists (Gonzales, 2019). However, the relaxed way in which image boards are moderated, combined with the sense of anonymity and the ability to share photographs and videos, has meant that this technology has been used to distribute CSAM. In 2019, the Internet Watch Foundation (2020) received over 500 reports of CSAM on image boards, although this accounted for less than 1 per cent of CSAM reports received. Similarly, in 2019 NCMEC received 1,380 reports from 4chan. While this accounted for less than 0.01 per cent of the reports received from ESPs, it was still the 24th highest number from the more than 140 organisations that submitted reports (NCMEC, 2020).

Forums have developed over time from simple text-based discussions (as with BBSs and Usenet groups), to more sophisticated multimedia platforms that allow photos and videos to be uploaded, making them closer to other social media platforms. However, they remain a relatively minor way in which CSAM is distributed. Bursztein et al. (2019) identified almost 31,000 reports of CSAM on forums that were made to NCMEC between 1998 and 2017. These accounted for just 0.1 per cent of reports made to the NGO during this time. There is also little sign of increasing use of forums for sharing CSAM.

As further evidence of their current limited use, the Internet Watch Foundation (2022) found that just 4 per cent of the URLs it examined in 2021 related to forums.

## Internet Relay Chat

CSAM distribution has been associated with Internet Relay Chat (IRC), which probably represents one of the most rudimentary and early forms of application. Initially developed to work in association with BBSs, IRC provides a medium of communication between users by using a locally installed program or a browser-based application. IRC allows users to share content on a one-to-one or one-to-many basis. It provides a slightly higher level of security (through anonymity) for the user by deploying handles (usernames) and private (invitation-only) channels for communicating. Anonymity is achieved by the server masking the user's IP address when the user connects to the server (Shao et al., 2018). IRC can also be encrypted using *Off the Record* (OTR), making it more secure. However, this would only appear to be functional for one-to-one chat, rather than multi-user chat[1].

Most IRC forums are text based (but may also allow images and videos to be shared) and work by sending messages to a central server, which relays the message to other users on the same channel. Messages will typically appear in a window that can be seen by all users, while another window will often show the users currently connected to the network.

Some networks also allow for direct client-to-client connections that use peer-to-peer connectivity to bypass servers (Etherton, 2001). IRC can be difficult to find unless one has an address and many will have controlled access, making them attractive to those wishing to share CSAM (Singletary, 2015). Unlike other methods of CSAM distribution, IRC remains largely unmonitored (Steel, 2015). Analysis by Bursztein et al. (2019) found that less than 0.2 per cent of CSAM reported to NCMEC between 1998 and 2017 related to IRC / chatrooms, although that still amounted to more than 36,000 reports. Although they seem to have peaked in use for CSAM around 2007, they appeared to have something of a resurgence around 2016–2017. However, the results presented by Bursztein et al. may have been the result of combining IRC with other types of chatroom and it may well have been these other forms of chatroom that have been popular in recent years.

## Instant messaging

Instant messaging, which does as it suggests and allows messages to be sent between users on a one-to-one basis and a one-to-many basis, has now become ubiquitous as a means of communication. While some messaging applications are designed solely for that purpose, it is now common for social media, videoconferencing and gaming applications to include instant messaging functions. This often allows for images and URLs to be shared between users. Sharing CSAM through this means is difficult to detect as the communications are not open to the public in the way that websites are for example. Detection will therefore rely on the other users to report, or instant messaging app administrators to detect, remove and report the sharing of CSAM – a job made more difficult when applications include built-in end-to-end encryption of messages. Operation Chemosh provides one example of a successful police operation that targeted the sharing of CSAM (mostly by children) on the instant messaging app WhatsApp. Led by Spain's Policia Nacional, Operation Chemosh led to 33 investigations involving a number of splinter groups involved in CSAM distribution using this method (Europol, 2019).

According to Bursztein et al. (2019), NCMEC received 36,086 reports of CSAM in instant messaging between 1998 and 2017. Of those reports, 32 per cent were received in the two most recent years (2016 and 2017), suggesting increases in the use of instant messaging. In 2019, Facebook's Messenger app was responsible for over 80 per cent of the images and videos containing CSAM reported to NCMEC, accounting for over 48 million individual items of CSAM, although noting that many items will be duplicates (Dance & Keller, 2020). Instant messaging is also a common means by which children *receive* CSAM. We Protect Global Alliance (2021) reported that 68 per cent of survey respondents who had received sexually explicit material online during childhood had received it through an instant messaging application.

## Computer games

Although playing a relatively minor role in CSAM distribution, the chat function in many online games has been reported as a means by which users can share material. Bursztein et al. (2019) reported 3,838 cases in which gaming platforms were reported to NCMEC between 1998 and 2017. Of those reports, 25 per cent were received in the two most recent years (2016 and 2017), suggesting this may be an increasingly popular way to share CSAM.

## File storage sites

File storage sites are divided here into cyber-lockers and image hosting sites. Cyber-lockers provide (typically encrypted) storage space to which users can upload files of any kind so that they can be accessed from anywhere (Zhang, 2018). Access to password-protected folders, or to the entire storage space, can be given to others, who can then download files that have previously been uploaded and stored by the user. This approach provides protection from web crawlers and law enforcement agencies searching for CSAM and at the same time gives easy access to files stored on these sites. This also means that a CSAM Consumer can access material without needing to store it on their own device (Steel et al., 2020). This approach has also been monetised with the use of premium file hosting sites that charge users to access material stored on a site. A survey of 450 police officers in 41 countries by Netclean (2019) found that 21 per cent believed there had been an increase in the use of file storage sites to store CSAM in the previous three years.

Six per cent of the CSAM reported by the Internet Watch Foundation (2020) in 2019 related to cyber-lockers. Of greatest concern was the finding that 30 per cent of the reports associated with babies (aged 0–2 years) were associated with cyber-lockers.

Image hosting sites allow for images and videos to be hosted by a third-party storage site which can then be easily shared with others, or found via search engines. Image hosting sites allow for the URL associated with a stored image to be shared, thereby making the sharing process simple and efficient in terms of data usage (only the URL needs to be shared, rather than sending a large image / video file). This allows others hosting CSAM on websites to embed links to the CSAM stored on image hosting sites. This means that the number of points of access to the CSAM for Consumers can be much larger than just the original hosting site. According to the Internet Watch Foundation (2022), image hosting sites accounted for 73 per cent of the CSAM identified by the organisation in 2021. They were also the most common way of sharing CSAM associated with children of all ages (Internet Watch Foundation, 2020). INHOPE (2022) found that 25 per cent of the reports its members received in 2021 related to image hosting sites. This high use of image hosting sites is likely to be due to their user-friendly design, allied with the simplicity with which links can be shared.

## Social media

As outlined in chapter 2, social media sites, which allow users to share media content with the world, are ubiquitous, with hundreds of applications now available, depending on preferred functionality and target group. The ease with which content can be shared (both publicly and privately) makes them particularly vulnerable to use by those wishing to share CSAM. Many social media sites allow for the creation of special interest groups and these can be used as a means for CSAM offenders to find each other and share information.

A 2020 *New York Times* article reported that in 2019, Facebook alone reported nearly 60 million photos and videos to NCMEC in the USA for containing CSAM. This accounted for more than 85 per cent of the photos and videos reported to the agency (Dance & Keller, 2020). This is partly a result of Facebook's dominant position in the social media market, but also a result of the company's investment in new algorithms and search technology to identify CSAM and other egregious material on their platform. One example of how Facebook has been used to share CSAM can be found in the 2017 case of an Indonesian Facebook group with over 7,000 members that was sharing CSAM and discussing how to approach and sexually abuse children without being discovered. The site was accidentally discovered by a group of Indonesian mothers who were sharing images of their children with an online parenting community. A police investigation led to the arrest of five suspects (United Nations Office on Drugs and Crime, 2021b).

In 2021, NCMEC (2022) received over 22 million reports from Facebook (each of which can contain multiple image and videos, but will also contain many duplicates). Other social media companies with high numbers of reports of CSAM images and videos to NCMEC included Instagram (3.4 million reports), Snapchat (512,000 reports) and TikTok (154,000 reports) (NCMEC, 2022).

## Sharing on the darknet

Sharing on the darknet appears to be somewhat more difficult than sharing on the open-net, due largely to information not being indexed as it is on the open-net, making it difficult to search for material in this environment (van der Bruggen & Blokland, 2020). Instead, new users to the darknet may need to seek advice and assistance from others in forums, who can give advice on how to find relevant sites (although even forums can be hard to find without the specific address being obtained). They may also need to use special software to gain access to darknet sites. Leclerc et al. (2021) used script analysis to describe the process by which new users accessed CSAM on the darknet. This typically started with accessing adult pornography and CSAM on the open-net and then seeking advice on how to access the darknet and, importantly, how to connect anonymously without leaving traces that could be followed by law enforcement investigators. Despite the anonymity of the darknet, the 'social' aspect of sharing in this environment can be extremely important, in the sense that gaining access to closed sites may need introductions from other users, or require new users to prove their credentials by providing newly created CSAM. In 2016, a man was convicted in the USA for sharing CSAM via the darknet. He was able to access a darknet site dedicated to trading CSAM only after he had shared CSAM from his own collection (United States Department of Justice, 2016).

Older technology is also being combined with darknet infrastructure to provide greater levels of anonymity (and therefore protection) to the user. For example, darknet peer-to-peer networks have emerged, which provide the same distributed sharing technology provided by open-net peer-to-peer networks. Indeed, TOR has a plug-in that allows peer-to-peer connections from its browser (Singletary, 2015). Freenet, another darknet environment, has its own peer-to-peer application called Frost, with numerous chatrooms dedicated to CSAM exchange (ECPAT Belgium, 2015).

There are fears that CSAM sharing on the darknet is growing at a rapid rate. For example, in 2019, the Internet Watch Foundation identified 288 new CSAM websites operating on the darknet, compared with 85 in 2018 (Internet Watch Foundation, 2020). This further increased to 734 websites in 2020 and 931 in 2021 (Internet Watch Foundation, 2022). Bursztein et al. (2019) identified over 4,000 reports submitted to NCMEC between 1998 and 2017 that were associated with CSAM on the darknet. Of those reports, 90 per cent were received in the three most recent years (2015–2017), indicating recent growth.

## Which countries share CSAM?

Not only is CSAM disproportionately shared through particular distribution channels online, its distribution is concentrated in a relatively small number of countries. The Internet Watch Foundation (2022) found that 72 per cent of the reports it actioned in 2021 (accounting for over 180,000 reports) related to CSAM hosted in Europe and 41 per cent were hosted in just one country – the Netherlands. While the USA accounted for the next largest contributor in 2021 (21%) (Internet Watch Foundation 2022), the Internet Watch Foundation (2020) reported that the proportion of CSAM hosted there had been declining, largely due to mandatory reporting requirements on ISPs and ESPs.

INHOPE (2022) found that the USA and Netherlands each hosted more than 15 per cent of the CSAM reported to its members in 2021. Within Europe, 76 per cent of reports related to CSAM hosted in the Netherlands, while a further 6 per cent was hosted in France.

Peer-to-peer networks show a different distribution of countries, with users in China sharing more CSAM than other countries, followed by Brazil, Mexico and the USA (Bissias et al., 2016). This difference may reflect either the international distribution of reporting centres (China is not currently part of the INHOPE network) or the preference for decentralised methods of distribution in those countries that do not result in reports being made to authorities.

## Summing up the ways in which CSAM is shared

Sharing CSAM on the internet can be achieved through an array of technologies and is subject to constant offender adaption as existing technologies are subject to greater attention by regulators and law enforcement agencies and new ones emerge that can be exploited for CSAM creation, sharing and viewing purposes. Currently, some are of more concern than others. Some methods of sharing (such as via BBSs and newsgroups) continue to be used by a minority, long after they have ceased to be fashionable – perhaps by a generation that grew up using these forms of technology. However, these methods of sharing would appear to be in decline and will probably be utilised by fewer and fewer users into the future, both for general use and for CSAM distribution. As a group of CSAM sharing methods, they probably represent a comparatively lower level of harm to the community, not only because of their relatively small and diminishing share of the CSAM market, but also because they are, on the whole, cordoned off (often through password protection) in a part of the open-net that most of us do not frequent.

By contrast, websites continue to be of concern because of their ubiquity. They are easy to create and publish with only a modicum of technical know-how, making it possible for almost anyone to share CSAM on their own website. There are of course multiple factors that curb their use including the ability of ISPs to remove the sites and report the publishers to law enforcement authorities (or at least report their IP address) and for search engine providers to program their algorithms to hide such sites in their search results. Approaches to tackling websites on the open-net will be discussed in more detail in later chapters and it is enough to note here that websites continue to be of concern as a channel for sharing CSAM by virtue of the large number of sites that could be discovered by both intentional CSAM Consumers and the general public.

Peer-to-peer networks are ideally suited to CSAM distribution because of their decentralised structure and their ability to avoid removal. However, they would appear to have been in declining use because of effective law enforcement action to identify and prosecute users. There appears to have been a resurgence in use of this technology on the darknet because it offers a means of distributing CSAM to a closed group in an efficient way, while also providing a level of anonymity unavailable on the open-net.

Perhaps of greatest concern is the proliferation of CSAM on applications that have been designed for their ease of use and capacity to hold vast amounts of data. This would particularly appear to be the case for both cyber-lockers and image hosting sites that are specifically designed to allow electronic files to be stored and shared. However, this problem also extends to social media sites and forums that allow users to publish material with ease to communities of like-minded individuals. It would seem likely that those platforms with the most users (and most content) are also the ones hosting the most CSAM. In a sense, the bigger the haystack, the more needles one is likely to find. An important implication of this assessment is that, while the scale of published content may be vast, it is controlled by relatively few corporations. As will be discussed later, this observation may offer insight into how to address this problem.

So, from an open-net perspective scale and ease of use are the key criteria that appear to drive CSAM sharing, allied it seems with low risk of detection. In contrast, CSAM sharing via the darknet is preserved for those willing to invest more effort in learning how to use services such as TOR and includes a greater proportion of content that depicts serious harm than found on the open-net. As we shall see later, the approach to addressing CSAM sharing via this vector is necessarily different to that required to address the open-net.

## Note

1 Further details on OTR can be found at https://en.wikipedia.org/wiki/Off-the-Record_Messaging.

## References

Akdeniz, Y. (2008). *Internet child pornography and the law*. Routledge.

Al Mutawa, N., Bryce, J., Franqueira, V.N.L. & Marrington, A. (2015). *Behavioural Evidence Analysis Applied to Digital Forensics: An Empirical Analysis of Child Pornography Cases using P2P Networks*. 10th International Conference on Availability, Reliability and Security (ARES 2015). https://doi.org/10.1109/ARES.2015.49

Bissias, G., Levine, B., Liberatore, M., Lynne, B., Moore, J., Wallach, H. & Wollak, J. (2016). Characterization of contact offenders and child exploitation material trafficking on five peer-to-peer networks. *Child Abuse and Neglect* 52, 185–199. https://doi.org/10.1016/j.chiabu.2015.10.022

Bursztein, E., Bright, T., Clarke, E., DeLaune, M., Eliff, D.M., Hsu, N., Olson, L., Shehan, J., Thakur, M. & Thomas, K. (2019, 13-17 May). Rethinking the Detection of Child Sexual Abuse Imagery on the Internet. In *Proceedings of the 2019 World Wide Web Conference (WWW '19), San Francisco, CA, USA*. https://doi.org/10.1145/3308558.3313482

Dance, G.J.X. & Keller, M.H. (2020, 7 February). Tech companies detect a surge in online videos of child sexual abuse. *The New York Times*. www.nytimes.com/2020/02/07/us/online-child-sexual-abuse.html

Durkin, K.F. & Bryant, C. (1999). Propagandizing pederasty: A thematic analysis of the online exculpatory accounts of unrepentant paedophiles. *Deviant Behaviour: An Inter-Disciplinary Journal* 20, 103–127 https://doi.org/10.1080/016396299266524

ECPAT Belgium (2015). *In the shadows of the Internet: Child sexual abuse material in the darknets*. ECPAT Belgium. https://ecpat.be/wp-content/uploads/2017/12/Analyse-6-CSAM-in-the-Darknets.pdf

Etherton, J. (2001). *Internet relay chat – pros, cons and those pesky bots*. Global Information Assurance Certification Paper, Sans Institute. www.giac.org/paper/gsec/717/internet-relay-chat-pros-cons-pesky-bots/101615#:~:text=Pros%20of%20IRC,the%20Internet%20Relay%20Chat%20network.

Europol (2019, 11 December). *Operation Chemosh: How encrypted chat groups exchanged emoji 'stickers' of child sexual abuse*. Europol. www.europol.europa.eu/newsroom/news/operation-chemosh-how-encrypted-chat-groups-exchanged-emoji-%E2%80%98stickers%E2%80%99-of-child-sexual-abuse

Gonzales, O. (2019, 7 November). 8chan, 8kun, 4chan, Endchan: What you need to know: 8chan, the site linked to mass-shooting screeds, has returned under a new name. *CNet*. www.cnet.com/news/8chan-8kun-4chan-endchan-what-you-need-to-know-internet-forums/

INHOPE (2022). *Annual report 2021*. INHOPE https://bit.ly/3797mhd

Internet Watch Foundation (2020). *The why. The how. The who. And the results: Internet Watch Foundation annual report 2019*. Internet Watch Foundation. www.iwf.org.uk/sites/defa ult/files/reports/2020-04/IWF_Annual_Report_2020_Low-res-Digital_AW_6mb.pdf

Internet Watch Foundation (2022). *The annual report 2021*. Internet Watch Foundation. https://annualreport2021.iwf.org.uk/pdf/IWF-Annual-Report-2021.pdf

Jenkins, P. (2001). *Beyond tolerance: Child pornography on the internet*. New York University Press.

Krone, T. (2005). *International Police Operations Against Online Child Pornography*. Trends and issues in crime and criminal justice 296. Australian Institute of Criminology. https://aic. gov.au/publications/tandi/tandi296

Leclerc, B., Drew, J., Holt, T., Cale, J. & Singh, S. (2021). *Child sexual abuse material on the darknet: A script analysis of how offenders operate*. Trends & issues in crime and criminal justice 627. Australian Institute of Criminology. https://doi.org/10.52922/ti78160

Lee, H.E., Ermakova, T., Ververis, V. & Fabian, B. (2020). Detecting child sexual abuse material: A comprehensive survey. *Forensic Science International: Digital Investigation* 34, 302022 https://doi.org/10.1016/j.fsidi.2020.301022

National Centre for Missing and Exploited Children (NCMEC) (2020). *2019 Reports by Electronic Service Providers (ESP)*. www.missingkids.org/content/dam/missingkids/geth elp/2019-reports-by-esp.pdf

National Centre for Missing and Exploited Children (NCMEC) (2022). *2021 CyberTipline reports by Electronic Service Providers (ESP)*. www.missingkids.org/content/dam/missingk ids/pdfs/2021-reports-by-esp.pdf

Netclean (2019). *Netclean Report 2019: A report about child sexual abuse crime*. www.netclean. com/wp-content/uploads/2017/06/Netclean_report_2019_A4.pdf

O'Halloran, E. & Quayle, E. (2010). A content analysis of a 'boy love' support forum: Revisiting Durkin and Bryant. *Journal of Sexual Aggression* 6(1), 71–85. https://doi.org/10.1080/ 13552600903395319

Quayle, E. & Taylor, M. (2011). Social networking as a nexus for engagement and exploit-ation of young people. *Information Security Technical Report* 16, 44–50. www.sciencedirect. com/science/article/abs/pii/S1363412711000574

Saboori, E. & Mohammadi, S. (2012). Anonymous communication in peer-to-peer networks for providing more privacy and security. *International Journal of Modelling and Optimization* 2(3), 217–221. https://doi.org/10.7763/IJMO.2012.V2.114

Shao, S., Tunc, C., Al-Shawi, A. & Hariri, S. (2018). Autonomic author identification in internet relay chat (IRC). *2018 IEEE/ACS 15th International Conference on Computer Systems and Applications (AICCSA)*. https://ieeexplore.ieee.org/document/8612780

Singletary, T. (2015). Dark Web and the rise of underground networks. In M. Bowers (Ed.), *Evolution of cyber technologies and operations to 2035* (pp.107–136). Advances in Information Security 63. Springer.

Steel, C.M.S. (2009). Web-based child pornography: Quantification and qualification of demand. *International Journal of Digital Crime and Forensics* 1(4), 58–69. https://doi.org/ 10.4018/jdcf.2009062405

Steel, C.M.S. (2015). Web-based child pornography: The global impact of deterrence efforts and its consumption on mobile platforms. *Child Abuse and Neglect* 44, 150–158. http:// dx.doi.org/10.1016/j.chiabu.2014.12.009

Steel, C.M.S., Newman, E., O'Rourke, S. & Quayle, E. (2020). An integrative review of historical technology and countermeasure usage trends in online child sexual exploitation material offenders. *Forensic Science International: Digital Investigation* 33, 2666–2817. https://doi.org/10.1016/j.fsidi.2020.300971

United Nations Office on Drugs and Crime (2021b). *UNODC Southeast Asia Pacific Written Submission to the Parliament of Australia Joint Committee on Law Enforcement.* Parliamentary Joint Committee on Law Enforcement Inquiry on Law enforcement capabilities in relation to child exploitation. Submission 7. www.aph.gov.au/DocumentStore.ashx?id= 84dfa4c8-c020-4e07-8ccd-d09b153187a6&subId=712049

United States Department of Justice (2016, 20 July). *Grand Rapids Man Sentenced For Distribution Of Child Pornography On The Dark Web.* [Press release]. www.justice.gov/usao-wdmi/pr/2016_0720_Piccolo

van der Bruggen, M. & Blokland, A. (2020). A crime script analysis of child sexual exploitation material fora on the darknet. *Sexual Abuse* 33(8), 950–974. https://doi.org/10.1177/1079063220981063

We Protect Global Alliance (2021). *Global threat assessment 2021: Working together to end the sexual exploitation of children online.* We Protect Global Alliance. www.weprotect.org/global-threat-assessment-21/#report

Wolak, J., Finkelhor, D. & Mitchell, K. (2011). Child pornography possessors: Trends in offender and case characteristics. *Sexual Abuse: A Journal of Research and Treatment* 23(1), 22–42. https://doi.org/10.1177/1079063210372143

Wolak, J., Liberatore, M. & Levine, B.N. (2014). Measuring a year of child pornography trafficking by U.S. computers on a peer-to-peer network. *Child Abuse and Neglect* 38(2), 347–356. http://dx.doi.org/10.1016/j.chiabu.2013.10.018

Wortley, R. & Smallbone, S. (2012). *Internet Child Pornography: Causes, Investigation and Prevention.* Praeger.

Zhang, H. (2018, 25 January). How secure is your data when it's stored in the cloud? *The Conversation.* https://theconversation.com/how-secure-is-your-data-when-its-stored-in-the-cloud-90000

# 5

# HOW IS CSAM CONSUMED?

## Introduction

So far, we have examined how CSAM is produced and distributed. Next, we turn attention to how it is consumed. More specifically, we focus on the situations in which CSAM is viewed, including when and where it is viewed. Measures taken to prevent others from discovering that CSAM is being viewed are also discussed.

## How is CSAM viewed?

As a starting point to this discussion, we need to differentiate between modes of viewing, with material being accessed via sites that either display or host CSAM (Guerra & Westlake, 2021). CSAM can be viewed online by accessing websites that display such material, with Consumers browsing the pages of interest, in much the same way as any website is browsed. This does not mean that the images are downloaded on to the Consumer's device, although their browsing history will store which pages have been accessed. Consumers may also choose to view the livestreaming of CSAM in real time, which also does not require material to be stored on their device (Acar, 2017).

### Storing CSAM to view later

Consumers may also choose to download CSAM from sites that host such material and store it for later viewing (Guerra & Westlake, 2021). The benefit of this approach is that they have access to the material whenever they want it, without fear of it being removed from websites, or no longer being available when stored remotely by others (for example on peer-to-peer networks). For some, the process of collecting and exchanging material is all-important, likened to collecting baseball cards

DOI: 10.4324/9781003327264-6

(Lanning, 1986). This can result in large collections being amassed by Consumers (Krone, 2004). CSAM collections have been characterised by a number of features. They are often the most important thing in a Consumer's life, with them going to significant effort to build a collection; collections are permanent in the sense that they are unlikely to be disposed of and Consumers seldom have enough, needing to continually accumulate more; collections are often carefully organised; a collection may be concealed, but this needs to be weighed against easy access; and it will often be shared with other Consumers (Lanning, 1986). Trading and sharing may occur directly on a one-to-one basis (e.g. via email or instant messaging) (Martellozzo & DeMarco, 2020) without it ever appearing in places where it can be downloaded by others. In some cases, Consumers will also be Content Producers, collecting CSAM associated with children they have sexually abused (Mitchell et al., 2005; Salter, 2013). In all these examples of collecting, there will be a need for the Consumer to store the CSAM. This could be on a computer (or phone), on an external storage device or on an online file storage site (Netclean, 2019).

Storage for subsequent viewing introduces a degree of vulnerability for CSAM Consumers as this may create opportunities for discovery by family members or by the police (Jones et al., 2021). To prevent this happening, Consumers may encrypt devices and password-protect access to file storage sites (Netclean, 2019).

## What is being viewed?

The description of the typical Victim / Survivor in chapter 2 provides an indication of the demographics associated with CSAM. In this section, we examine further the severity of the material being viewed and how that can escalate as Consumers view more CSAM.

### Severity of material

An analysis of almost 250,000 URLs containing CSAM that were reported to the Internet Watch Foundation (2022) found that 18 per cent of URLs reported in 2021 contained 'Category A' content. This included sexual activity between adults and children, including rape or sexual torture. This had declined from 21 per cent in 2019. 'Category B' (images involving non-penetrative sexual activity) material accounted for 20 per cent of reports (the same as in 2019). In contrast, 'Category C' (indecent images of children not falling into Categories A or B) increased from 59 per cent in 2019 to 62 per cent in 2021. CSAM involving babies and toddlers (aged up to 2 years old) is more likely to involve Category A (78%) than other age categories (Internet Watch Foundation, 2022).

### Escalation in viewing

Escalation in viewing can occur because of a transition from adult pornography to CSAM, as Consumers seek images and videos that depict more graphic content.

This can result from a desensitisation to adult pornography, feeding a desire for new experiences that leads to problematic internet use (Quayle & Taylor, 2002; Quayle & Taylor, 2003; Schell et al., 2007). Hanson (2019) has argued that the categorisation of different types of adult pornography on websites can mean that different categories are just seen as masturbatory aids. It might then be just a small step to choosing CSAM as another category for this purpose. Quayle and Taylor's (2002) qualitative study of 13 CSAM Consumers described the compulsive, addictive nature of collecting such material, which could lead to more extreme material being accessed.

Escalation, in terms of the seriousness of the content viewed, can also be facilitated by the mode of technology employed. Davis et al. (2018) found that CSAM Consumers who viewed videos preferred more graphic imagery (as measured by the COPINE scale) than offenders who solely viewed photographic CSAM.

In relation to livestreaming of CSAM, there is some evidence of escalation in the seriousness of content demanded. In examining the financial transactions of Australians who viewed the livestreaming of CSAM in the Philippines, Brown et al. (2020) found that the amount that Consumers were willing to pay increased the more that Consumers purchased such services. While the average for the first ten transactions made was AUS $60, for transactions 41 to 50 the average was AUS $120. The authors concluded that this could be an indication of escalation in harm, with offenders requesting more extreme content, which came at a higher premium (Brown et al., 2020).

## Situations in which CSAM is viewed

Wolak et al. (2011) have previously documented the changing locations where CSAM Consumers have viewed material. Examining the locations of the computers primarily used in CSAM offending by over 1,000 possessors of CSAM arrested by the police in the USA, they found that the proportion of computers used in the home declined from 91 per cent in 2000 to 77 per cent in 2006. Similarly, the proportion of computers used at work declined from 7 per cent to 3 per cent. In contrast, the proportion using a computer in an 'other' location (including multiple locations) increased from 2 per cent to 19 per cent (Wolak et al., 2011). These changes signalled a shift to greater mobility (with laptops and tablets and then mobile phones) in the way in which CSAM was consumed. Among convicted CSAM Consumers in Australia, almost all were found to view material at home (n=66, 97%), although nine (13%) also viewed it at work (Krone et al., 2017).

## Technology used to view CSAM

Mobile phone technology has developed significantly in the last decade, changing the way in which CSAM is consumed. An analysis of popular CSAM search terms on Google, Bing and Yandex by Steel (2015) found that desktops and laptops remained the most popular devices for CSAM searching, accounting for two-thirds of such searches in 2014.

More recently, there has been a shift away from desktop computers to laptops and tablets and then to mobile phones for viewing CSAM. This has coincided with improvements in the speed of mobile networks, cheaper mobile phone plans and improvements in phone design allowing high-quality videos to be played (Steel et al., 2020). These changes have made the viewing of CSAM easier and cheaper. With encryption included as the default on both Apple and Android platforms, it has also become more secure (Steel et al., 2020). A survey of 450 police officers from 41 countries found that CSAM was most commonly found on computers / laptops (97%) and mobile phones (93%). USB sticks and portable hard drives were also common (89%) (Netclean, 2019). A third (33%) of police officers reported that there had been an increase in the use of mobile phones to store CSAM in the last three years, while 22 per cent reported an increase use of computers / laptops (Netclean, 2019).

## Security measures to prevent disclosure

CSAM Consumers may take a range of measures to prevent others (particularly law enforcement) from becoming aware of their viewing activities, ranging from behavioural to technical solutions. Holt et al. (2010) described how the management of security, both online and offline, was a recurring theme in online forums for paedophiles.

Simple behavioural security methods included ensuring a computer screen was out of sight of doors and windows when being used, locking the computer when not in use, ensuring no external copies of files were kept, making sure no CSAM was on the hard drive or in memory caches, and using a laptop that could be disposed of quickly if needed (Holt et al., 2010).

Technical security solutions employed by CSAM Consumers can be divided into those associated with disclosing their identity while operating online and those associated with securing the physical equipment used by Consumers to prevent others gaining access to its content. While the former addresses concern over the *risk of detection* for Consumers operating online, the latter aims to *increase the effort* associated with gaining access to sensitive material.

Ensuring anonymity when operating online is a key feature of the behaviour of CSAM Consumers (Taylor & Quayle, 2008). CSAM Consumers have employed various methods to avoid disclosing their IP address, which would typically be left in all online transactions on the World Wide Web, like a digital trail of breadcrumbs leading the police back to the Consumer's computer (or at least as far as their router). Different anonymising methodologies have been employed with varying degrees of success. Older methods include remailers that strip identifiable information from emails (Steel et al., 2020). More contemporary approaches include the use of Network Address Translation (which allows multiple private IP addresses to be merged into a single public IP address, making it hard to identify the original address); Dynamic Host Configuration Protocol (which temporarily assigns an IP address to a device on a network from a pool of addresses held on a server, which can also be removed and reassigned); proxy servers (which channel data through a server that changes the IP address, as well as providing security through firewalls); virtual private networks (which act as a kind of forwarding proxy server, giving transmitted data a different sending IP address that could be from anywhere in the world); and The Onion Router (TOR) network (which transmits data through multiple servers, each of which change the IP address as the data are forwarded on) (Lee at al., 2020). All these methods serve to hide the electronic breadcrumbs that could lead authorities back to the CSAM Consumer when operating online.

Other approaches aim to prevent CSAM content being identified and / or linked to the Consumer. These approaches have included engaging in forums and chatrooms where pseudonyms / usernames are used (Jenkins, 2001); the use of encrypted messaging so that conversations cannot be intercepted by others (Europol, 2019; Netclean, 2019); using web-based email (rather than storing emails on a computer) (Krone et al., 2017); and the use of password-protected file storage sites that allow material to be stored remotely, rather than on the Consumer's device (Netclean, 2019; Steel et al., 2020).

Where securing the physical equipment is concerned, a range of measures have been employed to restrict access to a Consumer's hardware (Islam et al., 2019b). These have included encrypting and password-protecting hard drives to prevent CSAM from being accessed or identified (Holt et al., 2010; Casey et al., 2011). Almost half (49%) of police officers surveyed by Netclean (2019) reported that encryption was the biggest hurdle to investigating CSAM cases. 14 per cent specifically mentioned the challenge posed by locked and encrypted smartphones and computers.

As CSAM Consumers move from being browsers to collectors (Krone, 2004), they will learn from others in online forums about how to protect their identity and how to prevent others from discovering their activity (van der Bruggen & Blokland, 2020). This will mean that the most harmful Consumers are also likely to be the most difficult to detect from a law enforcement perspective.

Despite the range of security methods available to Consumers, many fail to take precautions to avoid detection (Guerra & Westlake, 2021). Among a sample of convicted Australian CSAM Consumers, Krone et al. (2017) found that only ten (8%) of the 130 offenders examined had encrypted their CSAM. However, it is important to note that these offenders were convicted between 2005 and 2011 and anonymising and encrypting technologies have become more readily available since then. Beyond encryption, it was still apparent that many Consumers took no precautions. Among a subsample of 68 Consumers for whom concealment methods were known, over half (n=37, 54%) were found to make no effort to conceal their activities. A quarter (n=17, 25%) were found to hide CSAM after viewing it and a quarter (n=18, 27%) saved the material to an inconspicuously named folder on their computer (Krone et al., 2017).

## Summing up the ways in which CSAM is consumed

The increasing scale with which CSAM is being discovered online is probably a good indication that it is also being viewed by more people, more often. However, the proportion of content that is of the most severe kind (involving sexual activity between adults and children, including rape or sexual torture) that is found on the open-net would appear to be in decline. This may be due to a shift towards the darknet, with Consumers who seek the most severe content moving in greater numbers to the more anonymous darknet environment. This assumes that the distribution (in terms of magnitude of different types and seriousness) of what is available online is an indicator of what is generally consumed. What we do know is that, when CSAM is consumed, it often leads to an escalation in the severity of the material viewed.

In terms of where and how CSAM is consumed, viewing material at home would appear to be the most popular location. However, as smartphones have become faster, cheaper and ubiquitous there would appear to have been a shift towards using these devices, although more traditional desktops and laptops are also still commonly used. The increasing prevalence of smartphone use means that location no longer becomes a barrier to viewing CSAM content and means it can be readily available at all times for Consumers, wherever they may be.

The CSAM ecosystem offers choices for the way in which CSAM is consumed and the consequent security measures that may be taken to avoid detection. For some, all CSAM activity may occur within the confines of the ecosystem. At its simplest, this may involve Consumers searching and browsing websites on the open-net with no content being saved. Consumers may use anonymising technologies, such as proxy servers and virtual private networks, to avoid the identity of their IP address from being left behind as they browse websites. They may also decide to save CSAM accessed through crypto-lockers (often paying for access to premium hosting sites) and save that material in their own crypto-locker, which may be encrypted and / or not routinely checked for CSAM by the ESP hosting the file storage site. In other cases, the CSAM ecosystem may be used to discover and share CSAM, but consumption may occur in an offline environment. In these cases, CSAM may be downloaded to the Consumer's device where it is stored for later viewing. Peer-to-peer networks are a hybrid of the two, where material will be stored on a local device, but made available to others to download via the CSAM ecosystem. Consumers viewing material stored on their devices will often take additional precautions to avoid detection by using encryption to prevent others from accessing the material.

Despite the range of security features available to prevent detection, it is apparent that many CSAM Consumers fail to take security seriously. However, this is largely based on what we know from detected offenders and may represent a self-selecting sample – they are detected because they failed to take adequate precautions, while the more security savvy Consumers go undetected. Indeed, security would appear to be a popular topic in discussions on CSAM forums, suggesting that at least some CSAM Consumers take this issue seriously.

# References

Acar, K.V. (2017). Webcam child prostitution: An exploration of current and futuristic methods of detection. *International Journal of Cyber Criminology* 11(1), 98–109. http://dx.doi.org/10.5281/zenodo.802941

Brown, R., Napier, S. & Smith, R.G. (2020). *Australians who view livestreaming of child sexual abuse: An analysis of financial transactions.* Trends and issues in crime and criminal justice 589. Australian Institute of Criminology. www.aic.gov.au/publications/tandi/tandi589

Casey, E., Fellows, G., Geiger, M. & Stellatos, G. (2011). The growing impact of full disk encryption on digital forensics. *Digital investigation* 8(2), 129–134. https://doi.org/10.1016/j.diin.2011.09.005

Davis, N., Lennings, C. & Green, T. (2018). Improving practice in child sexual abuse image investigations through identification of offender characteristics. *Sexual Abuse in Australia and New Zealand* (Jan), 1–12

Europol (2019, 11 December). *Operation Chemosh: How encrypted chat groups exchanged emoji 'stickers' of child sexual abuse.* Europol. www.europol.europa.eu/newsroom/news/operation-chemosh-how-encrypted-chat-groups-exchanged-emoji-%E2%80%98stickers%E2%80%99-of-child-sexual-abuse

Guerra, E. & Westlake, B.G. (2021). Detecting child sexual abuse images: Traits of child sexual exploitation hosting and displaying websites. *Child Abuse & Neglect* 122, 105336. https://doi.org/10.1016/j.chiabu.2021.105336.

Hanson, E. (2019). 'Losing track of morality': understanding online forces and dynamics conducive to child sexual exploitation. In J Pearce (Ed.), *Child sexual exploitation: Why theory matters* (pp.87–117). Policy Press.

Holt, T.J., Blevins, K.R. & Burkert, N. (2010). Considering the Pedophile Subculture Online. *Sexual Abuse: A Journal of Research and Treatment* 22(1), 3–24. https://doi.org/10.1177/1079063209344979

Internet Watch Foundation (2022). *The annual report 2021.* Internet Watch Foundation. https://annualreport2021.iwf.org.uk/pdf/IWF-Annual-Report-2021.pdf

Islam, M., Watters, P., Mahmood, A.N. & Alazab, M. (2019b). Toward detection of child exploitation material: A forensic approach. In M. Alazab & M. Tang (Eds.), *Deep Learning Applications for Cyber Security, Advanced Sciences and Technologies for Security Applications* (pp.221–246). https://doi.org/10.1007/978-3-030-13057-2_10

Jenkins, P. (2001). *Beyond tolerance: Child pornography on the internet.* New York University Press.

Jones, C., Woodlock, D. & Salter, M. (2021). Evaluation of PartnerSpeak. Research Report. University of New South Wales. https://malesurvivor.nz/wp-content/uploads/2021/11/Evaluation_of_PartnerSPEAK.pdf

Krone, T. (2004). *A Typology of Online Child Pornography Offending.* Trends and issues in crime and criminal justice 279. Australian Institute of Criminology. www.aic.gov.au/publications/tandi/tandi279

Krone, T. & Smith, R.G. (2017). *Trajectories in online child sexual exploitation offending in Australia.* Trends and issues in crime and criminal justice 524. Australian Institute of Criminology. www.aic.gov.au/publications/tandi/tandi524

Krone, T., Smith, R.G., Cartwright, J., Hutchings, A., Tomison, A. & Napier, S. (2017). *Online child sexual exploitation offenders: A study of Australian law enforcement data. Report to the Criminology Research Advisory Council: CRG 58/12–13.* www.aic.gov.au/sites/default/files/2020-05/58-1213-FinalReport.pdf

Lanning, K.V. (1986). *Child molesters: A behavioral analysis for law-enforcement officers investigating cases of child sexual exploitation.* National Centre for Missing and Exploited Children. www.ojp.gov/pdffiles1/Digitization/102031NCJRS.pdf

Lee, H.E., Ermakova, T., Ververis, V. & Fabian, B. (2020). Detecting child sexual abuse material: A comprehensive survey. *Forensic Science International: Digital Investigation* 34, 302022 https://doi.org/10.1016/j.fsidi.2020.301022

Martellozzo, E. & DeMarco, J. (2020). Exploring the removal of online child sexual abuse material in the UK: Processes and practice. *Crime Prevention and Community Safety* 22, 331–350. https://doi.org/10.1057/s41300-020-00099-2

Mitchell, K.J., Finkelhor, D. & Wolak, J. (2005). The internet and family and acquaintance sexual abuse. *Child Maltreatment* 10(1), 49–60.

Netclean (2019). *Netclean Report 2019: A report about child sexual abuse crime.* www.netclean.com/wp-content/uploads/2017/06/Netclean_report_2019_A4.pdf

Quayle, E. & Taylor, M. (2002). Child pornography and the internet: perpetuating a cycle of abuse. *Deviant Behaviour: An Interdisciplinary Journal* 23, 331–361. https://doi.org/10.1080/01639620290086413

Quayle, E. & Taylor, M. (2003). Model of problematic internet use in people with sexual interest in children. *Cyber Psychology and Behaviour* 6(1), 93–106. https://doi.org/10.1089/109493103321168009

Salter, M. (2013). *Organised sexual abuse.* Glasshouse / Routledge.

Schell, B.H., Martin, M.V., Hung, P.C.K. & Rueda, L. (2007). Cyber child pornography: A review paper of the social and legal issues and remedies – and a proposed technological solution. *Journal of Aggression and Violent Behaviour* 12(1), 45–63. https://doi.org/10.1016/j.avb.2006.03.003

Steel, C.M.S. (2015). Web-based child pornography: The global impact of deterrence efforts and its consumption on mobile platforms. *Child Abuse and Neglect* 44, 150–158. http://dx.doi.org/10.1016/j.chiabu.2014.12.009

Steel, C.M.S., Newman, E., O'Rourke, S. & Quayle, E. (2020). An integrative review of historical technology and countermeasure usage trends in online child sexual exploitation material offenders. *Forensic Science International: Digital Investigation* 33, 2666–2817. https://doi.org/10.1016/j.fsidi.2020.300971

Taylor, M. & Quayle, E. (2008). Criminogenic qualities of the internet in the collection and distribution of abuse images of children. *Irish Journal of Psychology* 29(1–2), 119–130. https://doi:10.1080/03033910.2008.10446278

van der Bruggen, M. & Blokland, A. (2020). A crime script analysis of child sexual exploitation material fora on the darknet. *Sexual Abuse* 33(8), 950–974. https://doi.org/10.1177/1079063220981063

Wolak, J., Finkelhor, D. & Mitchell, K. (2011). Child pornography possessors: Trends in offender and case characteristics. *Sexual Abuse: A Journal of Research and Treatment* 23(1), 22–42. https://doi.org/10.1177/1079063210372143

# 6
# UNDERSTANDING CSAM PROBLEMS

## Introduction

What should be clear from the discussion so far is that there is no *one* problem with CSAM. Instead, there are numerous, related problems that exist simultaneously in the CSAM ecosystem. This chapter provides a summary of these problems in the context of the CSAM ecosystem.

Where the production of CSAM is concerned, it is clear that there are behaviours that occur offline that lead to the creation of such material. This includes situations in which the perpetrator exploits the child in their care, where they exploit a child with whom they are in an intimate relationship (whether that be as another child or as an adult), where they target children who are not in their care and where they pay for access to children. All these tactics can be employed in the offline world to sexually abuse children. The internet may be employed to facilitate these perpetrator behaviours, but equally it may not. Sexual abuse may be undertaken with the intention of producing CSAM, or such material may be the by-product of the sexual abuse. Alternatively, sexual abuse may occur without CSAM being produced. Therefore, much of the child sexual abuse that is perpetrated will have an offline, real-world dimension and it follows that responses will need to be situated in the real world too. This is important to keep in mind. Addressing the production of CSAM will not solve the problem of child sexual abuse on its own. However, there are some forms of CSAM production that rely on internet use. For example, self-produced CSAM, where a Victim / Survivor may consensually share images with a (sometimes prospective) intimate partner, or where they are encouraged or coerced to provide such material by an online perpetrator who they may not know in the offline world, will rely on the internet for that type of CSAM to come into existence.

DOI: 10.4324/9781003327264-7

Where the distribution of CSAM is concerned, the role of the internet comes into its own. While CSAM can be shared offline, the internet makes this so much easier, offering a variety of channels for sharing quickly, cheaply and seemingly with impunity. In sharing CSAM, the number of perpetrators multiplies for any given Victim / Survivor, as the material is shared and shared again.

Closely related to the distribution of CSAM is its consumption. It goes without saying that most of those that share it will also consume it. However, those that consume it will not necessarily share it with others. They may be casual browsers or collectors of CSAM (Krone, 2004), who do not share with others what they find online. As such, production, distribution and consumption are closely related, but distinct behaviours and perpetrators can exhibit any combination of these behaviours.

## Classifying problem facilitators

One way to think about how we might intervene to address these problem behaviours is to consider the online facilitators that make the production, distribution and consumption of CSAM easier. Table 6.1 shows the problem facilitators, based on the discussion in the preceding chapters. This examines each of the three key behaviours in the CSAM process (production, distribution and consumption).

Examining CSAM production first, we can see from Table 6.1 that file storage sites (including image hosting) offer a potentially safe place to store CSAM, while social media and instant messaging provide avenues for extracting self-produced CSAM. Computer games (through their chat function) can also be a means of contacting children, grooming them and extracting self-produced CSAM. However, they also offer a means of CSAM production through online role-playing games, without children necessarily having been involved directly. Livestreaming creates

**TABLE 6.1** Location of problem facilitators in the CSAM ecosystem

*CSAM Process*

| Production | Distribution | Consumption |
| --- | --- | --- |
| File storage | Email | Websites |
| Forums | Websites | Computer games |
| Social media | Darknet | Livestreaming |
| Instant messaging | Forums | |
| Livestreaming | Social media | |
| Computer games | Instant messaging | |
| | File storage | |
| | Internet relay chat | |
| | Peer-to-peer networks | |
| | Computer games | |

a different set of circumstances in which CSAM is produced and simultaneously consumed, but without it being distributed beyond those directly consuming it. It should also be noted that livestreaming typically relies on the financial system because it usually involves CSAM that is monetised for profit by third parties. Therefore, within the production processes depicted in Table 6.1, we have a series of facilitators which allow CSAM to be created without the presence of a real Victim / Survivor, to be stored in a safe place, to be created through direct online contact with strangers, to be consumed live at the point of production and to be monetised through the financial system.

The distribution of CSAM is characterised in Table 6.1 by the wide variety of ways in which sharing can be facilitated. This ranges from long-standing methods of distribution (e.g. email and websites), through to more recent developments (e.g. social media, darknet and computer games).

In Table 6.1, problem facilitators shown in relation to consumption relate solely to those that are intrinsically related to the consumption of CSAM, rather than, for example, its storage. Indeed, CSAM will often be produced and distributed but this does not mean it will necessarily be contemporaneously consumed. Rather, it may be stored for later consumption. Websites and livestreaming have been classed as facilitators of CSAM consumption in Table 6.1. This is because consumption is a significant benefit of these technologies. Websites act as locations where CSAM can be viewed without it being stored for later use. Livestreaming relies on contemporaneous production and viewing. While CSAM could be downloaded and stored using both technologies, this will often not be the case. Computer games are included under consumption, because the very act of role-playing (and therefore consuming) CSAM through playing such games is also the means by which it is produced.

Based on this list of CSAM ecosystem facilitators, we can begin to define a number of specific problems that make up the more generic problem of CSAM. These only account for problems embedded within the ecosystem itself. They ignore problems associated with how perpetrators successfully find opportunities for contact offending and / or CSAM creation outside of internet-related facilitation.

For the purposes of this analysis then, we can identify 15 problems that warrant further attention. Addressing these 15 problems would go a significant way to solving CSAM, at least in its current guise. These problems include the following:

## *Production-related problems*

1. File storage sites (including image hosting) to store CSAM once it has been produced (which also aid distribution).
2. Forums (including bulletin boards, newsgroups, image boards and the latest generation of forums) that assist in creating cognitions / justifications among perpetrators to engage in child sexual abuse and to create CSAM.

3. Social media sites and instant messaging as the locations for perpetrators to locate, groom and exploit children and young people to self-produce CSAM.
4. Livestreaming technology to simultaneously produce, distribute, consume and monetise CSAM.
5. Computer games that are designed to depict or facilitate role play of child sexual abuse.
6. Computer games chat function as the location for perpetrators to locate, groom and exploit children and young people to self-produce CSAM.

## Distribution-related problems

7. Forums (including bulletin boards, newsgroups, image boards and the latest generation of forums) to distribute CSAM (both directly and through links).
8. Social media sites to distribute CSAM (both directly and through links).
9. Instant messaging to distribute CSAM (both directly and through links).
10. Internet relay chat to distribute CSAM links.
11. Peer-to-peer networks to distribute CSAM directly.
12. Computer game chat function to distribute CSAM (both directly and through links).
13. Email to distribute CSAM (both directly and through links).
14. Websites that host and (sometimes) monetise CSAM.
15. Darknet use (through TOR) to distribute CSAM (via websites and forums).

Note that some of the problems identified in Table 6.1 are repeated under different headings but only shown once in the list of 15. This is for ease of classification, with each being shown at the first point in the aetiology of the problem. For example, the CSAM ecosystem first facilitates the use of file storage sites and livestreaming at the production stage, although both are also problematic at the distribution stage. They are only shown once in the list of 15 because they involve one activity (e.g. uploading files to a file storage site / livestreaming) that has multiple implications (for production, distribution and consumption). In contrast, forums, instant messaging, social media and computer games are listed separately under production and distribution because they involve *different* activities. In the case of forums, they provide a meeting place for (potential) perpetrators to meet, where their feelings towards children can be shared and justified and thereby indirectly leading to child sexual abuse and the creation of CSAM. They are also used to share CSAM, links to file storage sites, or websites hosting such material, thereby directly playing a role in the distribution of CSAM. Where social media sites and gaming chat functions are concerned, they are used to target and groom young people to provide self-produced CSAM and they are also used to distribute CSAM – often in closed groups. Where instant messaging is concerned, its role in facilitating the self-creation of CSAM is very different from its role in sharing CSAM that has already been produced with other users and is therefore also shown twice in the list of 15. In each of the three cases described (forums, social media and instant messaging), the particular type of application is used in more than one way to facilitate CSAM.

Although an integral CSAM process, consumption is not a primary problem listed in the group of 15 (unlike production and distribution). This is because consumption (such as by viewing websites, viewing livestreaming and role play in computer games) is only made possible by other problem facilitators associated with production and distribution. Remove these facilitators and consumption becomes much more difficult.

These 15 problems share the characteristic that they are all facilitated by the internet, without which these problems would not exist. Obviously, we cannot just turn off the internet and, at the same time, we cannot just allow these problems to persist. So, we must seek solutions that aim to address one or more of these problems with the intention of reducing or eliminating their existence.

## Features of the 15 problems

A cursory reading of these problems shows they are quite disparate in nature, but there are some common features that might allow for rudimentary categorisation. This may in turn assist with prioritising preventative activity.

### *Facilitating access to saved material*

Many of the problems listed above relate to the storage and distribution of CSAM that has previously been created (problems 1, 7, 8, 9, 10, 11, 12, 13, 14, 15). Here the remedial task must be to locate and destroy material already in the system and prevent new material from entering the ecosystem.

### *Facilitating access to Victims / Survivors*

Social media platforms, and specifically the way in which they allow people to connect with each other, provide the virtual location in which perpetrators can anonymously or pseudonymously contact potential victims, in ways that would be much more difficult in the real world. This allows for a grooming process that ends in the self-production of CSAM by child Victims / Survivors.

Social media platforms also provide the location for Consumers to meet the facilitators of livestreaming of child sexual abuse. This can occur in both directions. The Consumer may seek out existing facilitators, or (with some encouragement) individuals who might be willing to facilitate livestreaming. Conversely, facilitators may trawl social media sites with the intention of finding potential Consumers (Napier et al., 2021). These are two different scenarios from a preventative perspective. In the case of social media, the prevention task lies in stopping a perpetrator from making contact and engaging with a potential victim. In the case of livestreaming, preventative effort needs to be applied to stopping the Consumer from engaging with a facilitator. In both cases, intervention needs to address the transactional nature of the problem, but each needs a different response given the differences between the transactions.

## Facilitating access to a community of perpetrators

Many of the problems in the list of 15 (problems 2, 7, 8, 9, 10, 11, 12, 13, 14, 15) facilitate access to a community of perpetrators. The CSAM ecosystem makes it easier for perpetrators to share CSAM with each other, without knowing with whom they are sharing it. This sharing can be on a one-to-one or one-to-many basis. Regardless of style of distribution, none of this sharing would be possible without the internet playing an intermediary role between people. Online forums allow perpetrators to communicate in ways that would be difficult in the real world – a real world where anonymity cannot be assured and risk of being caught will be higher.

## The failure of guardians

As outlined in Table 6.1, applications facilitate a range of problems. Many of these applications (including those associated with problems 1, 2, 3, 4, 5, 6, 7, 8, 9, 12, 13, 14) have a centralised structure and are designed, managed and promoted by a corporation – many of which are private enterprises with shareholders. These corporations should (at the very least from a moral perspective) have a respon-sibility for ensuring the customers who use their services have a safe experience. Risk should be minimised and, indeed, the very way in which these services are designed should have the safety of their users embedded as a core principle. Just as the managers of shopping malls, business parks, theme parks and sports stadiums have a responsibility to ensure the risks of bad things happening to their patrons are minimised (whether that be from a health and safety or security perspective), so too should the managers of applications ensure that their services are safe to use. Being vigilant to the possibility that CSAM will be produced and / or distributed on their applications is one of the risks that corporations should be aware of, at both the design and ongoing management stages. In this sense, application managers can be viewed as guardians who watch over their customers to ensure nothing adverse arises (we will discuss the role of guardians in more detail later). The fact that so much CSAM proliferates via commonly available applications suggests a failure of guardianship on the part of the application managers and simultaneously offers an opportunity to reduce risk through improved design and greater surveillance.

## Not all problems are equal

While the list of 15 problems identifies a range of ways in which the CSAM eco-system can flourish, it is important to note that these problems do not carry equal weight. The preceding chapters have highlighted how some problems are clearly more serious (either in terms of their volume or harm caused) than others. For example, older forms of forums (BBSs and newgroups) are now less of a problem than social media or peer-to-peer networks. According to analysis by Bursztein et al. (2019), even peer-to-peer networks may have had their heyday, with reports to authorities peaking more than 15 years ago.

So, on what criteria might we prioritise these 15 problems? There are at least four different ways to think about prioritisation and the selection of those which are most salient may differ from place to place and from time to time. These ways of thinking about priorities include:

- **CSAM volume.** Problem facilitators responsible for the production / distribution of large volumes of CSAM should be prioritised over those that account for smaller volumes.
- **CSAM growth.** Problem facilitators responsible for the fastest growth in production / distribution of CSAM should be prioritised over those that grow at a slower rate.
- **CSAM harm.** Problem facilitators responsible for the most harmful CSAM being produced / distributed should be prioritised over those responsible for less harmful CSAM.
- **Community expectation.** As with all matters involving law and order, there will be societal expectations over how problem facilitators are prioritised that may need to be considered. These expectations may well be based on considerations of volume, growth and harm, but they may also be based on other less tangible and, indeed, subjective factors, that could range from sentiments towards the companies responsible for the technologies, the countries in which Victims / Survivors and / or perpetrators are located, the impact of a recent news report and so forth.

If decisions need to be made on where to focus preventative efforts, consideration needs to be given to where the greatest threats lie in the proliferation of CSAM. Based on the earlier analysis of problem facilitators, we can begin to score them against the prioritisation measures (Table 6.2). What becomes clear is how poor our current understanding of these problems is. The ticks in Table 6.2 show those problems where there is evidence to support the prioritisation measure. One tick indicates there is any evidence to support a measure, two ticks indicate that there are two or more sources to support the measure. Similarly, one cross suggests there is evidence to contradict a measure and two crosses indicate two or more sources to contradict a measure. A cross and a tick means there was evidence in both directions.

Table 6.2 shows that, from a prioritisation perspective, we know nothing about what the community expects the focus of attention to be and was therefore not included as a column. That may be because of how the question is framed, with a focus on facilitators within the CSAM ecosystem. This is not a standard way to

**TABLE 6.2** Evidence to support the prioritisation of the 15 problem facilitators for intervention

| Problem facilitators | Prioritisation measures[a] | | |
| --- | --- | --- | --- |
| | Volume[b] | Growth | Harm[c] |
| File storage sites | ✓✓[d] | | ✓[e] |
| Forums (for production) | | | |
| Social media sites and instant messaging for grooming | | | ✓[f] |
| Livestreaming | ✓✓[g] | | ✓✗[h] |
| Computer game chat for grooming | | | |
| Forums (for distribution) | ✓✓[i] | | |
| Social media sites (for distribution) | ✓✓[j] | | |
| Instant messaging (for distribution) | ✓✓[k] | ✓✓[l] | |
| Internet relay chat (for distribution) | ✓[m] | ✓[n] | |
| Peer-to-peer networks (for distribution) | ✓✓[o] | ✗✗[p] | |
| Computer games (for distribution) | ✓[q] | | |
| Computer game play | | | |
| Email (for distribution) | ✓[r] | ✗[s] | |
| Websites | ✓✓[t] | ✗[u] | ✓[v] |
| Darknet | ✓[w] | ✓✓[x] | |

Key: ✓ = one positive source; ✓✓ =two or more positive sources; ✗= one negative source; ✗✗=two or more negative sources; ✓✗=mixed evidence

Table notes:
a The community expectation measure is excluded from Table 6.2 because no studies were identified that related to this priority measure.
b Volume was defined as any source that reported more than 1,000 cases, regardless of whether that was in a single year, or over multiple years.
c Harm was defined as evidence indicating babies / young children, torture or penetrative sexual acts were more likely to be involved.
d Internet Watch Foundation (2021); INHOPE (2020); Internet Watch Foundation (2020).
e The Internet Watch Foundation (2020) found that 30 per cent of the reports associated with babies (aged 0–2 years) were associated with file sharing sites (particularly cyber-lockers).
f Wolak et al. (2018).
g Terre des Hommes (2014); Brown et al. (2020).
h Terre des Hommes (2014)(✓); Ramiro et al. (2019) (✗).
i Bursztein et al. (2019); NCMEC (2020).
j Dance & Keller (2020); NCMEC (2020); NCMEC (2021).
k Bursztein et al. (2019); Dance & Keller (2020); NCMEC (2020).
l Bursztein et al. (2019); Dance & Keller (2020); NCMEC (2020); NCMEC (2021).
m Bursztein et al. (2019).
n Bursztein et al. (2019).
o Bissias et al. (2016); Bursztein et al. (2019).
p Bissias et al. (2016); Bursztein et al. (2019).
q Bursztein et al. (2019).
r Bursztein et al. (2019).
s Bursztein et al. (2019).
t Bursztein et al. (2019); Internet Watch Foundation (2019); Internet Watch Foundation (2020).
u Bursztein et al. (2019).
v Internet Watch Foundation's (2020) found that banner sites were more likely to involve babies and young children.
w Bursztein et al. (2019).
x Bursztein et al. (2019); Internet Watch Foundation (2020).

think about CSAM, which may reflect the lack of literature found on this topic. In contrast, if the question had been framed in terms of which perpetrators to focus on, which types of behaviour to prevent or which children to safeguard first, it is likely that more literature would have been found.

There is also an over-reliance on a small number of papers in Table 6.2. For example, Bursztein et al. (2019) appear 12 times in the table. This is because there is generally a lack of material that quantifies the volume that measures change over time associated with these 15 problems. However, if we take those problems with at least one priority tick and exclude those with evidence of a diminishing problem (peer-to-peer networks, email and websites), we can narrow the focus of concern to nine contemporary problems in the CSAM ecosystem. These include[1]:

1.  File storage sites (including image hosting) to store CSAM once it has been produced (which also aid distribution).
3.  Social media sites and instant messaging as the locations for perpetrators to locate, groom and exploit children and young people to self-produce CSAM.
4.  Livestreaming technology to simultaneously produce, distribute, consume and monetise CSAM.
7.  Forums (including bulletin boards, newsgroups, image boards and the latest generation of forums) to distribute CSAM (both directly and through links).
8.  Social media sites to distribute CSAM (both directly and through links).
9.  Instant messaging to distribute CSAM (both directly and through links).
10. Internet relay chat to distribute CSAM links.
12. Computer game chat function to distribute CSAM (both directly and through links).
15. Darknet use (through TOR) to distribute CSAM (via websites and forums).

On reviewing this list, it would appear to address the major ways in which material currently enters and circulates around the CSAM ecosystem. If one were to be critical, one might question why internet relay chat is on the list of problems to address, given that this is a comparatively old technology. This is, perhaps, a function of relying on a small number of sources for the prioritisation exercise, with the internet relay chat conclusion reliant on just one source (Bursztein et al., 2019). This highlights a weakness of exercises of this kind and suggests that lists like this one need to be treated as a guide, rather than as a rigid template.

While this prioritisation is rudimentary and no doubt open to criticism, it provides a working basis for triaging the problem facilitators in the CSAM ecosystem. Tackling these nine problems should arguably go a considerable way to addressing the overall problem with CSAM on the internet.

## Next steps

Now that the specific problems have been identified, we can begin to explore approaches that are being taken to address them and other possible approaches that could be undertaken into the future. The following chapter therefore provides an outline of the crime science discipline and its relevance to tackling CSAM. Chapter 8 then explores how this approach can be applied to the production of CSAM, while chapters 9 and 10 deal respectively with its distribution and consumption.

## Note

1 The numbering in the following list reflects the same numbers as those used in the earlier list of 15 problems for consistency.

## References

Bissias, G., Levine, B., Liberatore, M., Lynne, B., Moore, J., Wallach, H. & Wollak, J. (2016). Characterization of contact offenders and child exploitation material trafficking on five peer-to-peer networks. *Child Abuse and Neglect* 52, 185–199. https://doi.org/10.1016/j.chiabu.2015.10.022

Brown, R., Napier, S. & Smith, R.G. (2020). *Australians who view livestreaming of child sexual abuse: An analysis of financial transactions.* Trends and issues in crime and criminal justice 589. Australian Institute of Criminology. www.aic.gov.au/publications/tandi/tandi589

Bursztein, E., Bright, T., Clarke, E., DeLaune, M., Eliff, D.M., Hsu, N., Olson, L., Shehan, J., Thakur, M. & Thomas, K. (2019, 13–17 May). Rethinking the Detection of Child Sexual Abuse Imagery on the Internet. In *Proceedings of the 2019 World Wide Web Conference (WWW '19), San Francisco, CA, USA.* https://doi.org/10.1145/3308558.3313482

Dance, G.J.X. & Keller, M.H. (2020, 7 February). Tech companies detect a surge in online videos of child sexual abuse. *The New York Times.* www.nytimes.com/2020/02/07/us/online-child-sexual-abuse.html

INHOPE (2020). *Annual report 2019.* INHOPE. https://inhope.org/media/pages/the-facts/download-our-whitepapers/009c452175-1595854476/annualreport_inhope_2019.pdf

Internet Watch Foundation (2019). *Once upon a year: The Internet Watch Foundation annual report 2018.* Internet Watch Foundation. www.iwf.org.uk/sites/default/files/reports/2019-04/Once%20upon%20a%20year%20-%20IWF%20Annual%20Report%202018.pdf

Internet Watch Foundation (2020). *The why. The how. The who. And the results: Internet Watch Foundation annual report 2019.* Internet Watch Foundation. www.iwf.org.uk/sites/default/files/reports/2020-04/IWF_Annual_Report_2020_Low-res-Digital_AW_6mb.pdf

Internet Watch Foundation (2021). *Face the facts: The annual report 2020.* Internet Watch Foundation. https://annualreport2020.iwf.org.uk/

Krone, T. (2004). *A Typology of Online Child Pornography Offending.* Trends and issues in crime and criminal justice 279. Australian Institute of Criminology. www.aic.gov.au/publications/tandi/tandi279

Napier, S., Teunissen, C. & Boxall, H. (2021). *Live streaming of child sexual abuse: An analysis of offender chat logs.* Trends and issues in crime and criminal justice 639. Australian Institute of Criminology. https://doi.org/10.52922/ti78375

National Centre for Missing and Exploited Children (NCMEC) (2020). *2019 Reports by Electronic Service Providers (ESP).* www.missingkids.org/content/dam/missingkids/gethelp/2019-reports-by-esp.pdf

National Centre for Missing and Exploited Children (NCMEC) (2021). *2020 Reports by Electronic Service Providers (ESP).* www.missingkids.org/content/dam/missingkids/gethelp/2020-reports-by-esp.pdf

Ramiro, L.S., Martinez, A.B., Tan, J.R.D., Mariano, K., Miranda, G.M.J. & Bautista, G. (2019). Online child sexual exploitation and abuse: A community diagnosis using the social norms theory. *Child Abuse and Neglect* 96, 104080. https://doi.org/10.1016/j.chiabu.2019.104080

Terre des Hommes (2014). *Webcam child sex tourism: Becoming Sweetie: A novel approach to stopping the global rise of webcam child sex tourism.* Terre des Hommes. www.terredeshommes.org/wp-content/uploads/2013/11/Webcam-child-sex-tourism-terre-des-hommes-NL-nov-2013.pdf

Wolak, J.D., Finkelhor, D., Walsh, W. & Tritman, L. (2018). Sextortion of minors: Characteristics and dynamics. *Journal of Adolescent Health* 62(1), 72–79. https://doi.org/10.1016/j.jadohealth.2017.08.014

# PART II
# Addressing the problem

# 7
# TAKING A CRIME SCIENCE APPROACH

## Introduction

Chapter 1 introduced some of the basic ideas associated with crime science to demonstrate how it might be used to address CSAM, especially from the viewpoint of designing out crime. In this chapter, we explore in greater detail some of the most important tools and concepts that have been adopted by crime science and which can be used to reduce CSAM.

## Some theory

Any discussion of crime science should start with an understanding of some of the theory that underpins it. As noted in chapter 1, we need to take account of the role of rational choice, situational crime prevention and environmental criminology when we think about the genealogy of crime science. But we should also consider the role of routine activity theory that can legitimately be included under the banner of crime science for the additional tools it provides in understanding crime situations.

### Rational choice

Rational choice theory provides the fundamental framework for understanding offender decision-making (Clarke & Cornish, 1985; Cornish & Clarke, 1986). Originally drawing on a wide range of research from psychology, Clarke and Cornish (1985) argued that offenders were typically rational decision makers, weighing up the costs and benefits associated with any course of action to engage in crime. While the decision to offend may be made with incomplete information (e.g. of the likely rewards or risk of detection) or affected by distorted cognitions

DOI: 10.4324/9781003327264-9

(e.g. due to mental illness or substance use) it would typically be made in a rational (and therefore predictable) way, with the expectation of a certain positive outcome (whether that be in an instrumental or expressive sense) as a result of an illegitimate course of action. While not denying the role of other social, economic and psychological factors that may influence motivations to offend (which Cornish and Clarke (1986) described as factors associated with *criminal involvement*, as opposed to *criminal events*), rational choice theory focuses on the point at which the decision to offend is made (the criminal event). The task then becomes one of understanding the circumstances in which individuals decide to offend in any given context.

Related to rational choice theory is a body of work broadly known as opportunity theory. This demonstrates how crime occurs when opportunity is present. Some types of crime are more likely to occur in busy places and at busy times when there are more targets to choose from and where the potential for getting away with the crime is greatest. For example, pickpocketing and shoplifting may benefit from busy places with lots of targets to choose from. Other types of crime may benefit from seclusion or the absence of people. For example, burglary and vehicle theft tend to occur at times when there are few people around. When crime is hard to commit, it tends to occur less often. Just think about how less often one hears about armed robberies, vehicle thefts, burglaries, or even mobile phone theft, than one did a few years ago. Opportunity theory offers a plausible explanation. Some of this may be due to a reduction in target availability due to improved security (and therefore fewer opportunities for crime) and some of it may be due to easier targets being available elsewhere. In both cases, offenders make rational choices to stop committing one type of crime and to start committing another.

From a CSAM perspective, rational choice theory does not explain why some individuals may have paedophilic or hebephilic tendencies towards children (factors explaining their *criminal involvement*), but it may help to explain why they choose to target one child over another and why they choose to use certain applications to share CSAM and not others. Relatedly, opportunity theory helps to explain why CSAM has grown so rapidly in recent years and why most CSAM offenders would not be classed as paedophiles. The availability of CSAM, thanks to the internet, has created the opportunity for perpetrators to make a rational choice to search for CSAM (perhaps as a progression from adult pornography) and then to make a rational choice to store, share and, ultimately, in some cases, to produce such material. The opportunities to commit these crimes (especially those related to accessing, storing and sharing CSAM) are so much more apparent than they used to be because there is more CSAM available than ever before and the tools to make this happen are at the perpetrators' fingertips.

The rational choice perspective therefore has much to offer in both understanding why people offend in this way and for devising ways to reduce offending by altering the factors that would otherwise render individuals to consider such behaviour to be rational.

## *Situational crime prevention*

Situational crime prevention builds upon the rational choice perspective with a framework that describes a range of mechanisms by which the decision-making processes of an individual may be influenced to avoid them from choosing to engage in crime, when confronted with a given set of circumstances. Developed and refined over more than 40 years, situational crime prevention has become what must be the most widely used and successful criminological theory of all time. Like crime science, situational crime prevention offers a change-oriented perspective. It focuses on how crime can be prevented by altering the environment in which it would otherwise occur, thereby reducing the opportunity for crime commission. This is a result of changing the decision-making process for a would-be offender when encountering a situation.

Cornish and Clarke (2003) developed the situational crime prevention framework into 25 techniques that described the circumstances in which a situation could be changed to prevent crime. This focused on five[1] mechanisms of change associated with an offender's decision-making. These included increasing effort, increasing risk, reducing reward, removing excuses and reducing provocation. Each of these decision-making mechanisms were assigned five examples of changes to the environment that would elicit the mechanism in question. For example, increasing effort could result from target hardening, controlling access, screening exits, deflecting offenders and controlling tools. Increasing risks could be elicited by extending guardianship, assisting natural surveillance, reducing anonymity, utilising place managers and strengthening formal surveillance. Reducing rewards could result from concealing targets, removing targets, identifying property, disrupting markets and denying benefits. Reducing provocations could result from reducing frustrations and stress, avoiding disputes, reducing emotional arousal, neutralising peer pressure and discouraging imitation. Finally, removing excuses could result from setting rules, posting instructions, alerting one's conscience, assisting compliance and controlling drugs and alcohol. Each of these 25 techniques deserves more attention than there is room to explore here, although it is also important to note that the list is not exhaustive and other techniques may also be relevant for each of the five mechanisms. What should be clear is that this framework offers a very practical approach to thinking about how one might prevent crime in a wide range of situations.

Situational crime prevention has typically been used to explore how crime in the physical world might be reduced. This, for example, has included vehicle crime (Webb & Brown, 2017), burglary (Tilley & Webb, 1994), shoplifting (Ekblom, 1986), vandalism (Geason & Wilson, 1990) and alcohol-related crime (Homel et al., 1997; Graham & Homel, 2008) to name just a few. It has also been used to explore how sexual violence (Smallbone, 2016) and, more specifically, child sexual abuse (Smallbone et al., 2008) and child sexual abuse material (Wortley & Smallbone, 2012) might be reduced

From a CSAM perspective, situational crime prevention, and particularly the 25 techniques, have much to offer when thinking about how this problem might be eliminated. Where increasing effort is concerned, there is a role for controlling access to platforms, or deflecting perpetrators away from accessing CSAM. Increasing risks can be applied at almost every part of the CSAM ecosystem, with the potential to increase guardianship and place management on social media platforms and by ISPs, and to reduce the degree of anonymity. Reducing rewards can be achieved by concealing where CSAM can be found and removing CSAM more effectively. Removing excuses may be possible by making the conditions of use of online services much clearer and making sure they spell out their position in relation to CSAM. Posting instructions (such as 'posting of CSAM will not be tolerated') could also help to remove excuses. Of the five mechanisms, reducing provocation is probably the least useful in this context, although even here there may be a role for approaches that aim to reduce emotional arousal to CSAM, or that remove justifications and online subcultural support such as might be found in online forums.

## Environmental criminology

Environmental criminology explores how the physical world affects crime. It examines how the environment influences crime, how offenders travel through time and space, the spatial distribution of crime, risk factors and protective factors that affect the geographic distribution of crime, and changes in the distribution of crime over time. As such, environmental criminology is synonymous with understanding why crime occurs in some places more often than in other (Brantingham & Brantingham, 1981).

This at first sight may seem to have little relevance for CSAM. That is, unless one understands the CSAM ecosystem in a similar way to physical space, with the virtual distribution of CSAM influenced by risk and protective factors, in a similar way that crime in the physical world is a product of risk and protective factors. For example, some applications will be more popular than others for the distribution of CSAM, either because they offer functionality that is favoured by CSAM perpetrators, or because security is not as strict as elsewhere in the ecosystem. Crime opportunity structures create crime signatures, with the distribution of CSAM in the ecosystem reflecting the opportunities for it to flourish (Eck & Madensen, 2009). These crime signatures can be picked up through crime analysis, allowing for greater understanding about how crime opportunities are distributed. This is why articulating the 15 CSAM problems (and the prioritised list of nine problems) in the previous chapter was so important. Each of these will create different crime signatures that will lead to parts of CSAM ecosystem that most need to be addressed from a prevention perspective.

In understanding how crime opportunities are distributed in time and space, it is useful to think about how some places will be *crime attractors*. These are places where criminal opportunities are known to exist and to which motivated offenders will be attracted, in the hope that their search for a suitable target or victim will be successful. Other places will be crime *generators,* characterised as locations where large numbers of people tend to gather for non-crime-related purposes and where, because of the size of the group, criminal opportunities will arise. Thirdly, there are crime-neutral places that are neither attractors nor generators and where crime is infrequent and usually the result of local insiders (Brantingham & Brantingham, 2008).

From a CSAM ecosystem perspective, we can view some parts of the ecosystem as more prone to CSAM distribution because of the sheer size of the user population. For example, it should probably be no surprise that Facebook reports more CSAM to NCMEC than any other ESP, given it has far more users than any other platform, making it a significant crime generator[2]. Other online sites will be crime attractors because they bring together offenders who hope to find suitable targets / victims. For example, CSAM Consumers may seek out forums, peer-to-peer networks and internet relay chat groups that are known to share CSAM between group members. Similarly, banner sites may be sought out because they offer links to multiple sites holding CSAM material.

Understanding which sites are generators and which are attractors may help in devising interventions. For example, requesting users to report any CSAM they find on social media sites to the relevant platform's administrators is more likely to be a successful strategy on sites that are frequented by large numbers of law-abiding users, who will be keen to see such material removed. In contrast, users frequenting crime-attracting sites on the darknet are unlikely to report to a site's administrators if the very reason for them being at the site is for nefarious purposes.

Focusing on crime decision-making processes, Brantingham and Brantingham (1978; 1981) also outlined a model of crime site selection. This model included a number of propositions. Individuals are motivated to commit specific kinds of offences; the commission of an offence involves multiple decisions by an offender that leads to the identification of an victim in a given time and space; an environment emits many cues about its characteristics; an offender uses these cues (through learned experience) to locate victims; learned experience over time leads to an improved understanding of patterns of cues, which are used to develop general templates that assist in victim selection; once formed, a template becomes relatively fixed and influences subsequent offence decision-making; although many templates can be formed, the distribution of offenders, victims and opportunities tends to be clustered in time and space and this means that individual templates often have similarities that can be identified.

From a CSAM perspective then, the perpetrator decision about which sites to frequent will first depend on what they are seeking to achieve there. This might be receiving and consuming CSAM distributed by others, or to share CSAM in one's possession (as in problems 1, 4, 7, 8, 9, 10, 12, 15 from the nine priority problems in chapter 6). It might be to find a safe place to store CSAM (as in problem 1 from the nine priority problems in chapter 6). Alternatively, it might be to identify potential child Victims who can be groomed to provide self-produced CSAM (as in problem 3 from the nine priority problems in chapter 6). These are three very different motivations for visiting a site and will shape subsequent interactions with that site. These motivations address the first step in Brantingham and Brantingham's (1978; 1981) model of crime site selection – that individuals commit specific types of offences.

We have previously noted certain subcultural aspects to CSAM offending. The use of a common language for CSAM terms that regularly changes to evade web crawlers and search engine filters is something that will be learned through frequenting online forums and from noting the terms used in other CSAM sites frequented by Consumers. Once the language is learned, finding new CSAM sites is likely to become easier. This learning from experience with the environment is central to Brantingham and Brantingham's (1978; 1981) model.

Their model also suggests that, once a successful approach to CSAM perpetration has been developed (whether that be as a means of storing, sharing or finding CSAM, or grooming children online), then perpetrators will stick with that approach, even if other more effective approaches exist. This may explain why BBS and internet relay chat continue to be used long after technology has moved on.

### Routine activity

The routine activity approach[3] drew on the observation that crime was often the result of mundane, everyday actions. Cohen and Felson (1979) recognised the importance of opportunity in the crime commission process and noted that changes in lifestyles were leading to an increase in crime thanks to a growing number of crime opportunities. Property crimes like burglary rose in the post-World War II era because households (which, thanks to a rise in consumerism, often contained a greater abundance of stealable possessions than in earlier times) were increasingly left unoccupied during the day due to an increase in female participation in the labour force. This created opportunities for burglars to target unoccupied houses in the knowledge that they would probably find goods they could sell.

A crime opportunity was said by Cohen and Felson (1979) to require the availability of an attractive target and the absence of guardianship. In this context, a guardian is an individual who has ownership, control or authority over a target or location and can protect it from being subject to crime. Target attractiveness combined with the absence of guardianship therefore create the conditions in which a motivated offender could make the decision to engage in crime by choosing the target in question. Recognition of these three ingredients for a successful crime – a suitable target, the absence of a capable guardian and a motivated offender – while simple in its formulation, has allowed for significant development in understanding how crime occurs and how it can be controlled.

Developing the *chemistry for crime* further, Felson (2002) added camouflage, props and audiences to the mix, as three often important elements to add to the existing three almost always present factors. Therefore, predatory-type crimes will involve:

- A likely offender.
- A suitable target.
- The absence of a capable guardian.

And may often include:

- Props that help produce or prevent a crime, including weapons or tools.
- Camouflage that helps the offender avoid unwanted notice.
- Any audience the offender wants to impress or to intimidate.

In the context of the CSAM ecosystem, props and camouflage offer useful additions for thinking about how crime is facilitated. Depending on the problem considered, different tools (both hardware and software may be used). In grooming offences, this might include image capture software to allow livestreamed chats to be recorded. Where sharing is concerned, many of the legitimate applications we have already discussed (from social media to file storage sites) are used for CSAM distribution purposes and are therefore essential tools. Websites developed solely to distribute CSAM can also be considered tools of the trade.

Given the importance of anonymity to CSAM offenders, tools that also provide camouflage (thereby disguising who the user is and where they are) have proven particularly useful. Indeed, built-in camouflage is a key reason for using internet relay chat and the darknet to distribute CSAM. Other problem facilitators among the priority nine listed in chapter 6 will often need additional measures to be taken to provide camouflage. For example, this might include using pseudonyms when signing up as a user and deploying virtual private networks to hide an IP address.

Taking a wider perspective, the routine activities approach may help to explain the distribution of some crime opportunities in the CSAM ecosystem. Understanding guardianship may be one of the keys to unlocking approaches to reducing CSAM. For example, seven of the nine priority problems identified in chapter 6 (problems 1, 2, 4, 7, 8, 9, 12) are subject to some form of central online guardianship (or could be). As noted above, applications, especially those related to social media platforms, will often have the potential for some form of guardian (or moderator) to monitor activity and to ensure that the terms of use are being followed by customers. Unfortunately, the guardianship role in these settings is often inadequate, leaving opportunities for perpetrators to produce, distribute, store and consume CSAM. In fact, historically, guardianship was the very thing that electronic service providers relaxed, thanks to Section 230 of the Communications Decency Act (1996) in the USA, which, by designating them as non-publishers of content, made them exempt from liability for the content they carried. This overtly laissez-faire approach to content meant that guardianship was not of upper most concern in the design of applications. Therefore, like the soaring property crime rates in postwar Western countries, the growth in CSAM can be viewed as a product of its environment, characterised by an abundance of crime opportunities and an absence of sufficient capable guardianship.

## Some tools

Based on these general theories underlying the crime science approach, a number of helpful conceptual tools have been developed to understand the nature of crime in more detail. Some of these will also be useful in our exploration of ways to tackle CSAM and these are discussed briefly here. This is in no way intended to be comprehensive and is highly selective in the choice of tools. However, those that are discussed here each have a role to play in understanding how we might reduce CSAM.

### The crime triangle

Based on routine activity theory, Eck and Clarke (2003) and Eck (2003) developed the crime triangle (evolving from one triangle to two triangles over the course of the two papers), as shown in Figure 7.1. The inner triangle indicates the key ingredients of a crime event, involving the conjunction of a motivated offender and suitable target / victim in the same place. In this version, the role of the guardian (almost always present in Felson's version) is moved to the outer triangle, which depicts controllers of problems, who can exert influence to prevent a crime from occurring. For example, a guardian is someone who provides protection over the target / victim. This might be a neighbour, bystanders or anyone else present and willing to intervene to provide a protective role. Managers refer to those with control over the place where the crime may occur. These may be the owner of a property, a lessor or some other role that is able to change the environment where

**FIGURE 7.1** Routine activity theory's crime triangles

Source: Eck, 2003.

the crime may occur. A handler is someone who might be able to exert influence over the decision making of an offender. This might be a friend, a family member or someone in a formal role, such as a probation officer. So, while a crime may occur when an offender comes into contact with a suitable target in the same place, there is a range of external controllers that may act to prevent a crime from occurring by exerting pressure in different ways.

Eck and Clarke (2003) also developed a system-level version of the crime triangle, replacing 'place' with 'network'. The managers of those networks (e.g. telecommunications companies and banks) would then be responsible for controlling how the networks were used, changing their systems to make those environments less attractive to offenders.

From a CSAM perspective, the network version of the crime triangle has relevance – particularly where predatory crimes are involved. For example, the use of social media sites and instant messaging to groom children and young people into self-producing CSAM (problem 6 in chapter 6) can be viewed in the context of the crime triangle. A young person (target / victim) uses a social media application (the networked place) and is contacted and befriended by an offender posing as a young person. The offender builds rapport with the young person to a point where the young person is asked for nude or sexually explicit photos or videos. In this scenario, there is a place manager (the social media site developers) who could potentially target harden the location by making it impossible for adults to contact young people within the application. The target / victim in this scenario could have multiple guardians. These could include a site administrator, who monitors interactions, perhaps based on machine learning algorithms, and steps in to warn the young person or stop the interaction. Other members of the social media site could act as guardians by warning other users in general of a particular user's behaviour, warn the particular victim / target (if there is any public chat to indicate an approach by an offender) or warn the site administrator about a predator on their site. Friends and family in the real world may also act as guardians if they are able to monitor the online activity of the target / victim. Handlers of the offender will include site administrators who, on becoming aware of the offender's behaviour, can issue warnings, or ban the user from their site. Other handlers will include intimate partners in the real world who may become aware of the activity of the offender and notify authorities, or who are asked by the offender to monitor their online behaviour to prevent them from recidivist behaviour. Criminal justice agencies (police, corrections) will act as handlers in cases where offences are detected and may be able to prevent recidivism.

## Crime scripts

Crime scripts start with an understanding of how knowledge tends to be put into practice through routinised procedures (Cornish, 1994). For example, visiting a restaurant[4] typically involves a well-understood procedure that includes entering, waiting to be seated, receiving the menu, ordering, eating, requesting the bill, paying and exiting. The procedures we follow tend to be improved over time as we learn what works well and what doesn't, modifying our practice as we go. The same goes for understanding crime events, which typically follow routinised procedures once a successful method has been found[5]. Recognising these routine procedures in crime events means it is possible to write a script that typifies the common ways in which any given type of crime is executed. Cornish (1994) noted that scripts could be written at different levels of abstraction, from the very general (universal scripts) to the very specific (tracks).

Scripts are typically written in a sequential way for a crime event and typically from the offender perspective. They show the planning process leading up to an event, the process followed at the crime scene itself and the process followed after the crime and on leaving the crime scene. This approach has been widely used to unpack in detail how crime events unfold, ranging from fraud (Hardy et al., 2020) and money laundering (Gilmour, 2014), to domestic violence (Boxall et al., 2018), sexual assault (Chiu & Leclerc, 2019) and sex trafficking (Brayley et al., 2011).

Crime scripting has also been used to understand the crime commission processes associated with CSAM. Focusing on analysis of darknet forums, van der Bruggen and Blokland (2020) documented the script associated with participating in a CSAM forum on the darknet, starting with the preparations necessary to enter the forums through to the procedures necessary to leave the darknet without leaving a trail for law enforcement to follow. Similarly, Leclerc et al. (2021) examined the high-level steps followed in relation to first consuming and then sharing and producing CSAM on the darknet. Importantly, scripts of this kind allow for points of intervention to be identified. These might be situational measures that can be taken to change the decision-making process, or they may be law enforcement interventions which take advantage of vulnerable points in a script where offenders are at greater risk of leaving identifiable information that could lead to their arrest.

## Arms races

Arms races in a crime science context refer to how offenders adapt their criminal behaviour in response to external changes in the environment. These may be changes to the situation that make crime more difficult, or more risky, or changes in the behaviour of others (e.g. law enforcement, capable guardians) that influence the criminal decision-making process (Ekblom, 1997; 1999; 2012a; 2012b). As a result, responses to crime problems need to continually evolve to address countermoves by offenders. For example, Shover (1996) showed how money safe design evolved over time to address changing offender modi operandi used to break into them. Brown (2017) has similarly shown how vehicle security evolved over time in response to offenders finding ways to overcome it.

In relation to CSAM, offender adaptation is common, often taking advantage of new technology. For example, the development of hidden websites that can only be found by visiting a series of other websites (thereby sequentially collecting a series of cookies) is an offender adaptation to web crawlers that seek out and report CSAM (Internet Watch Foundation, 2019). Similarly, the use of closed forums on the darknet by CSAM offenders is an adaptation designed to increase anonymity online and avoid law enforcement detection as methods on the open-net have proven vulnerable to law enforcement tactics (e.g. peer-to-peer networks that are frequently monitored by law enforcement). These examples highlight the fact that no single, one-time intervention will solve the problem. Rather, changes will need to be made incrementally, with the expectation that offenders will adapt to the situation.

Offender adaptation should also be expected by ESPs. New technology designed to improve functionality for most users will quickly be adopted by offenders and this suggests that monitoring should be built into the roll-out of new developments and changes made quickly if they are found to be used by some to the detriment of other users.

While arms races of this kind may seem frustrating and seemingly futile, they can serve a useful crime reduction role. With each iteration of an arms race, the knowledge and resources needed from an offender perspective are likely to increase and this means that not all of those who might have previously committed a crime using existing technology will be able to in future. So, the increased effort required will deter some offenders – at least until knowledge about how to overcome the new technological change has become widespread. So, arms races can suppress the prevalence of offending which may help to reduce crime. For example, if the next iteration in the CSAM arms race results in an increase in darknet use, it is unlikely that all of those who casually browse for CSAM on the open-net, or who migrate to it from freely available adult pornography, are likely to acquire the knowledge and skills required to operate securely on the darknet.

## The 11 Ds

Ekblom and Hirschfield (2014) developed a set of 11 principles that described how intervention could operate to change the offender decision-making process to engage in crime. These principles built upon Cornish and Clarke's (2003) 25 techniques of situational crime prevention, elaborating on the five underlying mechanisms (increasing effort, increasing risk, reducing reward, removing excuses and reducing provocation), which were considered to insufficiently capture the full range of mechanisms by which offenders may choose not to commit crime. Each beginning with a letter 'D', these 11 principles included:

- **Defeat / delay.** This might be achieved by blocking access or movement required to complete an offence. This might also be achieved by blocking access to information sought by offenders. As such, this would fall into the category of *increasing effort* in situational crime prevention terms.
- **Disable / deny.** This might be achieved by removing / reducing the availability of an item targeted or used by an offender. It might also mean modifying

or securing an item in a way that means it cannot be used in the way intended. This could either relate to an object targeted in a crime, or a tool used to facilitate the crime. As such, this would also fall into the category of *increasing effort* in situational crime prevention terms.

- **Direct / deflect.** This might be achieved by altering a situation in such a way that an offender decides to offend elsewhere, regardless of whether the information used to make that decision was true or false. This may be due to perceived *increased risk, increased effort* or *reduced reward* in situational crime prevention terms.

- **Deter-known.** This relates to situations in which an offender can observe and judge the risk of engaging in a crime and decide the risks outweigh the rewards. This could result from either *increased risk* or *reduced rewards* in situational crime prevention terms.

- **Deter-unknown.** This relates to situations in which the offender is unable to observe or judge the perceived risk and will be uncertain about the measures taken to control crime opportunities, with uncertainty resulting in a decision to avoid offending. Here there is no direct comparison with situational crime prevention as the lack of information means that a rational choice to offend or not cannot be made.

- **Discourage.** This involves a direct attempt to change an offender's decision to commit a crime. From a situational crime prevention perspective, it could result from *increased risk, increased effort, reduced rewards* or a *removal of excuses*.

- **Demotivate.** This involves prompting motives or emotions that are opposed to committing crime. From a situational crime prevention perspective, this could be through removing excuses. However, demotivation as a tactic goes beyond situational crime prevention mechanisms and can involve other factors such as creating empathy for the Victim or eliciting a guilty conscience.

- **Deceive.** This can involve purposely imparting false information to an offender. This may have a situational crime prevention impact by increasing perceived *risk* or *effort*, or reducing perceived *rewards*. It could also have an impact on detection and arrest by encouraging offenders to make a false move in the belief that risks are lower than they in reality.

- **Disconcert.** This involves creating confusion in the mind of the offender that leads them to make decisions or involuntary movements that make it easier for them to be detected. Here, there is no direct connection with situational crime prevention.

- **Detect.** This is intended to make offenders self-expose their intentions to commit crime, or actions subsequent to a crime event, that make it easier to identify them. Again, there is no direct link with situational crime prevention as it assumes the offender has made the decision to commit a crime that is subject to detection.

- **Detain.** This involves capture and detention following the detection of an offender. There is no direct link to situational crime prevention here.

These were subsequently grouped into three categories, which described the modes of action, noting that some fell into more than one category. Defeat / delay, disable / deny, direct / deflect, discourage, deter-known, deter-unknown were included under the heading of 'Practical'. This described mechanisms that limit what an offender can do by changing the environment and its contents. Detain, detect, direct / deflect, disconcert, deter-known and deter-unknown were included under the heading of 'Personal'. These are mechanisms that are focused on the individual. They aim to spot, identify, catch and track individuals. Deceive, demotivate, discourage, disconcert, deter-known and deter-unknown were included in the 'Psychological' category, which aim to change how offenders see, think and feel.

For a given problem, interventions can be devised that seek to use one or more of these modes of action by employing specific intervention principles. From a CSAM perspective, we can imagine the principles being applied to each of our nine priority problems. For example, if we were to focus on just one problem – *livestreaming technology to simultaneously produce, distribute, consume and monetise CSAM* – we can explore how some of the Ds could potentially be deployed in future. Not all of these may currently be legal, ethical or technologically possible, but they nonetheless illustrate how the 11 Ds may be relevant:

- **Defeat / delay:** block access of IP addresses to livestreaming sites for both facilitators and Consumers of livestreaming of CSAM. Restrict internet bandwidth for IP addresses (or for whole communities if IP addresses cannot be identified) for facilitators attempting to use the internet for livestreaming of CSAM.
- **Disable / deny:** deny access to banking services needed to buy / sell livestreaming of CSAM. Build artificial intelligence algorithms into smartphone cameras and other digital cameras that detects potential CSAM and refuses to record.
- **Direct / deflect:** redirect livestreaming consumers away from social media sites / chatrooms where they meet and negotiate with facilitators, towards websites offering psychological help for CSAM viewing, or towards law enforcement pages that remind them of the risk of detection.
- **Deter-known:** raise the risk of law enforcement detection for livestream CSAM consumption by sharing information on increased law enforcement activity with those previously convicted of child sexual abuse-related cases. Or banks sending SMS to customers they suspect of sending payments to facilitators, that outline increased checks being undertaken on payments being made. Target areas where facilitators operate for more police patrols. Seek anonymous tip-offs of facilitators of livestreaming CSAM in local communities.
- **Deter-unknown:** use media to raise profile of law enforcement activity aimed at prosecuting Consumers who purchase livestreaming of child sexual abuse. Raise confusion over whether the facilitators that Consumers meet online are in fact law enforcement officers operating covertly.

- **Discourage:** use targeted social media campaigns to highlight significantly increased surveillance of chatrooms / social media sites where Consumers meet facilitators. Emphasise the negative impact on the lives of those that are caught purchasing the livestreaming of CSAM.
- **Demotivate:** challenge in online forums the fantasies that CSAM offenders hold about children and raise awareness about the real harm it causes.
- **Deceive:** Encourage CSAM Consumers to download software that allows law enforcement to track their movements and potentially allowing Consumers to be identified. Covertly operating in social media / chatrooms, police could seek to scam first-time consumers, thereby dissuading them from participating again.
- **Detect:** employ tools available through the financial system to detect those making payments to known facilitators. Provide this intelligence to the police for further investigation.
- **Detain:** use policing methods to identify the name and address of CSAM livestreaming facilitators and Consumers and execute search warrants, seeking to make arrests.

Where *disconcert* is concerned, Ekblom and Hirschfield (2014) described an example of a knife-detection arch being used in random locations at a music entertainment complex. Customers would queue along corridors to enter the venue and on turning a corner would be confronted by an arch. Security staff would be looking out for suspicious reactions from customers that might suggest they were unwilling to go through the arch. Operating in the online world, it is difficult to imagine a circumstance in which a facilitator or Consumer of CSAM livestreaming would reveal their identities in a similar way because of being disconcerted online.

## The hierarchy of intervention

Originally developed by Herman Goldstein (presented in Scott, 2005) in the context of problem-oriented policing, the hierarchy of interventions provides a scale of interventions that can be applied to deal with problems, starting with the least intrusive at the bottom of the hierarchy, the most intrusive at the top. This was subsequently modified by Brown (2013) by incorporating lessons from Clarke and Newman's (2005) eight roles of government in encouraging design into products. Brown's hierarchy was focused on product design. However, this has been modified further in Figure 7.2 below to reflect pressure that might be applied by governments on ESPs. At the lowest level of pressure applied (the bottom of the list), governments might seek to educate ESPs about the problem of CSAM and its impacts on the community, and outline the expectations on them to address the problem. This awareness raising is intended to spur the ESPs into action voluntarily, with companies seeking to address the problems about which they were previously unaware.

The next step up the hierarchy involves calling on ESPs to do more to address the problem of CSAM, given they are likely to have the capability and resources

| Pressure applied | Government interventions with ESPs |
|---|---|
| High | Bringing civil action to compel ESPs to take responsibility for the problem |
| | Introducing legislation to regulate preventative action by ESPs |
| | Providing tax incentives or subsidies to encourage ESPs to take responsibility for the problem |
| | Focusing government procurement on online services that incorporate the desired design changes |
| | Supporting research and development efforts by ESPs to find solutions to the problem |
| | Pressing for the creation of a new organisation to take responsibility for the problem |
| | Creating a climate in which control of CSAM becomes a significant feature in the consumer's decision to use an online service, thereby creating competition between ESPs |
| | Naming and shaming ESPs to raise public attention of their failure to address the problem |
| | Collaborating with advertisers to demand that ESPs provide online services that are CSAM free |
| | Raising public expectations that the online service they use will be sufficiently free from CSAM, thereby exerting market pressure on ESPs |
| | Targeted confrontational request to ESPs to take responsibility for the problem |
| | Straightforward, informal request to ESPs to take responsibility for the problem |
| Low | Educating ESPs about their responsibility for CSAM in their online services |

**FIGURE 7.2** Hierarchy of government interventions to encourage electronic service providers to incorporate CSAM prevention measures into their online services

Sources: Scott, 2005; Clarke & Newman, 2005; Brown, 2013.

to make a difference. This approach is closely followed by more targeted, confrontational calls for ESPs to take responsibility for the CSAM problem. Given the concentrated nature of the problem, this might involve targeting the one or two ESPs that are responsible for the most CSAM on their platforms. The first three measures involve direct engagement with the ESPs. From step four onwards, the engagement shifts to involving other third parties who may be able to influence the activities of ESPs indirectly. Step four seeks to raise awareness and expectation among users of ESP platforms that they should be able to use the ESP services free from the possibility that they might discover CSAM during their legitimate use and free from the knowledge that they may be supporting a means by which others may seek to exploit children using the same platforms. This step is intended to influence market forces by encouraging customers to demand CSAM-free services and to ultimately move to other services that may be working harder to eradicate CSAM. This in turn could result in CSAM prevention being taken seriously by ESPs as an important consumer requirement that influences demand and therefore usage of their platforms. This obviously depends on the availability of other ESP services that are sufficiently similar, to convince customers to transfer their loyalty.

Step five on the hierarchy involves engaging with advertisers to convince them of the importance of investing advertising expenditure in online services that are known to be free from CSAM. This potentially has a more direct impact on ESP profitability as large online services are typically reliant on advertising revenue. However, advertisers may be unwilling to cease using services of concern if they clearly have market dominance and are the most cost-effective way to reach their intended target audiences.

Step six involves naming and shaming ESPs that fail to adequately protect against their services from being used to produce and distribute CSAM. This is a more aggressive approach than previous steps because, by definition, it involves targeting particular corporations who are likely to respond with defensive positions. It is, however, more of a broadcast intervention in that the messaging is likely to be targeted at the general community, via the media, some of whom may then choose to change the services they use.

Step seven involves creating a climate in which the presence of CSAM is a significant issue in consumers' decisions to use particular services. In a sense, this is similar to earlier interventions, in that it seeks to encourage a change in attitude and behaviour by both ESPs and consumers, which, in turn, may result in action that prevents CSAM production and distribution on those services. As such, it marks the last of the persuasion-focused interventions and is intended to create public pressure to leverage change among ESPs. A range of measures could be taken to assist in the creation of a suitable climate, ranging from engagement with the tech industry, creating and supporting champions to call for change, and creating media campaigns to raise awareness and call for change.

Step eight involves pressing for the creation of a new organisation to take responsibility for the problem. This could be a new government agency or NGO focused on CSAM prevention that can devote its resources to promoting change in practice by ESPs and to keep the issue high on the agenda for media and the public. This could also be a kind of watchdog that takes reports of CSAM found on ESP platforms and that could also proactively search for such material, and thereby identify emerging problems that need to be addressed.

Step nine focuses on building capacity to tackle the problem by investing in research and development efforts to tackle CSAM. This could be research that aims to better understand the problem but could also lead to the development of tools that could be used by ESPs to identify, block and remove CSAM content on their sites and for law enforcement agencies to detect CSAM perpetrators (both Producers and Consumers).

Step ten focuses on influencing investment decisions by government when procuring IT solutions. Procurement guidelines could be amended to take due regard for the likelihood that new IT solutions might facilitate CSAM. This could also be taken a step further by requiring procurement teams to take into consideration the activities of vendors in other spheres outside of government IT contracts that might facilitate CSAM. For example, an ESP may offer cloud solutions that are attractive to government while at the same time their public versions (e.g. file storage sites) are used for CSAM distribution because of inadequate preventative measures being taken by the ESP to remove the problem.

Step eleven sees the introduction of legislation by government to regulate ESPs to ensure they take measures to prevent CSAM being produced and distributed through their services. This could be supported by regulatory activity to ensure ESPs are following the legislation. Currently, this is likely to be heavily opposed by ESPs because of its impact on increasing costs associated with regulatory compliance. It would challenge the notion that service providers are not publishers of content and should therefore not be held responsible for the material found on their sites, although there has generally been more acceptance of the need to remove CSAM (and some other abhorrent material).

The final step relates to the possibility of taking civil action against ESPs for the harm they cause in perpetuating the existence of CSAM by failing to take enough action to prevent the production and distribution of CSAM on their sites. This could result in significant penalties being imposed on ESPs as restoration for Victims / Survivors of CSAM. If sufficiently large, these penalties could encourage shareholders to force their corporations to take preventative action in future.

These are just some of the measures that could be taken to leverage change by those that have ownership over a significant portion of the CSAM ecosystem. While presented as a hierarchy, this does not mean that intervention needs to start at the bottom step and work upwards. Subject to the nature and extent of the problem, a decision can be made to jump up to any step without having previously tried lower steps. The hierarchy is also intended to be bidirectional – the intensity of intervention can go up or down depending on understanding of the current problem. Chapter 11 develops some of these ideas further when proposing priorities for further action.

## A word on displacement

Before concluding this section, it is worth briefly touching on the issue of displacement. Displacement refers to the migration of crime away from its original target, towards other suitable targets because of intervention that changes the opportunity for crime commission associated with the original target. Displacement is commonly considered in relation to geographical targets / interventions, but it can also refer to other forms of displacement including, among others, temporal displacement, target group displacement, switching to other forms of crime and switching to other modi operandi to execute the same type of crime. Situational crime prevention approaches are often criticised for their perceived tendency to simply displace crime. The same arguments may also be made in relation to the CSAM ecosystem. In response to approaches to suppress CSAM production and distribution in one part of the ecosystem (for example, by increasing effort, increasing risk or reducing the rewards associated with offending), this activity may simply be deflected to other, less secure parts of the ecosystem where there are more opportunities to create and share such material.

However, the evidence suggests that displacement is not as common as critics of situational crime prevention would have one believe. For example, a review of 55 situational crime prevention studies by Hesseling (1994) found that displacement was present in 33 studies, but in no case was there complete displacement, meaning there was an overall positive effect on crime, even if a portion of it moved elsewhere. A systematic review of displacement and diffusion of benefit (the opposite of displacement, characterised by a benefit from the intervention that extends beyond its intended target) associated with situational crime prevention measures found that displacement only occurred in about a quarter of observations. Importantly, diffusion of benefit was equally as likely as displacement and, overall, the systematic review showed a positive net effect from situational crime prevention measures (Guerette & Bowers, 2009). These findings suggest that, even if displacement were to occur as a result of applying one of the broad suite of situational crime prevention, or more broadly, crime science approaches, one would still expect to reduce crime. Crime reduction could also be further boosted by a diffusion of benefit that extended the impact beyond its intended target.

## Bringing it all together

This chapter has introduced the building blocks of crime science that we can use to explore opportunities for addressing the CSAM ecosystem. It has outlined some of the key theoretical perspectives that help us to think differently about crime issues, and it has introduced some tools that can be used to unpack the nature of criminal events which, in turn, will help with the task of identifying opportunities to reduce the scale of the problem.

This crime science thinking will help in shaping the remainder of the book, which will focus on exploring how different aspects of the CSAM problem can be addressed. Chapter 7 explores approaches taken to address the production of CSAM, while chapters 8 and 9 deal with the distribution and consumption of CSAM respectively. These chapters not only aim to review, from a crime science perspective, what is being done already, but, where possible, to offer up other approaches that have yet to be tried or tested.

## Notes

1 The original formulation consisted of three mechanisms – *increasing effort, increasing risk* and *reducing reward*. Following further developments in thinking and debate between scholars (Wortley 1998; 2001;Cornish & Clarke, 2003), two additional mechanisms were added – *removing excuses* and *reducing provocation*.
2 According to Statista.com in January 2021, Facebook had over 2.7 billion users. This was 400 million more users than its nearest rival, YouTube, which had almost 2.3 billion users. www.statista.com/statistics/272014/global-social-networks-ranked-by-number-of-users/
3 Felson (2008) explained that he originally expressed a preference for the term *approach*, rather than *theory*, because he did not consider it a full-blown theory in the first instance and also because he attempted to avoid confrontation with conventional criminologists, who disliked the work and preferred that it be subsumed within existing theory.
4 This is an often-quoted example and one used by Cornish (1994) himself.
5 This is similar to Brantingham and Brantingham's (1981) idea that offenders develop templates in their target selection decision-making process, based on previous experience and knowledge gained from others.

## References

Boxall, H., Boyd, C., Dowling, C. & Morgan, A. (2018). *Understanding domestic violence incidents using crime script analysis.* Trends & issues in crime and criminal justice 558. Australian Institute of Criminology. www.aic.gov.au/publications/tandi/tandi558

Brantingham, P.J. & Brantingham, P.L. (1978). A theoretical model of crime site selection. In M. Krohn & R.L. Akers (Eds.), *Crime, law and sanction: theoretical perspectives* (pp. 105–118). Sage Publications.

Brantingham, P.J. & Brantingham, P.L. (1981). *Environmental criminology.* Waveland Press.

Brantingham, P. & Brantingham, P. (2008). Crime pattern theory. In R. Wortley & L. Mazerolle (Eds.), *Environmental criminology and crime analysis* (pp. 78–93). Willan Publishing.

Brayley, H., Cockbain, E. & Laycock, G. (2011). The value of crime scripting: Deconstructing internal child sex trafficking. *Policing* 5(2), 132–143. https://doi.org/10.1093/police/par024

Brown, R. (2013). *Regulating crime prevention design into consumer products: Learning the lessons from electronic vehicle immobilisation.* Trends & issues in crime and criminal justice 453. Australian Institute of Criminology. www.aic.gov.au/sites/default/files/2020-05/tandi 453.pdf

Brown, R. (2017). Vehicle crime prevention and the co-evolutionary arms race: recent offender countermoves using immobiliser bypass technology. *Security Journal* 30(1), 60–73. https://doi.org/10.1057/s41284-016-0001-1

Chiu, Y.N. & Leclerc, B. (2019). Scripting Stranger Sexual Offences Against Women. *Sexual Abuse* 33(2), 223–249. https://doi.org/10.1177/1079063219889055

Clarke, R.V. & Cornish, D. (1985). Modelling offenders' decisions: a framework for research and policy. In M. Tonry & N. Morris (Eds.), *Crime and justice: A review of research, Volume 6* (pp.147–185). The University of Chicago Press.

Clarke, R.V. & Newman, G. (2005). Modifying criminogenic products: What role for government? In R.V. Clarke & G. Newman (Eds.), *Designing out crime from products and systems* (pp.7–83). Crime Prevention Studies 18. Willan Publishing.

Cohen, L. & Felson, M. (1979). Social Change and Crime Rate Trends: A Routine Activity Approach. *American Sociological Review* 44(4), 588–608. https://doi.org/10.2307/2094589

Cornish, D. (1994). The procedural analysis of offending and its relevance for situational prevention. In R.V. Clarke (Ed.), *Crime Prevention Studies, Volume 3* (pp.151–196). Criminal Justice Press.

Cornish, D.B. & Clarke, R.V. (1986). *The reasoning criminal: Rational choice perspectives on offending.* Springer-Verlag

Cornish, D.B. & Clarke, R.V. (2003). Opportunities, precipitators and criminal decisions: A reply to Wortley's critique of situational crime prevention. In M. Smith & D.B. Cornish (Eds.), *Theory for situational crime prevention* (pp. 41–96). Crime Prevention Studies 16. Criminal Justice Press.

Eck, J. (2003). Police problems: The complexity of problem theory, research and evaluation. In J Knutsson (Ed.), *Problem-oriented policing: from innovation to mainstream*, (pp. 79–113). Crime Prevention Studies 15. Willan Publishing

Eck, J. & Clarke, R.V. (2003). Classifying Common Police Problems: A Routine Activity Approach. In M. Smith & D. Cornish (Eds.), *Theory for Practice in Situational Crime Prevention* (pp.7–39). Crime Prevention Studies 16. Criminal Justice Press.

Eck, J.E. & Madensen, T. (2009). Using signatures of opportunity structures to examine mechanisms in crime prevention evaluations. In J. Knutsson & N. Tilley (Eds.), *Evaluating crime reduction initiatives* (pp.59–84). Crime Prevention Studies 24. Willan Publishing.

Ekblom, P. (1986). *The prevention of shop theft: An approach through crime analysis.* Crime Prevention Unit Series 5. Home Office Crime Prevention Unit. www.researchgate.net/publication/247953176_The_Prevention_of_Shop_Theft_An_Approach_Through_Crime_Analysis

Ekblom, P. (1997). Gearing up against crime: A dynamic framework to help designers keep up with the adaptive criminal in a changing world. *International Journal of Risk, Security and Crime Prevention* 2(4), 249–265. www.researchgate.net/profile/Paul-Ekblom/publication/291456106_Gearing_up_against_crime_A_dynamic_framework_to_help_designers_keep_up_with_the_adaptive_criminal_in_a_changing_world/links/56b4b1ab08ae83713174a339/Gearing-up-against-crime-A-dynamic-framework-to-help-designers-keep-up-with-the-adaptive-criminal-in-a-changing-world.pdf

Ekblom, P. (1999). Can we make crime prevention adaptive by learning from other evolutionary struggles? *Studies on crime and crime prevention* 8(1), 27–51.

Ekblom, P. (2012a). The private sector and designing products against crime. In B.C. Welsh & D.P. Farrington (Eds.), *The Oxford handbook of crime prevention* (pp.384–403). Oxford University Press.

Ekblom, P. (2012b). Happy returns: ideas brought back from situational crime prevention's exploration of design against crime. In G. Farrell & N. Tilley (Eds.), *The reasoning criminologist: Essays in honour of Ronald V. Clarke* (pp.52–63). Crime Science Series. Willan Publishing.

Ekblom, P. & Hirschfield, A. (2014). Developing an alternative formulation of SCP principles – the Ds (11 and counting). *Crime Science* 3(2). https://doi.org/10.1186/s40 163-014-0002-5

Felson, M. (2002). *Crime and everyday life.* Third Edition. Sage

Felson, M. (2008). Routine activity approach. In R. Wortley & L. Mazerolle (Eds), *Environmental criminology and crime analysis* (pp.70–77). Willan Publishing

Geason, S. & Wilson, P.R. (1990). *Preventing graffiti and vandalism.* Australian Institute of Criminology. www.aic.gov.au/sites/default/files/2020-05/cpgraffiti.pdf

Gilmour, N. (2014). Understanding money laundering: A crime script approach. *The European Review of Organised Crime* 1(2), 35–56. https://standinggroups.ecpr.eu/sgoc/wp-content/uploads/sites/51/2020/01/gilmour.pdf

Graham, K. & Homel, R. (2008). *Raising the bar: Preventing aggression in and around bars, pubs and clubs.* Willan Publishing

Guerette, R.T. & Bowers, K. (2009). Assessing the extent of crime displacement and diffusion of benefits: A review of situational crime prevention evaluations. *Criminology* 47(4), 1331–1368. 10.1111/j.1745-9125.2009.00177.x

Hardy, J., Bell, P. & Allan, D. (2020). A crime script analysis of the Madoff Investment Scheme. *Crime Prevention and Community Safety* 22, 68–97, https://doi.org/10.1057/s41 300-019-00082-6

Hesseling, R. (1994). Displacement: A review of the empirical literature. In R.V. Clarke (Ed.), *Crime Prevention Studies, Volume 3* (pp.197–230). Criminal Justice Press.

Homel, R., Hauritz, M., Wortley, R., Mcllwain, G. & Carvolth, R. (1997). Preventing alcohol related crime through community action: The Surfers Paradise Safety Action Project. In R. Homel (Ed.), *Policing for prevention: Reducing crime, public intoxication and injury* (pp.35–90). Crime Prevention Studies 7. Criminal Justice Press.

Internet Watch Foundation (2019). *Once upon a year: The Internet Watch Foundation annual report 2018.* Internet Watch Foundation. www.iwf.org.uk/sites/default/files/reports/2019-04/Once%20upon%20a%20year%20-%20IWF%20Annual%20Report%202018.pdf

Leclerc, B., Drew, J., Holt, T., Cale, J. & Singh, S. (2021). *Child sexual abuse material on the darknet: A script analysis of how offenders operate.* Trends & issues in crime and criminal justice 627. Australian Institute of Criminology. https://doi.org/10.52922/ti78160

Scott, M. (2005). Shifting and sharing police responsibility to address public safety problems. In N. Tilley (Ed.), *Handbook of crime prevention and community safety* (pp.385–410). Willan Publishing.

Shover, N. (1996). *Great Pretenders: Pursuits and careers of persistent thieves.* Westview Press.

Smallbone, S. (2016). Situational prevention approaches. In E.L. Jeglic & C. Calkins (Eds.) *Sexual violence: Evidence based policy and prevention* (pp.146-160). Springer International Publishing.

Smallbone, S., Marshall, W.L. & Wortley, R. (2008). *Preventing child sexual abuse: Evidence, policy and practice.* Willan Publishing.

Tilley, N. & Webb, J. (1994). *Burglary reduction: Findings from Safer Cities schemes.* Crime Prevention Unit Series 51. Home Office Police Research Group. www.ojp.gov/pdffiles1/Photocopy/149304NCJRS.pdf

van der Bruggen, M. & Blokland, A. (2020). A crime script analysis of child sexual exploitation material fora on the darknet. *Sexual Abuse* 33(8), 950–974. https://doi.org/10.1177/1079063220981063

Webb, B. & Brown, R. (2017). Preventing vehicle crime. In N. Tilley & A. Sidebottom (Eds.), *Handbook of crime prevention and community safety* (pp.354–372). Second edition. Routledge.

Wortley, R. (1998). A two-stage model of situational crime prevention. *Studies on crime and crime prevention* 7, 173–188. https://discovery.ucl.ac.uk/id/eprint/1301891/1/1301 891.pdf

Wortley, R. (2001). A classification of techniques for controlling situational precipitators of crime. *Security Journal* 14(4), 63–82. https://doi.org/10.1057/palgrave.sj.8340098

Wortley, R. & Smallbone, S. (2012). *Internet Child Pornography: Causes, Investigation and Prevention*. Praeger.

# 8

# APPROACHES TO REDUCING THE PRODUCTION OF CSAM

## Introduction

Before we explore potential approaches that could reduce the production of CSAM, it is worth revisiting the vulnerabilities and behaviours associated with this activity, as these will give clues as to how to address this problem, although it also highlights the daunting range of ways in which a child may become a Victim / Survivor of CSAM. Chapter 3 highlighted six high-level scripts (to use the terminology of Cornish (1994) discussed in chapter 7) that describe ways in which CSAM is extracted from children.

The first script is associated with the abuse of a child by a caregiver. This can be subdivided into three common tracks that involve parents who abuse their own children, family friends and acquaintances who find situations in which they can abuse a child known to them, and employees of institutions (schools, care homes, sports clubs etc.) who abuse a child in their care.

The second script involves perpetrators extracting CSAM from children with whom they are in a relationship. This may involve either a child or adult perpetrator and can be consensual or coerced from a child (representing four different tracks – child perpetrator / consensual, child perpetrator / coerced, adult perpetrator / consensual and adult perpetrator / coerced).

The third script involves perpetrators who predate on children who are not in their care and this can involve tracks that include kidnapping a child, a child being recruited by an organised crime group or images being taken without the child's awareness or consent (such as at swimming pools, the beach, or with hidden cameras in public toilets or changing rooms).

The fourth script involves perpetrators paying to gain access to a child for sexual purposes. This may involve tracks that include paying to access a child who has been

DOI: 10.4324/9781003327264-10

kidnapped and held against their will, paying a parent, paying a facilitator who can provide access to a child or, indeed, paying a child themselves for sex.

The fifth script involves perpetrators who groom children online to gain access to CSAM. Here, possible tracks include engaging with a child online to provide CSAM images, coercing more extreme images from the child by threatening to release prior images to friends / family and blackmailing the Victim / Survivor into meeting the perpetrator and being subject to sexual abuse.

The sixth script involves the livestreaming of child sexual abuse. Here, possible tracks can include a parent who facilitates the abuse, a friend or other family member as part of a cottage industry, or more organised abuse in a sex den. Types of livestreaming can involve abuse watched by many consumers simultaneously, or abuse that is purchased and directed by a single Consumer. As noted earlier, livestreaming is somewhat of a hybrid because of the active roles played by the facilitator and the viewer in the abuse of the child, with both targeting a child from their own perspectives before an incidence of abuse takes place. This script can also contain elements that may be like other scripts, including the role of caregivers (script one), the recruitment of a child by an organised crime group (script three) and perpetrators paying for (virtual) access to children (script four).

This list is by no means exhaustive, but it highlights at least 20 different ways in which CSAM may be produced. It also ignores methods that do not involve an actual child, such as through computer games and cartoons. It demonstrates the scale of the task in preventing the production of CSAM as each track is an avenue for it to enter the CSAM ecosystem. It is also clear that, apart from CSAM that involves the grooming of children online (an admittedly growing problem that was addressed by problem no. 3 in chapter 5[1]) CSAM production script tracks typically involve direct abuse of a child in the real world. This would first and foremost call for solutions that prevent the sexual abuse of the child in these circumstances.

Given the complexity of this situation, it may be worth considering these problems at a higher level of resolution by distilling the different tracks into a high-level crime script that consists of just four stages. First, there is the process of *target selection* in which a perpetrator meets a child that they intend to abuse in circumstances where there is a lack of capable guardianship to protect them from being victimised. Reviewing the tracks above, target selection clearly comes in a variety of ways, ranging from direct contact by the perpetrator (either physically or virtually), or the use of an intermediary / facilitator who provides access to the child (either for financial gain or voluntarily).

The second stage in this high-level script involves *preparation* for the abuse. This involves the perpetrator manipulating the situation to make the sexual abuse possible. This preparation stage can vary in complexity and duration. For example, it can involve conversations with the target in which they are groomed to act in a way that the perpetrator requests; or gaining trust from a target's capable guardians (e.g. parents) so that guardianship is lowered and then offering to babysit; or the perpetrator planning a time when their partner is away from the home and they are alone with their child; or planning the kidnap of a child; or negotiating the circumstances of livestreamed child abuse with a facilitator; or arranging with a facilitator the time and place to meet a child they are paying to directly abuse. In each case, there is a set of circumstances associated with time and place that might be manipulated (for example by applying the 25 techniques of situational crime prevention, or the 11 Ds discussed in chapter 7) to disrupt or prevent the preparation process.

The third stage in this crime script involves the *perpetration* of the sexual abuse. This may involve direct contact sexual assault, sexual abuse by a third party that is controlled by the perpetrator, or self-produced abuse that is requested or directed by the perpetrator. As this is a CSAM crime script, this sexual abuse will always involve the creation of images (which may or may not be recorded / stored).

The final stage in this crime script is the *completion* of the event, which results in the creation of (typically digital) images for further distribution and consumption. This event completion stage may mark the end of the relationship between the Victim / Survivor and perpetrator and they may have no further contact. This could be the case where children are groomed online to self-produce images, with the perpetrator ceasing contact once images have been acquired. Similarly, in cases where third parties are used to procure access to a child (either directly or via livestreaming) the completion of the sexual act with the child may be followed by no further contact with that Victim / Survivor. In other cases where the perpetrator is known to the child (as with parents, other family members, friends and teachers) there will be a continued relationship that will need to be maintained to ensure that the Victim / Survivor does not report to others that they have been sexually abused (Dorais, 2002). Completion of the event does not necessarily signal an end to the sexual abuse and will often lead to repeated behaviour against the same child (in which case the script may start again at the preparation stage) or against a different child (in which case the script will start with target selection).

The high-level crime script to produce CSAM therefore involves target selection – preparation – perpetration – completion. Examining CSAM offending at this level of abstraction allows us to consider how existing interventions designed to keep children safe play a role in combatting the production of CSAM. The following paragraphs therefore examine interventions relevant to each of the four stages in the crime script.

## Interventions that address target selection

Many of the interventions that currently exist to keep children safe from being a Victim / Survivor of child sexual abuse (and not just CSAM) are designed to impede the process by which a perpetrator is able to contact a child and select them as a target for victimisation. While this book is not intended to outline the entire child protection framework, it is worth examining how some of the most commonly used approaches play a role in addressing target selection.

## Incarcerating child sexual offenders

One way to stop child sexual offenders from targeting a child to victimise is to remove them from society through criminal justice action that detects, prosecutes, convicts and sentences offenders to periods in custody. Incarcerating offenders provides an incapacitation effect for the duration of the time that an offender is in prison as they will be unable to target child Victims / Survivors during that time. This approach has the added benefit of bringing justice for Victims / Survivors, which may help in the healing process. Indeed, justice for Victims / Survivors should be at the centre of any child sexual abuse-related prosecution.

From a crime science perspective, criminal justice action of this kind changes the risk–reward ratio. It can increase both the actual and perceived risk of detection and subsequent conviction. This may have a specific deterrent effect on a convicted offender, who decides the risk of future detection is far too great to continue to offend. And it may have a general deterrence effect on society, preventing would-be perpetrators from targeting children to abuse for fear of detection and subsequent sanction.

There are two fundamental issues with this argument which mean that traditional criminal justice responses of this kind are unlikely to entirely solve the problem of children being targeted by sexual offenders – the problems of attrition and low recidivism rates.

## Attrition in the criminal justice system

If we planned to reduce child sexual abuse by locking up offenders, we would want to be certain first that perpetrators would be brought to justice and would then receive long custodial sentences on conviction – the longer the better if the intention is to stop other children from being victimised. However, attrition in the criminal justice system makes this very difficult. Not all Victims / Survivors come forward and report their experiences to the police. When they do, the police may decide there is insufficient information on which to investigate, or prosecutors may decide there is insufficient evidence to achieve a conviction or jurors may decide there is too much reasonable doubt to find a defendant guilty. The fact is, very few cases of child sexual abuse result in a perpetrator going to prison. Examining 453 cases[2] of child sexual abuse in the USA, Block and Williams (2019) found that just 57 (13%) cases resulted in either a guilty plea or a finding of guilt by a jury. Indeed, only 89 (20%) cases proceeded to a prosecution. In New South Wales, Australia, 6,872 incidents of child sexual assault were reported to the police in 2019, yet criminal proceedings were undertaken against only 922 people and only 504 people were found guilty of such offences[3]. These findings suggest that when a case of child sexual abuse is reported to the police, an accused perpetrator has only a one-in-five to one-in-seven chance of being prosecuted and a one-in-eight to one-in-thirteen chance of being convicted.

This of course assumes that a child sexual abuse offence is reported to the police in the first instance. Yet we know that, for all kinds of reasons, Victims / Survivors often fail to report (or significantly delay reporting) their experiences to the police. For example, the Royal Commission into Institutional Responses to Child Sexual Abuse in Australia found that only 19.2 per cent of Victims / Survivors who participated in a private session with the Commission reported having previously disclosed the abuse to the police. If an incident is reported to the police, it can be many years after the abuse, although there is evidence to suggest this gap is getting shorter (Royal Commission into Institutional Responses to Child Sexual Abuse, 2017b).

Noting these figures still exclude those who have yet to disclose abuse in any way, we can estimate that possibly less than 3 per cent of cases of child sexual abuse result in a conviction[4]. We can of course argue over the precise proportions, but the contention that only a small proportion of child sexual abuse results in a conviction holds.

While important from a justice perspective, from a crime-reduction perspective, criminal justice responses that aim to incarcerate child sexual abuse offenders would appear to be inefficient, given that most cases do not result in a conviction. Even based on these somewhat shaky estimates, it would be fair to suggest that even a large increase in criminal justice resources devoted to incarcerating offenders would have only a modest impact on reducing the degree to which children are targeted by recidivist child sexual offenders. This also assumes we know how best to improve criminal justice responses to this problem. A systematic review of criminal justice responses to CSAM found very little evidence of effective practice, largely due to a lack of robust research in this area (Eggins et al., 2021).

## Low recidivism rates

One way to consider the efficacy of incarcerating child sexual offenders is to examine the counterfactual. Would convicted sex offenders commit further offences once they were caught and prosecuted? If they were to continue to offend on release from prison, then this might justify long periods of incarceration on the basis that incapacitation prevented recidivism. The problem is that this does not in fact appear to be the case. Rates of child sexual offender recidivism tend to be low – at least when measured by criminal justice outcomes. A review by Dowling et al. (2021) found that recidivism rates varied according to the length of follow-up period and specific measure of recidivism used. Among studies that used reports to the police, arrest or charge as the outcome measure, there were 35 studies with follow-up periods of two years or less and sexual offence recidivism rates of between 0 per cent and 31 per cent. Those with similar designs that followed up for four years or more (four studies) demonstrated sexual offence recidivism rates of between 0 per cent and 3 per cent. Among studies of adult offenders that used conviction or sentence as the outcome measure, one study followed up for less than two years and found that just 3 per cent were reconvicted for a further sexual offence. There were also 16 studies that examined conviction / sentence for sexual offending over a period of four years or more and found that recidivism rates were between 0 per cent and 31 per cent. Therefore, taken together, Dowling et al. (2021) found that sexual offence recidivism was up to 31 per cent. However, in 33 of the 39 samples of child sexual offenders examined by Dowling et al. (2021), the sexual offence recidivism rates were 15 per cent or less.

These recidivism rates suggest that 70 per cent or more of child sexual offenders may not go on to commit a further sexual offence. Given these figures include both adult and child sexual offence recidivism, it is highly likely that the proportion of child sexual offenders that are not proceeded against for another child sexual offence is likely to be higher than 70 per cent. On this basis, incarcerating child sexual offenders with the intention of preventing them from targeting further children in future (presumably as a result of activating specific deterrence) is a fairly inefficient means of reducing the problem, given that at least seven in ten were unlikely to go on to commit a further offence anyway. However, this argument needs to be weighed against evidence that suggests a significant portion of CSAM offenders have also committed contact child sexual abuse that has been undetected. Seto et al. (2011) examined six studies based on self-report surveys and interviews and found that over half (55%) reported previously committing a contact child sexual offence. This might support the argument for incarceration if it prevented offending that would otherwise not be subject to criminal justice sanction.

### Treatment programmes for child sexual offenders

Another means by which the potential for target selection could be reduced is to treat the underlying motivations that drive perpetrators to commit sexual offences against children. Treatment can be either medical or psychological and can be undertaken in prison or in the community.

Medical forms of treatment for sexual offenders that are mandated in some jurisdictions (e.g. some US states) involve hormonal medication or surgical castration (Reed, 2017). Hormonal medication involves an offender being treated with chemicals (typically an injection of drugs such as medroxyprogesterone acetate, cyproterone acetate or LHRH agonists) that reduce their level of testosterone, which in turn reduces sexual urges. However, it has been known to be accompanied with serious side effects including osteoporosis and heart disease (Lee & Cho, 2013). Surgical castration involves the removal of the offender's testicles, thereby reducing the production of testosterone[5]. This too can have negative side effects including hair loss, weight gain and suicidal tendencies (Reed, 2017).

Psychological treatment often involves participating in programmes that involve cognitive behavioural therapy (CBT), multi-systemic therapy (MST) and / or Risk-Need-Responsivity (RNR) approaches. Delivered either in groups or in individual sessions, CBT involves helping offenders to recognise distorted thinking patterns that lead to them deciding to offend and teaching coping strategies that will result in more prosocial courses of action. MST, typically focused on adolescents, aims to treat a range of offending risk factors associated with the individual, family, peer, school and community settings (often by employing CBT and other psychological therapies tailored to the problem). RNR approaches to treatment provide a framework within which psychological services (such as CBT) can be delivered. It aims to match the type and dosage of treatment to the level of risk posed by the treatment recipient, recognising that offender treatment programmes are most effective when targeting those most likely to offend (i.e. risk). Treatment should also target the criminogenic factors that influence offending (i.e. need). Finally, treatment should be tailored to the offenders' learning styles and abilities (i.e. responsivity) (Hanson et al., 2009).

Systematic reviews of treatment outcomes have shown overall positive impacts on reducing recidivism among sexual offenders (Lösel & Schmucker, 2005; Schmucker & Lösel, 2008; Soldino & Carbonell-Vayá, 2017; Lösel & Schmucker, 2017). Medical treatments (surgical castration and hormonal medication) have previously been shown to be more effective than psychological treatments (Lösel & Schmucker, 2005; Schmucker & Lösel, 2008), although they have generally fallen out of popularity due to legal, ethical (lack of informed consent and coercion) and health concerns (Reed, 2017). A systematic review that excluded medical treatments due to their failure to meet the strict study inclusion criteria[6] found that psychological treatment was associated with a 26 per cent reduction in sexual offence recidivism (Lösel & Schmucker, 2017). A further systematic review of more recent studies also found that psychological treatment had a positive impact on sexual reoffending (Soldino & Carbonell-Vayá, 2017).

Psychological treatment involving MST was found to be highly effective, while CBT was also found to be effective in reducing sexual offence recidivism (Lösel & Schmucker, 2017; Soldino & Carbonell-Vayá, 2017). Other forms of psychological treatment, such as therapeutic communities and insight-oriented treatments, were not found to have a significant impact on reoffending by Lösel & Schmucker (2017). This study also showed that psychological treatment that was only conducted in groups had no impact on recidivism, while individual-based and mixed (group and individual sessions) treatment approaches had a positive impact on recidivism (Lösel & Schmucker, 2017). Further, Soldino and Carbonell-Vayá (2017) found that individualised treatment was more effective than mixed treatment approaches. Treatment programmes that included volunteer peer support were also effective in reducing sexual offending (Soldino & Carbonell-Vayá, 2017)

Lösel and Schmucker (2017) also found that psychological treatment in the community was effective, while prison-based programmes had no impact on recidivism[7]. A similar finding has been noted in individual studies of programmes. In the UK, an evaluation of the prison-based Sex Offender Treatment Programme found that rates of sexual offending were significantly higher for those receiving treatment than for a matched control group (Mews et al., 2017)[8]. A study of sex offender treatment in Bavarian prisons, which tested alternative methods of control group selection, found that sexual reoffending was not significantly different for those receiving treatment compared with a control group (regardless of the method for selecting a control group) (Lösel et al., 2020)[9].

A systematic review examining the impact of RNR models used to address sexual reoffending found a positive impact on recidivism (Hanson et al., 2009). Sexual offence recidivism was found to be lower for those treated with RNR approaches (10.9%) compared with those in control groups (19.2%). Positive results were also found for any recidivism (31.8% vs 48.3%).

To sum up what works in treating sexual offenders, psychological treatment options (e.g. MST, CBT and RNR) that work with the individual (and not solely groupwork settings), that are delivered in the community and that offer volunteer peer support, stand the best chance of reducing sexual offence recidivism among convicted sex offenders. Castration, while effective (and probably politically appealing in some jurisdictions), is problematic from an ethical, legal and medical perspective, which has resulted in this option largely falling out of favour. Treatment may therefore help in reducing the likelihood of sexual reoffending by as much as half. However, in the context of preventing the targeting of children for sexual abuse, there are some caveats to note. Most notably, treatment is typically targeted at those that have already been reported, investigated, prosecuted and found guilty of child sexual offences. Yet, we know that most instances of abuse will not result in a conviction. Therefore, as a means of preventing children from being targeted, treatment provides an important, if small, contribution to addressing this problem.

## Sex offender registries

Sex offender registries are designed to activate increased surveillance on convicted sex offenders – by the police and/or the community. Such registries are used in several countries, including Australia, Canada, France, Ireland, Japan, South Korea, the UK and the USA (Day et al., 2014; Christensen, Sanchez de Ribera et al., 2021). They typically involve a database containing the details of convicted sexual offenders who meet the criteria for registration, as established by a jurisdiction's legislation. Criteria vary between jurisdictions with differences in the types of offences included, whether offences against adults as well as children are also covered and variations in the length of time that registration is required.

Offenders may be required to register with the police and to inform the police of any change in living circumstances, such as change in address and contact with children. Police may also conduct checks on sex offenders to ensure they abide by the conditions of the registration (Plotnikoff & Woolfson, 2000). In some jurisdictions, a range of additional restrictions may be imposed on registered sex offenders, including restrictions on the areas where they live, restrictions on the types of employment in which they can work (e.g. excluding employment that may bring offenders in close contact with children) and restrictions on access and use of the internet (Reed, 2017).

Non-public forms of registries have been shown to be effective in assisting the police with the ongoing management of sex offenders by both improving surveillance and intelligence and assisting with investigations (Day et al., 2014). They have also been shown to reduce sexual offending targeted at Victims / Survivors known to the offender (family / friends / acquaintances), but not where strangers are concerned (Prescott & Rockoff, 2011). However, the crime prevention effects may be associated with adult Victims / Survivors, rather than children (Agan & Prescott, 2014).

Sex offender registries may also be open to the public (Napier et al., 2018). These are typically intended to alert the community about sex offenders that live in their neighbourhood so that they can be vigilant to avoid children encountering those on the register. This may be in the context of strangers living locally, but may also include new intimate partners who may seek access to a mother's children. Some schemes (such as those in the UK and Western Australia) provide limited disclosure for parents, carers and guardians concerned about contact with a certain individual. These schemes require applications to be made with the police, who then decide whether information is provided and in what form. However, such registries often have poor take-up by the community, with few applications for information disclosure being accepted. In other countries, such as in the USA, information is made available through the media, on public websites and, in some cases, through letters sent to neighbours of registered sex offenders. These schemes have largely proven to be unsuccessful in reducing recidivism of child sexual offenders (Drake & Aos, 2009; Napier et al., 2018; Zgoba & Mitchell, 2021). However, there is modest evidence to suggest they prevent the onset of sexual offending, thereby providing a degree of general deterrence (Letourneau et al., 2010; Napier et al., 2018). The limited success of public sex offender registries is, perhaps, unsurprising given that many child sexual abuse Victims / Survivors are offended against by someone they know and (as noted earlier) the fact that reoffending rates of contact child sexual offending tend to be low anyway (Napier et al., 2018; Dowling et al., 2021). These findings suggest that, as a means of preventing child sexual offenders from targeting child Victims / Survivors, sex offender registers are likely to be of limited use.

## Employee criminal record checks

From an organisational perspective, conducting criminal record checks on employees and prospective employees, combined with rules about the types of historical offences that would prohibit an employee from working with the organisation (or performing certain functions as an employee), provides a means by which organisations may become aware of risk from employees and act to prevent children in their care from being targeted. Criminal record checks typically involve making an application to a central government authority requesting the disclosure of the previous criminal history of an individual. Depending on the jurisdiction, this application may be made by an individual requesting their own recorded criminal history, or by a third party (typically an organisation seeking to employ the individual) with the consent of the individual concerned. As part of, or in addition to, the criminal record check, the central authority may also maintain a register or a flag on the record to indicate that individuals should not be placed in positions where they work with children or vulnerable adults. In Northern Ireland, for example, it is illegal for individuals who are placed on a barred list maintained by the Disclosure and Barring Service[10] to work with children or vulnerable adults, or indeed to apply for such a position (Lipman & Manthorpe, 2016). In the USA, checks extend to the fingerprinting of employees who work in organisations that provide social or medical care and receive funding from Medicaid or Medicare[11].

In many other countries, there is no requirement for employers to check the criminal record of their employees. Indeed, there is a tension between the *right to know* and the *right to be forgotten*, due to concerns with the rehabilitation of offenders and their ability to integrate back into society. For example, in France and Germany, employers are not permitted to collect sensitive information of this kind on employees (Herzog-Evans, 2011; Lipman & Manthorpe, 2016). Although criminal record checks as a means of preventing the targeting of children for abuse may have a degree of face validity, there is little empirical evidence to show that the measure works (South et al., 2015). Davis and Wells (1994–1995) (reported in South et al., 2015) surveyed organisations that undertook criminal record checks and those that undertook other types of pre-employment screening. They found little difference between the two in terms of their ability to screen out unsuitable candidates and in terms of the reports of child abuse reported by the two types of organisation[12].

## *Raising awareness of risk among children and young people*

The final intervention discussed here, that is aimed at preventing the targeting of children by perpetrators, focuses on strategies that can be employed by potential victims of child sexual abuse (and / or CSAM). These interventions aim to raise awareness among children of the dangers of engaging with others who may seek to sexually exploit them. Unlike the previous interventions discussed in this section (which focused solely on offline behaviours), this may include both offline and online encounters with potential perpetrators.

Where offline encounters are concerned, awareness strategies typically involve teaching children about appropriate behaviour, how to recognise signs that contact with an adult may not be appropriate, how to deal with situations and how to tell a trusted adult about an encounter they were concerned about. There are numerous initiatives around the world that aim to increase awareness among children and parents of the dangers of engaging with Content Producers[13] and offer strategies about how to deal with these risks. For example, in the USA, NCMEC provides classroom resources, guidance for parents, and cartoon videos aimed at children through its Netsmartz portal[14]. Similar resources are provided in Australia by the e-Safety Commissioner[15] and by the Daniel Morecombe Foundation[16]; in Canada by the Canadian Centre for Child Protection[17]; in France by Association Une Vie[18]; and in the UK by the Lucy Faithful Foundation[19]. The Lucy Faithful Foundation also hosts a website with searchable details of over 200 interventions of this kind[20]. These resources typically also address online encounters that often occur on social media sites and chat sites where Content Producers groom children for self-produced content. More recent developments have included the launch of the E-Himaya platform in Morocco in December 2021, which aims to improve online education and awareness of children and parents[21].

There is some evidence to suggest that increasing awareness of child sexual abuse among children and young people can reduce their risk of victimisation. A systematic review of school-based reduction programmes to prevent child sexual abuse found that such programmes significantly increased knowledge of child sexual abuse and preventative strategies. They also increased protective behaviours aimed at dealing with situations when they were targeted for sexual abuse (Walsh et al., 2015).

## Online moderation by social media platforms

Online moderation on social media platforms can provide a degree of capable guardianship through surveillance that identifies Content Producers attempting to engage with children. This may occur because of user complaints that report inappropriate engagement with another user, or through proactive review of chatlogs held by the platform that are alert to inappropriate conversations. Automated algorithms can be used to detect potential situations in which grooming may be occurring (Gunawan et al., 2018; Suhartono et al., 2019). However, this can be difficult due to the speed with which grooming interactions can occur, the changing nature of slang used and different languages that must be considered (We Protect Global Alliance, 2021). Currently, only about a third of technology companies deploy algorithms of this kind (We Protect Global Alliance, 2021).

Once a potential grooming situation has been identified, action can be taken by the moderators to warn, suspend or ban a user on the platform. They can also report a user to a relevant law enforcement or regulatory agency. In one example, a man travelled from Australia to the Philippines to meet a 13-year-old girl he had allegedly paid for sex. He was arrested by Filipino authorities after Facebook monitoring of chatlogs identified the man engaging with the girl, who sent explicit naked photos to him via a messaging services in return for payment. He then travelled to the Philippines where he was arrested (Murdoch, 2016).

Unfortunately, action by moderators may have limited effect because experienced Content Producers will often lure unsuspecting children on to encrypted chat or livestreaming platforms where interactions are not monitored by moderators. If a Content Producer is identified and subsequently suspended or banned, the relative anonymity of the online environment means that they may rejoin under a different username, using a different email address and disguising an IP address with a commercial VPN service. Indeed, it is just as likely that a Content Producer will already operate online with multiple usernames, creating multiple personas, so that if one is lost (due to moderator enforcement) they can continue to operate on the same platform. For example, one convicted online sex offender was found to have up to

40 fake Facebook accounts that he used to groom children into providing him with self-produced CSAM (Donald, 2017).

## Interventions that address preparation

Interventions that address offence preparation are somewhat more difficult to identify, partly because those interventions that address target selection are indistinguishable from those that address offence preparation. For example, offender treatment and rehabilitation may address both the targeting and offence preparation using psychological techniques that help offenders to retrain their thinking. In the online environment, target selection and preparation may also be indistinguishable, with a potential victim being identified at random and groomed for CSAM immediately.

### *Situational prevention of preparation in the offline environment*

There are, however, some measures that can be taken to reduce the potential for preparation in both the offline and online environment. In the offline world, Smallbone and Wortley (2001) have demonstrated the situationally specific conditions in which child sexual abuse often takes place. For example, where familial child sexual abuse was concerned, they showed that the most common means of organising time alone with the child involved being home alone with the child with the knowledge of the wife / girlfriend (58%) and watching television with the child (37%). For extrafamilial victimisation, the most common scenarios for organising time alone involved watching television with the child (32%), letting the child sleep in the same bed (31%) and going for car rides with the child (31%) (Smallbone & Wortley, 2001). These offer potentially risky situations in which offenders prepare to sexually abuse children. Therefore, limiting the circumstances in which adult males are alone with children in these circumstances (even in the case of family members) may help to reduce the opportunity for child sexual abuse to occur.

### *Proactive law enforcement investigation of online grooming*

From an online preparation perspective, there are potential points of intervention in the process of grooming for self-produced CSAM. Significant effort is devoted by law enforcement agencies around the world to identifying and prosecuting Content Producers who engage in the grooming of children. One common approach is to operate undercover, pretending to be a child or young person, available to be groomed. This approach can be used to lure the Content Producer into either giving information that could lead to their detection, or to arrange to meet in the real world, where an arrest can be made. Although there are no formal evaluations of covert methods (because of the obvious sensitivity of sharing information with researchers), Christensen, Rayment-McHugh et al. (2021) suggest that such proactive policing methods are likely to be effective in resulting in prosecutions. As an example, Krone (2005b) described two Queensland cases (R V S [unreported]; R V

K [2004] QCA 162) in which police operated undercover, assuming the identities of young girls in chatrooms that resulted in them being groomed by perpetrators and invited to meet offline. Proactive investigations that result in arrest would appear to have a high prosecution rate. Analysis of 34 cases employing proactive investigation that resulted in arrests in the USA found that 33 (97%) resulted in conviction, most of whom pleaded guilty to the charges (31 cases, 91%) (Mitchell et al., 2005).

### Awareness raising to help children identify grooming

Awareness raising among children and young people is relevant not only to the targeting of Victims / Survivors but also during the preparation stage of grooming. Providing children and young people with the skills to identify and deflect perpetrators could help to reduce their vulnerability to exploitation, as noted earlier. There are also technical solutions that could be helpful. For example, machine learning algorithms could be built into online chat functions to detect when an adult is pretending to be a child online. This could be used to flag with the child user (and a capable guardian, such as a parent) that they are in fact speaking with an adult, even though they may have been led to believe it was another child. Raising awareness in this way may help to close down a conversation before it leads to self-produced CSAM being created (Meyer, 2015). However, care would need to be taken in how such a tool was made available, as this could also be used by perpetrators to identify whether the child they were attempting to groom was, in fact, an undercover police officer.

### Warnings for parents and guardians

Applications are also available to automatically monitor a child's social media and chat interactions to detect inappropriate, sexual or unsolicited language by reference to a database of commonly used terms and phrases. A parent can then be warned when, for example, a CSAM Producer approaches their child to potentially groom them for self-produced CSAM[22]

## Interventions that address perpetration

The perpetration stage relates to the production of CSAM, which may be either generated by a Content Producer abusing a child, or through self-creation by a child, after being groomed by a Content Producer. Unfortunately, once the targeting and preparation stages have been successfully performed, it is extremely difficult to prevent perpetration.

## Interventions that address completion

As with perpetration, there are relatively few tools available to address the completion stage of a CSAM incident. In a sense, this is could be viewed as appropriate, given that the event has already occurred and therefore much more attention is paid to preventing the event from occurring in the first place. However, addressing the completion stage is important to prevent repeat victimisation – either of the same child, or other children (although noting that the very process of reporting can itself be traumatising). Relevant interventions to this domain include establishing reporting and response frameworks, mandatory reporting, reactive police investigations (in contrast to proactive investigations used in the perpetration stage) and crowdsourcing of intelligence (which is really a subcategory of reactive investigation).

## Establishing reporting and response frameworks

While child protection systems are well developed in most Western countries, in many parts of the world, there is little or no capacity to respond to reports of child sexual abuse. In these circumstances, there is a need to establish basic frameworks that not only allow for cases of abuse to be reported, but for an adequate and safe response to be provided. For example, NGOs like Child Helpline International facilitate improved reporting mechanisms in developing countries. In 2018, the NGO partnered with ICMEC to deliver the Advocate, Collaborate & Train to End Violence Against Children (ACT to EVAC) programme in five countries – Jordan, Kenya, Peru, the Philippines and Tanzania. This sought to improve not only the reporting of online child sexual abuse, but to improve the services available to respond to victims[23].

## Mandatory reporting of child sexual abuse

Mandatory reporting in the offline world is the legislated requirement for certain groups to report suspected cases of child abuse and child neglect to the relevant authorities. The groups covered by such requirements will vary between jurisdictions and can include professions who regularly encounter children (such as teachers, social workers and medical professionals), although in some jurisdictions the onus will be placed on all adults to report (Australian Institute of Family Studies, 2020). The purpose of mandatory reporting is to increase the number of reports of child abuse and neglect and therefore increase the number of police investigations and subsequent prosecutions. This in turn is intended to prevent repeat victimisation and therefore reduce harm experienced by children.

There is evidence that mandatory reporting increases the flow of reports of child sexual abuse and the number of substantiated cases. Comparing the state of Victoria, Australia with the Republic of Ireland (jurisdictions of similar size), Mathews (2014) found that the rate of reporting and rate of substantiated cases of child sexual abuse was considerably higher in Victoria (where mandatory reporting was legislated) than in Ireland (where there was no mandatory reporting). Similarly, examining the impact of mandatory reporting pre / post implementation in Western Australia,

Mathews et al. (2016) found that both reporting and substantiated investigations increased over time.

However, mandatory reporting is not without its problems. A systematic review and meta-synthesis by McTavish et al. (2017) concluded that high-quality evidence was not available to show that mandatory reporting did more good than harm. The researchers documented a series of negative outcomes for the children concerned, including escalation in maltreatment, being placed in foster homes that were worse than the family home and being traumatised by the investigation process.

Mandatory reporting can also occur within and between organisations as a way of monitoring allegations of child sexual abuse in aggregate. For example, UN Iraq has introduced a policy for reporting de-identified information on allegations of child sexual exploitation involving aid workers that can allow for the analysis of patterns and trends, which can then be used to drive action[24].

## Reactive police investigation

A significant element of police work associated with child sexual abuse, in both the online and offline world, involves conducting painstaking reactive investigations to uncover the necessary evidence to prosecute perpetrators in cases reported to them. These may be cases of CSAM reported through centralised channels such as NCMEC, or cases of contact sexual abuse reported directly to the police. The intention of these investigations is to rescue children from harm, achieve justice for Victims / Survivors, reduce the risk of further harm to the community and increase the perceived risk of detection among perpetrators (from both a specific and general deterrence perspective).

Relatively little formal evaluation research has been undertaken to inform what works in reactive police investigations of these kinds, although there is some evidence to suggest that polygraphs (in jurisdictions in which they are permitted) can prove effective in eliciting information from perpetrators (Christensen, Rayment-McHugh et al., 2021; Eggins et al., 2021). For example, Bourke et al. (2015) described how the tactical use of polygraph procedures with a sample of 127 suspects with no prior history of contact child sexual offending resulted in over half disclosing prior offending of this kind (compared with only 5% prior to the polygraph procedure). Disclosure was found to be greatest 3–4 days after a search warrant was executed.

There is also evidence to suggest that training for officers can improve outcomes (Davidson et al., 2017; Eggins et al., 2021). A survey of police in the UK, Netherlands and Italy found that those who received specialist training in investigating online child sexual abuse were more knowledgeable and better equipped to conduct such investigations than were officers who received general training or no training (Davidson et al., 2017). Examining specialist Internet Crimes Against Children Taskforces in the USA, Marcum and Higgins (2011) found that task forces with more trained investigators tended to perform more computer forensic examinations. Marcum et al. (2010) also demonstrated that training on cybercrime increased the number of CSAM arrests made by a police department in the USA. However, there is evidence that officers working in specialist cybercrime investigation roles often do not have access to the training they require (Harkin et al., 2018; Holt et al., 2020).

Specialist task forces would appear to be important in conducting police investigations focused on CSAM (Christensen, Rayment-McHugh et al., 2021). For example, Marcum et al. (2010) found that police departments that employed specialist task forces tended to make more arrests for CSAM offences than departments without them. A systematic review of the role of specialist investigation units that respond to child sexual abuse found that they tended to have greater involvement of partner agencies (such as child protective services and medical services) and had higher arrest rates than traditional approaches. Child Victims / Survivors also showed a higher level of satisfaction with specialist units than with other approaches (Westera et al., 2016).

## Computer forensic examination

As part of an investigation into CSAM production, police may seize the computers used by a suspect (as well as other devices, such as smartphones, digital cameras and external storage devices) to gather evidence of offending behaviour. Computers can hold a great deal of information about sites accessed, files created, saved and opened etc. Even if files are deleted from hard drives, forensic examination tools can still be used to retrieve files (Wortley & Smallbone, 2012). It is important to note that forensic examination is relevant for production, distribution and viewing of CSAM, allowing these different activities to be identified, although in this section we are expressly interested in the role of forensics in the production process, with an investigation arising following a report. While integral to the investigation of CSAM, forensic examination has also become a blockage to investigation, with police digital forensics units often having a backlog of cases due to increased demand and resulting in long wait times to receive the results of examinations (Islam et al., 2019b).

## Crowdsourcing of intelligence

Linked with the investigation of child sexual abuse and the production of CSAM, crowdsourcing can be used to gain additional information from the public. Europol's *Stop Child Abuse – Trace an Object* initiative publishes online the images of objects such as, clothing, bedding, furniture, toys and room decoration that are found in CSAM and encourage the public to contact investigators with tips on to whom those items might belong. These images are typically uploaded when other lines of inquiry have been exhausted. To date, more than 18,000 tips from the public have been received since the initiative began in 2017[25], although it is unclear to what extent these lead to criminal justice outcomes.

## Summing up the evidence on approaches the reduce the production of CSAM

Preventing CSAM production is difficult. With more than 20 different script tracks for CSAM production, there would appear to be plenty of opportunity for images and videos to enter the CSAM ecosystem and subsequently be distributed to others. This chapter has attempted to describe the common measures taken to address child sexual abuse and CSAM by using a high-level crime script as the framework for understanding intervention points. This crime script consists of just four stages that describe how CSAM production events occur, including target selection, offence preparation, offence perpetration and offence completion.

At the target selection stage, there is limited evidence of effective measures in offline environments. Education and awareness raising aimed at children can help them to identify situations in which they may be targeted by an adult for sexual abuse and to employ tactics to avoid being a victim and to report when they have been.

Measures targeted at convicted sexual offenders can also be effective in helping to avoid further targeting of children. Psychological treatments that employ cognitive behavioural therapies may reduce subsequent reoffending by around a quarter, while non-public sex offender registries may help the police to manage sex offenders in the community by allowing for further surveillance. Perhaps the most effective method of preventing convicted sex offenders from reoffending against children is to incarcerate them, although this is problematic because most sex offenders are never convicted or incarcerated and there is (contentious) evidence to suggest that most would not go on to reoffend anyway.

Other measures aimed at preventing target selection in the offline world are less effective. While criminal record checks by employers are commonly used when employing staff to work with children, there is little evidence to show they work better than other methods of employment screening. However, they do at least force employers to undertake screening based on a criminal record and, as such, is better than no screening. Public sex offender registries, that are commonly used in some jurisdictions, have shown to be of limited use in preventing reoffending, although they may have prevented some first-time offending.

In the online world, measures that attempt to prevent target selection are seldom employed. That is, apart from site moderation which aims to block or suspend users if they are reported or identified for breaching community standards. However, it is unclear the extent to which this is standard practice among social media platforms, or how many adult users are blocked from grooming children in this way, or indeed how effective it is when there is the potential to circumvent the sanction with new user profiles that can flourish in an environment that is characterised by anonymity.

Overall then, it would seem difficult to prevent a perpetrator in either the offline or online world from targeting children as Victims. That which does appear to work focuses, on the one hand, on the very small proportion of child sex offenders who are convicted (via psychological treatment, sex offender registry management and incarceration) and, on the other hand, on children protecting themselves from being targeted, by raising their awareness of the risks.

At the preparation stage, there is a recognition that there are certain offline environmental situations in which child sexual abuse is more likely to occur. This can include watching television alone with a child, taking a child on car rides or sharing a bed with the child. However, knowing these are risky situations does not necessarily stop abuse from occurring as parental figures and guardians are often groomed into trusting a perpetrator in situations where they are left alone with a child.

In the online environment, considerable effort is made by law enforcement agencies to operate undercover to identify and pursue the most serious and persistent offenders. However, this is a resource-intensive police activity where the demand created by CSAM Content Producers is likely to far outweigh the available supply of undercover officers (Vedelago, 2020).

At the completion stage, the focus of attention shifts to increasing the likelihood that child sexual abuse comes to the attention of the authorities and that repeat victimisation (either of the same child or other children) is prevented. In this regard, mandatory reporting of child sexual abuse (and child neglect) forms an important part of the child protection framework and has been demonstrated to increase the number of verified cases of child sexual abuse. However, mandatory reporting needs to be supported by effective and safe practices to deal with Victims / Survivors once they have been identified.

Greater attention is also paid to the investigation, detection and prosecution of child sexual offenders at the completion stage. Specially trained police officers working in specialist task forces focused on investigating child sexual abuse, and drawing on the latest computer forensic technology, and crowdsourcing intelligence leads when necessary, are effective in rescuing children and bringing child sexual offenders to justice. But the problem remains that most child sexual offences are not reported to the authorities and many do not proceed to prosecution, either due to a lack of evidence, a lack of policing resources to investigate all cases, or both.

Overall then, there are significant amounts of energy and resources devoted to disrupting the child sexual offence commission process, although most (criminal record checks, sex offender registries, psychological treatment for sex offenders, mandatory reporting, police investigation for specially trained officers in task forces) all rely on child sexual offences having been committed and attempting to prevent repeat victimisation. There would appear to be relatively few interventions that are truly preventative in nature. Among these are education and training for young people to help them identify, repel and report attempts at being groomed and proactive policing methods that attempt to disrupt and detect online offenders from grooming children for sexual offences. So, in this environment, it would seem fair to conclude that the production of CSAM is stacked in favour of the Content Producer, with both plentiful opportunities to offend and relatively few (insufficient) effective interventions to stop the production from occurring.

# What more could be done to reduce CSAM production?

Let's return to Ekblom and Hirschfield's 11 Ds of crime prevention, introduced in chapter 7 and explore how these might be used to tackle CSAM production.

## *Age restrictions on social media platforms*

At the offence targeting stage in cases of online grooming that lead to self-produced CSAM, we could pay closer attention to approaches that aim to defeat / delay offending by blocking a perpetrator from finding a potential victim online. One approach would be to design social media platforms so that they are difficult for adult perpetrators to be in the same virtual space as children by using age verification technology. Many social media sites now include age restriction policies (sometimes known as age-gating) in their terms of use, to prevent children below a certain age from accessing the platforms. For example, Facebook, Twitter, Instagram, Snapchat, TikTok and others all require users to be at least 13 years old (and older in some jurisdictions)[26]. From a CSAM theory of change perspective (noting that this is not the primary reason for the age restriction), these policies aim to reduce the likelihood that a child below a certain age will frequent the same virtual space as a Content Producer and, in the absence of effective capable guardianship, subsequently becomes a Victim / Survivor of CSAM[27]. In the context of the 11 Ds of crime prevention, this can be viewed as directing / deflecting offenders away from places frequented by potential victims. However, such policies currently offer limited (insufficient) protection. One reason for this is that the age of users is seldom verified, so children may simply circumvent an age restriction policy by giving a false date of birth with no requirement to support this with evidence. Additionally, there are plenty of sites aimed at children and that could be frequented by Content Producers to mean that those intent on finding potential victims need not look far to find a suitable online location. There have also been concerns raised that age verification could impede privacy rights and also provide powerful ESPs with additional personal information that would be used for data analytic and marketing purposes (Joint Committee on the Draft Online Safety Bill, 2021). It could also lead to increased data leakages if data held by ESPs is hacked and stolen (Snow, 2022).

Despite these limitations and concerns, age verification could prevent children from encountering adults in online environments. This could require active age verification, perhaps with the use of a third-party company that specialises in online age verification. However, these services will often rely on either the user providing proof of identity to the third-party provider, or the provider checking the identity of the user against existing databases – such as the electoral roll. This is problematic as children will often not have formal identity documents (driver's license / passport) with which their identity can be checked and will be too young to appear on the electoral roll. As an alternative, age estimation can be made by algorithms that assess the other online services and sites visited by a user. Facial recognition can also be used with a high degree of accuracy. This could be used to log on to a site, providing both authentication and age estimation[28] (House of Representatives Standing Committee on Social Policy and Legal Affairs, 2020).

Age estimation tools of this kind could, then, be used in a routine activity sense to prevent adults from entering the same virtual space as children, thereby preventing opportunities for subsequent grooming. Similarly, they could be built into livestreaming applications to provide a warning sign if an adult was livestreaming with a child – perhaps automatically saving such sessions in an unencrypted format for subsequent review. It should be noted that it is currently unclear how effective such measures would be, especially while users could employ commercially available VPNs to operate in jurisdictions that fall outside of the use of such age verification technology. However, as noted earlier, this is unlikely to result in a 100 per cent displacement, suggesting there could still be a net gain. Responsibility for employing age verification technology would rest with ESPs to implement on their platforms, so could theoretically be voluntarily employed in all jurisdictions where it was legal to do so, thereby minimising the opportunities to circumvent the technology with VPNs. However, there are moves to legislate the requirement for ESPs to use age verification in some cases. For example, France and Germany both require adult pornography sites to verify age, while a number of other countries are considering similar proposals (McCabe, 2021).

## Making it harder to find friends

A significant part of the fun of social media for some people is the ability to contact new and interesting people. Yet this function can also serve as a means by which CSAM Content Producers can find children that they can target to groom for CSAM. This function is also used by livestreaming facilitators to find Consumers who may wish to purchase a livestreaming show, although negotiations are usually then undertaken in private chat sessions (Napier et al., 2021).

Potential options here would be to defeat / deny offenders access to this function (to use Ekblom & Hirschfield's (2014) 11 Ds) by turning off this function as a default setting, or limiting the number of people who can see a user's profile / contact a user as a default. This would mean that a user would need to take proactive action to be seen. Combined with age verification technology, this could be used to limit who can see the profile of a child as a default on a child's account.

## Disinformation in online forums

The targeting stage could also be addressed by focusing greater effort to deter, discourage, demotivate, deceive and disconcert (Ekblom & Hirschfield, 2014), by spreading disinformation in online forums frequented by individuals with paedophilic interests. This could include spreading information about heightened risks of detection due to increased / improved policing methods (whether real or not), sharing links to CSAM sites that are openly monitored by police, or providing information about the harm caused to children in an effort to engage the conscience of offenders and to demotivate them from offending. Messages that direct perpetrators to treatment might also be disseminated. This work could be undertaken by police, or it could be undertaken by private corporations or NGOs, as long as it could be done safely without online reprisals targeted at those engaged in this activity. However, it would ideally be undertaken with enough dosage (involve many active participants) to reach those that such a campaign would aim to target (multiple forums and multiple forum users).

No doubt those spreading disinformation in online forums would be targeted by forum moderators for expulsion from the site and could lead to greater security required to gain access, such as proving one's credentials as having an interest in paedophilia. However, that is not problematic if it is viewed as part of the intervention, aiming to increase the transactional costs associated with running a forum and potentially limiting access to individuals who might be on the fringe of being involved in child sexual abuse, thereby preventing them from gaining additional knowledge and peer approval for their actions and beliefs.

However, this approach would need to be balanced against the intelligence that may be harvested from such sites by law enforcement officers. This might include gaining information on forum participants, information on new and emerging methods and links to CSAM sites shared by other participants.

## Removing the profit from livestreaming

At the livestreaming offence preparation stage, a facilitator will negotiate a fee with a Consumer. Once a fee is agreed, the Consumer will arrange for the payment to be sent from their bank account to the account of the facilitator's choice. This may be through a standard bank, but will often involve a money service business (such as Western Union, or MoneyGram) to which funds can be instantly wired and withdrawn in cash from a local store, prior to the livestreaming offence being perpetrated (Brown et al., 2020). For example, AUSTRAC found that Australian bank, Westpac, had facilitated over 3,000 payments from Australian CSAM Consumers to livestreaming facilitators in the Philippines, through LitePay, the bank's low-cost, funds transfer service (Janda, 2019). This highlights again the central role of the financial system in supporting elements of the CSAM ecosystem, as noted in chapter 2.

Aware of these processes, banks and money service businesses are playing an important capable guardianship role in these routine financial activities, scanning accounts for suspicious patterns of transactions that may be associated with the consumption of livestreaming of child sexual abuse. Potential indicators of purchasing the livestreaming of child sexual abuse include small payments (AUS $15–$500) made on a frequent basis (sometimes multiple times a day) to different accounts, with descriptions such as 'accommodation', 'education', 'school', 'uniform' or 'medical bills' (AUSTRAC, 2019). Once identified, payments may be blocked, customers reported to financial authorities (for making suspicious transactions) and, in some cases, the accounts of customers attempting to make such transactions may be closed. Indeed, in recent years, the banking sector has been active in closing the accounts of those suspected to be involved in this business. In some cases, this has resulted in livestreaming facilitators evolving the ways in which funds are received. For example, a third party (friend or family member) may be recruited to open an account with a money service business, to which funds are sent by the livestream Consumer. The third party collects the money from the money service business and informs the livestreaming provider that the funds have been received. This can all occur within a short period of time as the third parties will be located close to a money service business, ready to withdraw the funds as soon as they arrive. If the money service business blocks an account on suspicion of funds being used for illicit purposes, the livestream facilitator may simply ask another friend / family member to receive the funds. However, each time an account is cancelled, it increases the effort associated with conducting the livestreaming business and may be enough to discourage some facilitators from continuing in this business.

Given the importance of the financial system for the continued success of livestreaming of child sexual abuse as an illicit business model, and the pivotal role of the banking sector as a capable guardian in identifying and preventing transactions made for this purpose, there is potentially more that can be done to increase the risk of detection at the offence preparation stage. This may mean the development of more effective financial algorithms for identifying transactions for livestreaming purposes by a bank's customers, the greater sharing of information between banks of emerging transaction pattern profiles and even the sharing of information on customers that have been blocked or banned for making payments to livestreaming facilitators (although noting the ethical and legal considerations that would accompany this approach). Indeed, banks are likely to be essential in reducing the extent of livestreaming of child sexual abuse by increasing the risk of detection (both real and perceived) of both CSAM Consumers and facilitators involved in this business, which may help to detect, discourage and deter offenders in the context of the 11 Ds discussed in chapter 7 (Ekblom & Hirschfield, 2014). We return to the importance of the financial system in the priorities for action in chapter 11.

As with other interventions, there is likely to be a degree of displacement that results from improved banking surveillance and activity. This may result in an increased use of cryptocurrencies to side-step centralised banking services. However, not all CSAM Consumers purchasing livestreaming of child sexual abuse will be willing to use cryptocurrencies. Indeed, given the still relative novelty of cryptocurrencies among the public, the transfer of funds from a bank account to a cryptocurrency exchange might be one indicator that a bank customer may be involved in an illicit transaction. This might be strengthened if the customer was also purchasing VPN services, screen-capture software, metadata-stripping software or anonymising software (AUSTRAC, 2019).

## Throttling internet speeds

As noted in chapter 7, it may be possible to disable / deny livestreaming perpetrators by reducing internet speeds to IP addresses that are known to be involved in such activity to the point where stable livestreaming connections cannot be established. This would have an impact on the offence perpetration stage of the CSAM production script. This intervention might extend to whole communities where livestreaming of child sexual abuse is known to occur. This could be based on intelligence from the police, or monitoring by the ESPs providing livestreaming platforms, working in partnership with ISPs providing the internet connection. However, this would prove ethically contentious and may not be legal in many jurisdictions. It may also disadvantage households in deprived communities, especially those that are not involved in livestreaming of child sexual abuse.

## Could cameras decide whether to record?

One possibility to avoid the production of CSAM (even though physical sexual abuse may not be prevented) may be to develop cameras that can identify whether the image is of a sexual nature or involves a naked child and simply refuse to record the images. As such, this would be another example of disabling / denying offenders access to facilitating equipment in the context of the 11 Ds (Ekblom & Hirschfield, 2014). This may currently be in the realms of science fiction, but the development of more sophisticated artificial intelligence applications will eventually allow cameras in smartphones and laptops to discern when CSAM is being filmed and simply not save what is being viewed. Imagine if three makes of smartphone (Apple, Samsung and Xiaomi) incorporated such technology? Given that they account for over half of worldwide smartphone sales[29], this could have a marked impact on the effort that Content Producers would need to exert to record CSAM using a mobile phone. Although the market is somewhat more fragmented, similar approaches could be applied to laptops and tablet devices with built-in cameras.

Similar technology is already available for identifying adult pornography and is routinely applied by social media platforms to flag and remove material that is in breach of community standards. It is also used by Facebook to detect revenge porn uploaded to its site (Cheung, 2020). New algorithms are also being developed that can differentiate a child's face from an adult's, which in turn could lead to the development of CSAM-specific identification tools (Islam et al., 2019a; 2019b). However, such technology is not without its problems. When Tumblr introduced an algorithm to remove all pornographic material from its site, there were complaints over its high rate of false positives, leading to seemingly innocuous material being removed (Matsakis, 2018).

## Notes

1 That is, social media sites and instant messaging as the location for perpetrators to locate, groom and exploit children and young people to self-produce CSAM.

2 See Figure 1 in Block and Williams (2019). The study started with a sample of 500 cases, but outcomes could not be identified for 47 cases, leaving a sample of 453.

3 Figures obtained from the New South Wales Bureau of Crime Statistics and Research – www.bocsar.nsw.gov.au/Documents/Landing_Pages/Sexual%20Assault%20CJS.pdf

4 I recognise that there are all kinds of limitations with this kind of back-of-an-envelope calculation. These include the fact that reports to the police in a given year will not necessarily result in court appearances in that same year, changes in willingness to disclose over time, changes in police practices over time, differences between institutional abuse and abuse in other settings, and differences between justice systems. However, they serve to highlight that when a perpetrator commits a sexual offence against a child, that individual has a very low likelihood of going to jail.

5 Noting that testosterone is also produced by the adrenal glands, so surgical castration does not eliminate the production of testosterone entirely.

6 Although Lösel and Schmucker (2017) note that in some cases additional medication was provided to some individuals in the studies examined, though this is not examined further in the systematic review.

7 However, Soldino and Carbonell-Vayá (2017) found treatment location (prison vs community) made no difference to treatment outcomes.

8 Although this section is about the *targeting* of children for contact child sexual offences and subsequent production of CSAM, it is also pertinent to note that Mews et al. (2017) found that child image reoffending was higher for those receiving treatment than those in the control group.

9 Lösel et al. (2020) found that when employing a control group based on exact matching using the Static-99 actuarial risk assessment tool variables, sexual offence recidivism rates for the treatment group were slightly higher (7.1%) than for the control group (5.9%). In contrast, when employing a propensity score weighting approach to control group selection, sexual offence recidivism was slightly higher in the control group (8.7%) than in the treatment group (7.3%). In neither comparison were the differences statistically significant.

10 The Disclosure and Barring Service operates across England, Wales and Northern Ireland. Indeed, the requirements for criminal record checks are largely similar in England and Wales to Northern Ireland.

11 Requirements for criminal record checks / fingerprints differ from state to state for organisations that do not receive funding from Medicare / Medicaid.

12 Although focused on a different population and based solely on aggregate-level data, Hughes et al. (2014) provide some further evidence of the lack of effectiveness of criminal record checks. Their study of criminal incidents on university campuses found that there was no difference in the level of crime on campuses that used criminal record checks to screen employees and those that did not employ such measures.

13 See chapter 2 for a description of Content Producers in the CSAM ecosystem.

14 Found at www.missingkids.org/netsmartz/home

15 Found at www.esafety.gov.au/educators

16 Found at https://danielmorcombe.com.au/keeping-kids-safe-resources/

17 Found at www.protectchildren.ca/en/programs-and-initiatives/

18 Found at https://1vie.org/en/#tools

19 Found at www.parentsprotect.co.uk/

20  Found at https://ecsa.lucyfaithfull.org/interventions
21  Found at www.e-himaya.gov.ma/
22  One such application can be found at www.keeperschildsafety.net.
23  Found at www.childhelplineinternational.org/wp-content/uploads/2021/08/Annual-Review-2020-Online-Version.pdf
24  Found at https://psea.interagencystandingcommittee.org/resources/iraq-information-sharing-protocol-sharing-sensitive-information.
25  Found at www.europol.europa.eu/newsroom/news/ten-child-victims-of-sexual-abuse-identified-thanks-to-international-taskforce-europol
26  It is no coincidence that all of these social media platforms set the same age restriction on the use of their sites. This will avoid the sites being required to comply with the Children's Online Privacy Protection Rule, as set out in the US Children Online Privacy Protection Act (COPPA). The Rule requires sites aimed at children under the age of 13 years to adhere to a number of conditions if they collect personal information. Further details can be found www.ftc.gov/tips-advice/business-center/guidance/complying-coppa-frequently-asked-questions-0
27  This draws on routine activity theory's crime triangles discussed in chapter 7 (Eck & Clarke, 2003; Eck, 2003).
28  Services of this kind are provided by companies like Yoti.com.
29  According to sales data for the first quarter of 2021 – www.idc.com/promo/smartph one-market-share.

# References

Agan, A.Y. & Prescott, J.J. (2014). Sex offender law and the geography of victimization. *Journal of Empirical Legal Studies* 11(4), 786–828. https://doi.org/10.1111/jels.12056

AUSTRAC (2019). *Combating the sexual exploitation of children for financial gain: Activity indicators*. AUSTRAC. www.austrac.gov.au/sites/default/files/2019-11/Fintel%20Allia nce%20-%20Indicators%20report%20-%20Combating%20sexual%20exploitation%20 of%20children.pdf

Australian Institute of Family Studies (2020). *Mandatory reporting of child abuse and neglect*. CFCA Resource Sheet – June 2020. Australian Institute of Family Studies https://aifs. gov.au/cfca/sites/default/files/publication-documents/2006_mandatory_reporting_ of_child_abuse_and_neglect.pdf

Block, S.D. & Williams, L.M. (2019). *The Prosecution of Child Sexual Abuse: A Partnership to Improve Outcomes: Final Summary Overview*. Office of Justice Programs. www.ncjrs.gov/ pdffiles1/nij/grants/252768.pdf

Bourke, M.L., Frogmeli, L., Detar, P.J., Sullivan, M.A., Meyle, E. & O'Riordan, M. (2015). The use of tactical polygraph with sex offenders. *Journal of Sexual Aggression* 21(3), 354–367. https://doi.org/10.1080/13552600.2014.886729

Brown, R., Napier, S. & Smith, R.G. (2020). *Australians who view livestreaming of child sexual abuse: An analysis of financial transactions*. Trends and issues in crime and criminal justice 589. Australian Institute of Criminology. www.aic.gov.au/publications/tandi/tandi589

Cheung, K.C. (2020, 27 May). Facebook using AI to detect 'revenge porn'. Algorithm-XLab. https://algorithmxlab.com/blog/facebook-using-ai-detect-revenge-porn/

Christensen, L.S., Rayment-McHugh, S., Prenzler, T., Chiu, Y.N. & Webster, J. (2021). The theory and evidence behind law enforcement strategies that combat child sexual abuse material. *International Journal of Police Science & Management* 23(4), 392–405. https://doi. org/10.1177/14613557211026935

Christensen, L.S., Sanchez de Ribera, O. & Trajtenberg, N. (2021). A systematic review of professionals' views about community management policies for individuals convicted of sexual offences. *Sexual Abuse* 34(2), 127–156. https://doi.org/10.1177/1079063221 1000369

Cornish, D. (1994). The procedural analysis of offending and its relevance for situational prevention. In R.V. Clarke (Ed.), *Crime Prevention Studies, Volume 3* (pp.151–196). Criminal Justice Press.

Davidson, J., DeMarco, J., Bifulco, A., Bogaerts, S., Caretti, V., Aiken, M., Cheevers, C., Corbari, E., Scally, M., Schilder, J., Schimmenti, A. & Puccia, A. (2017). *Enhancing police and industry practice: EU child online safety project.* www.mdx.ac.uk/__data/assets/pdf_file/0017/250163/ISEC-report-FINAL.pdf

Davis, N. & Wells, S. (1994–1995). Effective Screening of Child Care and Youth Workers. *Children's Legal Rights Journal* 15(1-2), 22–27.

Day. A., Carson, E., Boni, N. & Hobbs, G. (2014). The management of sex offenders in the community: From policy to practice. *Australian Journal of Social Issues* 49(3), 249–394.

Dorais, M. (2002). *Don't tell: The sexual abuse of boys.* McGill-Queens University Press.

Donald, K. (2017, 5 September). British paedophile Paul Leighton jailed for 16 years for rape. *The Guardian.* www.theguardian.com/uk-news/2017/sep/04/british-paedophile-paul-leighton-jailed-for-16-years-for-rape

Dowling. C., Boxall, H., Pooley, K., Long, C. & Franks, C. (2021). *Patterns and predictors of reoffending among child sexual offenders: A rapid evidence assessment.* Trends and issues in crime and criminal justice 632. Australian Institute of Criminology https://doi.org/10.52922/ti78306

Drake, E.K. & Aos, S. (2009). *Does sex offender registration and notification reduce crime? A systematic review of the research literature.* Washington State Institute for Public Policy www.wsipp.wa.gov/ReportFile/1043/Wsipp_Does-Sex-Offender-Registration-and-Notification-Reduce-Crime-A-Systematic-Review-of-the-Research-Literature_Full-Report.pdf

Eck, J. (2003). Police problems: The complexity of problem theory, research and evaluation. In J. Knutsson (Ed.), *Problem-oriented policing: from innovation to mainstream* (pp. 79–113). Crime Prevention Studies 15. Willan Publishing:

Eck, J. & Clarke, R.V. (2003). Classifying Common Police Problems: A Routine Activity Approach. In M. Smith & D. Cornish (Eds.), *Theory for Practice in Situational Crime Prevention* (pp.7–39). Crime Prevention Studies 16. Criminal Justice Press.

Eggins, E., Mazerolle, L., Higginson, A., Hine, L., Walsh, K., Sydes, M., McEwan, J., Hassall, G., Roetman, S., Wallis, R. & Williams, J. (2021). *Criminal justice responses to child sexual abuse material offending: A systematic review and evidence and gap map.* Trends & issues in crime and criminal justice 623. Australian Institute of Criminology. www.aic.gov.au/publications/tandi/tandi623

Ekblom, P. & Hirschfield, A. (2014). Developing an alternative formulation of SCP principles – the Ds (11 and counting). *Crime Science* 3(2). https://doi.org/10.1186/s40 163-014-0002-5

Gunawan, F.E., Ashianti, L. & Sekishita, N. (2018). A simple classifier for detecting online child grooming conversation. *Telkomnika* 16(3),1239–1248. https://doi.org/10.12928/TELKOMNIKA.v16i3.6745

Hanson, K.R., Bourgon, G., Helmus, L. & Hodgson, S.A. (2009). *Meta-analysis of the effectiveness of treatment for sexual offenders: Risk, need, and responsivity.* Public Safety Canada. www.publicsafety.gc.ca/cnt/rsrcs/pblctns/2009-01-trt/index-en.aspx

Harkin, D., Whelan, C. & Chang, L. (2018). The challenges facing specialist police cybercrime units: an empirical analysis. *Police Practice and Research: An International Journal* 19(6), 519–536. https://doi.org/10.1080/15614263.2018.1507889

Herzog-Evans, M. (2011). Judicial rehabilitation in France: Helping with the desisting process and acknowledging achieved desistance. *European Journal of Probation* 3(1), 4–19. https://doi.org/10.1177/206622031100300102

Holt, T.J., Cale, J., Leclerc, B. & Drew, J. (2020). Assessing the challenges affecting the investigative methods to combat online child exploitation material offenses. *Aggression and Violent Behavior* 55, 101464. https://doi.org/10.1016/j.avb.2020.101464

House of Representatives Standing Committee on Social Policy and Legal Affairs (2020). *Protecting the age of innocence: Report of the inquiry into age verification for online wagering and online pornography.* Parliament of the Commonwealth of Australia. https://parlinfo.aph. gov.au/parlInfo/download/committees/reportrep/024436/toc_pdf/Protectingtheage ofinnocence.pdf;fileType=application%2Fpdf

Hughes, S.F., Elliott, T.L. & Myers, M. (2014). Measuring the Impact of Background Checks on Reducing Crime in Higher Education. *Public Administration Research* 3(2), 154–170. http://dx.doi.org/10.5539/par.v3n2p154

Islam, M., Mahmood, A.N., Watters, P., & Alazab, M. (2019a). Forensic Detection of Child Exploitation Material Using Deep Learning. In M. Alazab & M. Tang (Eds.), *Deep Learning Applications for Cyber Security, Advanced Sciences and Technologies for Security Applications* (pp. 211–220). https://doi.org/10.1007/978-3-030-13057-2_10

Islam, M., Watters, P., Mahmood, A.N. & Alazab, M. (2019b). Toward detection of child exploitation material: A forensic approach. In M. Alazab & M. Tang (Eds.), *Deep Learning Applications for Cyber Security, Advanced Sciences and Technologies for Security Applications* (pp. 221–246). https://doi.org/10.1007/978-3-030-13057-2_10

Janda, M. (2019, 21 November). How Westpac's LitePay service inadvertently helped Australian paedophiles abuse Filipino children. *ABC News.* www.abc.net.au/news/2019-11-21/how-westpac-inadvertently-facilitated-paedophilia/11725414

Joint Committee on the Draft Online Safety Bill (2021). *Draft Online Safety Bill: Report of session 2020-21.* House of Lords and House of Commons. https://committees.parliam ent.uk/committee/534/draft-online-safety-bill-joint-committee/

Krone, T. (2005b). *Queensland Police stings in online chat rooms.* Trends and issues in crime and criminal justice 301. Australian Institute of Criminology. www.aic.gov.au/publications/ tandi/tandi301

Lee, J. & Cho, K. (2013). Chemical Castration for Sex Offenders: Physicians' Views. *Journal of Korean Medical Science* 28(2), 171-172. http://dx.doi.org/10.3346/ jkms.2013.28.2.171

Letourneau, E.J., Levenson, J.S., Bandyopadhyay, D., Armstrong, K.S. & Sinha, D. (2010). Effects of South Carolina's sex offender registration and notification policy on deterrence of adult sex crimes. *Criminal Justice and Behavior* 37(5), 537–552. https://doi.org/ 10.1177/0093854810363569

Lipman, V. & Manthorpe, J. (2016). *Better safe than sorry? Checking care workers: a scoping review of the international evidence.* Social Care Workforce Research Unit, The Policy Institute, Kings College. https://kclpure.kcl.ac.uk/portal/files/135864358/Better_safe_than_sor ry_2016.pdf

Lösel, F., Link, E., Schmucker, M., Bender, D., Breuer, M., Carl, L., Endres, J. & Lauchs, L. (2020). On the effectiveness of sexual offender treatment in prisons: A comparison of two different evaluation designs in routine practice. *Sexual Abuse* 32(4), 452–475. https://doi. org/10.1177/1079063219871576

Lösel, F. & Schmucker, M. (2005). The effectiveness of treatment for sexual offenders: A comprehensive meta-analysis. *Journal of Experimental Criminology* 1, 117-146. https://doi.org/ 10.1007/s11292-004-6466-7

Lösel, F. & Schmucker, M. (2017). Sexual offender treatment for reducing recidivism among convicted sex offenders: a systematic review and meta-analysis. *Campbell Systematic Reviews* 2017, 8. https://doi.org/10.4073/csr.2017.8

Marcum, C.D. & Higgins, G.E. (2011). Combating child exploitation online: predictors of successful ICAC task forces. *Policing: A Journal of Policy and Practice* 5(4), 310–316. https://doi.org/10.1093/police/par044

Marcum, C.D., Higgins, G.E., Freiburger, T.L. & Ricketts, M.L. (2010). Policing possession of child pornography online: investigating the training and resources dedicated to the investigation of cybercrime. *International Journal of Police Science & Management* 12(4), 516–525. https://doi.org/10.1350%2Fijps.2010.12.4.201

Mathews, B. (2014). Mandatory reporting laws and identification of child abuse and neglect: Consideration of differential maltreatment types, and a cross-jurisdictional analysis of child sexual abuse reports. *Social Sciences* 3, 460–482. https://doi.org/10.3390/socsci 3030460

Mathews, B., Lee, X.J. & Norman, R.E. (2016). Impact of a new mandatory reporting law on reporting and identification of child sexual abuse: A seven year time trend analysis. *Child Abuse & Neglect* 56, 62–79. https://doi.org/10.1016/j.chiabu.2016.04.009

Matsakis, L. (2018, 12 May). Tumblr's porn-detecting AI has one job – and it's bad at it. *Wired*. www.wired.com/story/tumblr-porn-ai-adult-content/

McCabe, D. (2021, 27 October). Anonymity no more? Age checks come to the web. *New York Times*. www.nytimes.com/2021/10/27/technology/internet-age-check-proof.html

McTavish, J.R., Kimber, M., Devries, K., Colombini, M., MacGregor, J.C.D., Wathen, C.N., Agarwal, A. & MacMillan, H.L. (2017). Mandated reporters' experiences with reporting child maltreatment: a metasynthesis of qualitative studies. *BMJ Open*, 7, e013942. https://doi.org/10.1136/bmjopen-2016-013942

Mews, A., Di Bella, L. & Purver, M. (2017). *Impact evaluation of the prison-based Core Sex Offender Treatment Programme.* Ministry of Justice Analytical Series. Ministry of Justice. https://assets.publishing.service.gov.uk/government/uploads/system/uploads/attachme nt_data/file/623876/sotp-report-web-.pdf

Meyer, M. (2015). *Machine learning to detect online grooming.* Department of Information Technology, Uppsala University. http://uu.diva-portal.org/smash/get/diva2:846981/FULLTEXT01.pdf

Mitchell, K.J., Finkelhor, D. & Wolak, J. (2005). The internet and family and acquaintance sexual abuse. *Child Maltreatment* 10(1), 49–60.

Murdoch, L. (2016, 1 September). Australian accused of child sex tourism arrested in the Philippines. *Sydney Morning Herald.* www.smh.com.au/world/australian-accused-of-child-sex-tourism-arrested-in-the-philippines-20160901-gr6x8x.html

Napier, S., Dowling, C., Morgan, A. & Talbot, D. (2018). *What impact do public sex offender registries have on community safety?* Trends and issues in crime and criminal justice 550. Australian Institute of Criminology. www.aic.gov.au/sites/default/files/2020-05/ti_what_impact_do_public_sex_offender_registries_have_on_community_safety_22051 8_0.pdf

Napier, S., Teunissen, C. & Boxall, H. (2021). *Live streaming of child sexual abuse: An analysis of offender chat logs.* Trends and issues in crime and criminal justice. 639. Australian Institute of Criminology. https://doi.org/10.52922/ti78375

Plotnikoff, J. & Woolfson, R. (2000). *Where are they now? An evaluation of sex offender registration in England and Wales.* Police Research Series 126. Home Office Policing and Reducing Crime Unit. www.researchgate.net/publication/265496371_Where_Are_They_Now_An_Evaluation_of_Sex_Offender_Registration_in_England_and_Wales

Prescott, J.J. & Rockoff, J.E. (2011). Do sex offender registration and notification laws affect criminal behavior? *Journal of Law and Economics* 54(1), 161–206. www.journals.uchicago. edu/doi/abs/10.1086/658485

Reed, P. (2017). Punishment beyond incarceration: The negative effects of sex offender registration and restrictions. *Journal of Law and Criminal Justice* 5(2),16–30. https://doi.org/ 10.15640/jlcj.v5n2a

Royal Commission into Institutional Responses to Child Sexual Abuse (2017b). *Final Report: Volume 4, Identifying and disclosing child sexual abuse.* Commonwealth of Australia. www.childabuseroyalcommission.gov.au/sites/default/files/final_report_-_volume_4_ identifying_and_disclosing_child_sexual_abuse.pdf

Schmucker, M. & Lösel, F. (2008). Does sexual offender treatment work? A systematic review of outcome evaluations. *Psicothema* 20(1), 10–19. www.psicothema.com/pmidlookup. asp?pmid=18206060

Seto, M.C., Hanson, R.K. & Babchishin, K.M. (2011). Contact sexual offending by men arrested for child pornography offenses. *Sexual Abuse: A Journal of Research and Treatment,* 23, 124–145. https://doi.org/10.1177/1079063210369013

Smallbone, S.W. & Wortley, R.K. (2001). *Child sexual abuse: Offender characteristics and modus operandi.* Trends and issues in crime and criminal justice 193. Australian Institute of Criminology. www.aic.gov.au/sites/default/files/2020-05/tandi193.pdf

Snow, J. (2022, 27 February). Why age verification is so difficult for websites. *Wall Street Journal.* www.wsj.com/articles/why-age-verification-is-difficult-for-websites-1164 5829728

Soldino, V. & Carbonell-Vayá, E.J. (2017). Effect of treatment on sex offenders' recidivism: a meta-analysis. *Anales de Psicología* 33(3), 578–588. http://dx.doi.org/10.6018/ analesps.33.2.267961

South, S., Shlonsky, A., Mildon, R., Pourliakas, A., Falkiner, J. & Laughlin, A. (2015). *Scoping Review: Evaluations of pre-employment screening practices for child-related work that aim to prevent child sexual abuse.* Royal Commission into Institutional Responses to Child Sexual Abuse. www.parentingrc.org.au/wp-content/uploads/2018/01/Scoping-review_Evaluations- of-pre-employment-screening-practices-to-prevent-csa.pdf

Suhartono, D., Gazali, W. & Mamahit, K.F. (2019). Analytic hierarchy process in detecting probability of online grooming using neural network. *ICIC Express Letters* 13(12), 1087– 1095. www.icicel.org/ell/contents/2019/12/el-13-12-01.pdf

Vedelago, C. (2020, 19 June). More than 7.4 million images of child abuse circulating in Victoria. *The Age.* www.theage.com.au/national/victoria/more-than-7-4-million-ima ges-of-child-abuse-circulating-in-victoria-20200619-p554dy.html

Walsh, K., Zwi, K., Woolfenden, S. & Shlonsky, A. (2015). School-based education programmes for the prevention of child sexual abuse. *Cochrane Database of Systematic Reviews* 2015, 4, CD004380. https://doi.org/10.1002/14651858.CD004380.pub3

We Protect Global Alliance (2021). *Global threat assessment 2021: Working together to end the sexual exploitation of children online.* We Protect Global Alliance. www.weprotect.org/glo bal-threat-assessment-21/#report

Westera, N., Darwinkel, E. & Powell, M. (2016). *A systematic review of the efficacy of specialist police investigative units in responding to child sexual abuse.* Royal Commission into Institutional Responses to Child Sexual Abuse. www.childabuseroyalcommission.gov. au/sites/default/files/file-list/Research%20Report%20-%20The%20response%20of%20 specialist%20police%20investigative%20units%20to%20child%20sexual%20abuse%20- %20Government%20responses.pdf

Wortley, R. & Smallbone, S. (2012). *Internet Child Pornography: Causes, Investigation and Prevention*. Praeger.

Zgoba, K.M. & Mitchell, M.M. (2021). The effectiveness of Sex Offender Registration and Notification: A meta-analysis of 25 years of findings. *Journal of Experimental Criminology*. https://doi.org/10.1007/s11292-021-09480-z

# 9
# APPROACHES TO PREVENTING THE DISTRIBUTION OF CSAM

## Introduction

The problem of CSAM distribution lies at the heart of the CSAM ecosystem. In chapter 5, seven distribution-related problems are identified as contemporary issues to be addressed. These include:

- File storage sites (including image hosting) to store CSAM once it has been produced (which also aid distribution).
- Forums (including bulletin boards, newsgroups, image boards and the latest generation of forums) to distribute CSAM (both directly and through links).
- Social media sites to distribute CSAM (both directly and through links).
- Instant messaging to distribute CSAM (both directly and through links).
- Internet relay chat to distribute CSAM links.
- Computer game chat function to distribute CSAM (both directly and through links).
- Darknet use (through TOR) to distribute CSAM (via websites and forums).

It therefore follows that any interventions aimed at preventing the distribution of CSAM should attempt to address one of these contemporary problems[1]. As in chapter 8, this chapter also draws on the 11 Ds of crime prevention to explain how CSAM may be prevented from flowing through the ecosystem.

## Search and destroy

Key to the international effort to prevent the distribution of CSAM is the ability to identify and remove material from the CSAM ecosystem. A significant infrastructure has been established to assist with the reporting and subsequent removal of

DOI: 10.4324/9781003327264-11

CSAM. From a prevention perspective, this falls firmly under the banner of defeat / delay in the 11 Ds framework (Ekblom & Hirschfield, 2014) by effectively blocking access and therefore increasing the effort to which Content Producers must go to share their material and to which Consumers must go to find it.

### Identifying CSAM to be removed

In the USA, NCMEC, through its CyberTipline, plays a central role in receiving reports of CSAM that have been identified by members of the public and by ESPs. Under Chapter 110, Title 18 of the US Criminal Code, ESPs that are registered in the USA are required to provide reports of CSAM they discover to NCMEC as soon as reasonably possible. Failure to do so can incur a fine. These reports provide details of the CSAM along with identifying information associated with a user, including IP address etc. NCMEC is permitted to forward reports to law enforcement agencies, both in the USA and overseas. As a result of this process, and given that many of the large ESPs are US-based, NCMEC has become a significant international hub for receiving and disseminating reports of CSAM to the relevant authorities.

This, however, is not the only coordination point for receiving CSAM reports. Indeed, many countries have their own infrastructure for receiving reports via law enforcement agencies, government regulators and NGOs. As noted in chapter 1, INHOPE represents a growing international network of hotlines that can receive and process CSAM reports (INHOPE, 2022).

In discharging their duties, ESPs often employ sophisticated algorithms to identify CSAM that is being shared on their sites. However, as noted earlier, this currently often occurs once on the site, rather than at the point of upload, with reluctance among ESPs to prescreen content prior to upload (Independent Inquiry into Child Sexual Abuse, 2020). Some ESPs also employ large workforces, often operating in developing countries, employed by third-party companies with poor conditions of service, to process content that has been alerted to them, removing that which breaches community standards (including CSAM). Indeed, humans are viewed as more effective at identifying abhorrent material quickly than are machines (Roberts, 2017), although poor mental health can be a common consequence of working in this profession (Krishna, 2021). Many ISPs will also play an active role in identifying and removing CSAM from their web servers. In some jurisdictions (such as in Australia), this will be a statutory obligation, with ISPs being given a specified time to remove material, while in others (such as in the UK) it remains a voluntary activity. European Directive 2000/31/EC requires ISPs registered in the European Union to take action to remove or disable access to relevant information once they become aware of illegal activity on their networks[2].

### Tools for identifying CSAM

One of the key tools in implementing a search and destroy policy has been the use of technology that can identify material in the CSAM ecosystem that has already been identified and classified as CSAM by trained experts. Using applications such as Microsoft's PhotoDNA[3], Google's CSAI Match[4] and Thorn's Scene-Setting Video Hashing[5], CSAM images and videos can be scanned and given a unique code, known as a hash. ESPs can then scan their servers on a routine basis to identify images with the same hash value, which will identify them as CSAM that has already been identified by accredited organisations. This can then be reported and removed by ESPs in the knowledge that the file concerned contains CSAM. This can be achieved without the staff of the organisation hosting the material having to view it. This latter feature is also important from a law enforcement personnel perspective, saving the need for CSAM to be viewed and classified if it has already been processed and given a hash value by another agency, thereby helping to save resources required to classify CSAM and reduce some of the trauma experienced by staff that continually view CSAM as part of their occupation. A survey of 32 ESPs by We Protect Global Alliance (2021) found that the use of hash technology was common, with 87 per cent and 76 per cent using it to detect images and videos respectively.

As an example of how hash technology is used by individual ESPs, AOL developed the Image Detection and Filtering Process (IDFP) that scans the attachments of all emails sent by AOL customers. Hash values are created for all files and these are compared to an internal library of CSAM-related hash values. When a match is found, the email is blocked and a report is made to NCMEC's CyberTipline (Martellozzo & DeMarco, 2020). However, implementing processes of this kind, that require integration of hash technology with internal removal and reporting systems, have been criticised for the increased technical and resource requirements they place on ISPs / ESPs (Martellozzo & DeMarco, 2020). In August 2021, Apple announced improvements to the way in which it aimed to tackle CSAM. One of the measures announced was the use of hash technology to scan a device for known CSAM before it was uploaded to Apple's encrypted iCloud environment. This would be achieved by the file to be uploaded first being given a hash value that would be compared with a database of hash values associated with CSAM files. If a match was identified, it would be sent to a monitoring centre for human review. If it was proven to be CSAM, it was proposed that a report would then be made to NCMEC (Apple, 2021)[6]. Unfortunately, these proposals were short-lived. Following public criticism that this would erode privacy standards and would be a back door to accessing files stored on an Apple device, the proposals were effectively shelved in early September 2021 (Peters, 2021).

Hash technology is also built into web crawlers used by organisations including the Internet Watch Foundation and the Canadian Centre for Child Protection to routinely identify CSAM hosted by other organisations online and to request its removal. For example, Project Arachnid works by searching URLs that have previously been reported to Cybertip.ca (a Canadian mechanism for reporting CSAM) or that have been reported directly to Project Arachnid. Files are then compared to an existing database of hash values to identify matches. Takedown notices are then issued (via a court process) to ISPs found to be hosting CSAM, requesting them to remove the material.

One disadvantage of this approach is that, with a proliferation of hashing technology (e.g. the Message-Digest Algorithm 5 is different to the Secure Digest Algorithm), the same image or video may be given multiple hash values. It is unclear to what extent these are currently comparable and subject to any form of de-confliction. For example, Project Arachnid uses multiple sources of CSAM content – its own hash list and those provided by law enforcement agencies such as the Royal Canadian Mounted Police and by Interpol. In general, CSAM previously identified by one application may not be picked up as CSAM by another application unless it has first been picked up as CSAM by a human operator and given a hash value associated with a particular application. Nevertheless, hash technology of this kind enables verified CSAM to be identified and removed from the ecosystem in a routinised way.

However, this means that CSAM that has yet to be identified by a human operative and subsequently given a hash value can continue to be distributed online until it is found. New algorithms are being used to automatically identify CSAM that has not previously been identified. For example, Schulze et al. (2014) developed a tool that included identification of both visual and audio content, which could differentiate between CSAM and adult pornography. Google, through its Content Safety API, uses machine learning classifiers to identify new CSAM on its platforms. Thorn's Safer API serves a similar function. This prioritises content that is most likely to be CSAM for review, although this process still needs confirmation by a human viewing the material. Commercial solutions that can scan collections for illicit content of this kind are also available, meaning that solutions that identify new CSAM could be purchased as a service by smaller ESPs / ISPs who may not have the internal capabilities to develop such algorithms[7]. These novel approaches to identifying new CSAM could in future be combined with web crawlers to search for material that is routinely identified for takedown notices.

## Ordering the removal of CSAM

While search and destroy tactics work well when capable guardianship results in organisations taking responsibility for both proactively identifying and removing CSAM from their own servers (and therefore the part of the CSAM ecosystem within their control), there will be other cases in which third-party organisations identify the material. As noted earlier, members of the INHOPE network play a crucial internet-level role in identifying URLs that contain CSAM. However, they have no direct way of removing the CSAM. Instead, they can send a takedown notice to the ISP or ESP where the CSAM is hosted if it is registered in that jurisdiction. The relevant law enforcement agency will also typically be notified of the CSAM content. The organisation hosting the CSAM will be expected to remove the material as soon as it becomes aware of it. In some jurisdictions, this needs to be supported by a court order that directs the ISP / ESP to remove the material and they may not be required to do so without that order.

When CSAM is located on servers registered in overseas jurisdictions, a report will be sent to the relevant INHOPE member, or a government / law enforcement authority where no INHOPE-affiliated organisation is present. The removal of the CSAM will then be dependent on action taken by that jurisdiction, which can vary depending on cultural, legal and resource constraints. Despite the growth of the INHOPE network, there remains a lack of standardised practice internationally. Indeed, it can prove difficult to enforce the removal of CSAM in some low-income countries, where police resources may be limited (Martellozzo & DeMarco, 2020).

Here, it is also worth highlighting the different motivations among ISPs and ESPs for removing CSAM from their servers. There is a distinction to be drawn here between removing CSAM to avoid reputational risk and removing it as a legal obligation. This distinction may determine the commitment shown to removing CSAM. Where social media platforms are concerned, CSAM images and videos and links to CSAM sites may be posted in public places that are accessible to anyone (although recognising that much will also be shared on a one-to-one basis or in closed, moderated groups). The open publication of CSAM will damage the reputation of the platform, which could in turn negatively affect the willingness of users to engage with the platform and impact revenue if advertisers become concerned about their reputation from using the platform in advertising campaigns. One can expect that outward-facing social media platforms will be proactive in scanning the content that users post to identify and remove offensive material that could create reputational damage.

This proactive, voluntary approach to searching out and destroying CSAM can be contrasted with other problem facilitators in the CSAM ecosystem, where a more reactive approach may be taken. For example, file storage sites offer the capacity for CSAM to be stored and for a URL to that location to be shared with others to access the material. This is less likely to be stumbled upon by members of the public, or by web crawlers trained to focus on websites of interest, unless the URL is known. To increase security from the CSAM Content Distributor's perspective, the site may also be password protected, with the password only provided to those that are granted access, making it even less likely to be stumbled across. Similarly, ISPs may host sites on the World Wide Web that contain CSAM. Yet to the public, the ISP largely remains unknown, providing the server on which the site is located, but not advertising that it does so. In both the file storage and ISP hosting cases, reputational damage is likely to be minimal, given that they can legitimately claim that, as facilitating intermediaries, they are not responsible for the content that users place on their sites. This, essentially, is the stance created by Section 230 of the Communication Decency Act (1996) in the USA, the jurisdiction where many of the ISPs and ESPs concerned are located, in part due to the safeguards offered by this legislation. In these cases, legal leverage is applied to remove CSAM within a reasonable time once the host becomes aware of it. This shows that the business model of the enterprise will often determine whether a proactive or reactive approach to CSAM removal is taken. Regardless, most ISPs and ESPs will affirm their commitment to removing CSAM that they are found to be hosting.

### *But removal is not always effective*

While CSAM search and destroy strategies would appear to be the simplest of approaches to preventing its distribution, it doesn't always work. Research by the Canadian Centre for Child Protection (2021) has demonstrated the high level of repeat distribution of the same CSAM files once an ISP or ESP has been requested to remove it. Based on data gathered by Project Arachnid on the nature of take down notices made to ESPs, 41 per cent of ESPs were found to have recidivist media on their servers that had previously been removed. Indeed, recidivist media accounted for almost half (48%) of all CSAM media previously taken down by ESPs between 2018 and 2020. This situation has got worse in recent years. In 2018, recidivist media accounted for 21 per cent of removed media. By 2019, this had increased to 49 per cent and by 2020 had reached 55 per cent[8]. With half of all CSAM reappearing on the servers of the same companies, the question must be asked how proactive they are as an industry at voluntarily searching for and removing CSAM of which they should already be aware. Beyond the obvious social responsibility of reducing the availability of CSAM, there is little incentive for a company to do so, given they are typically not liable for CSAM on their servers until they become aware of it (again) and the lack of reputational damage resulting from being found to host CSAM, given the relative anonymity of many ISPs / ESPs.

The Canadian Centre for Child Protection (2021) also found that the distribution of recidivist media was heavily skewed towards a small number of ISPs / ESPs. For example, CSAM appearing on ALFA TELECOM s.r.o and Serverel servers had recidivism rates of 94 per cent. In contrast, companies like ImgOutlet. com, ImgMaze.com and ImageBam had recidivism rates of under 5 per cent. This concentration of recidivist material offers a means of prioritising the way in which CSAM distribution is tackled, focusing the greatest efforts on sites with the most recidivist media.

## Taking down rogue servers

The removal of servers on which CSAM is shared is one means by which police can disrupt the activities of CSAM perpetrators. From the 11 Ds perspective, this approach would be an example of disabling / denying access to the equipment needed to offend. In this case, access to remotely located servers that can be used to distribute and consume CSAM.

However, this typically relies on police finding the physical location of the servers to be able to switch them off and this may only be a short-term solution if the servers are backed-up elsewhere, or the contents are mirrored on multiple servers in different locations. Nevertheless, takedown operations of this kind may be successful in defeating or delaying CSAM distribution for a time and may also result in important intelligence being collected by the police that can be used in enforcement operations, thereby helping to increase risk of detection for CSAM perpetrators, as well as increasing the effort involved in offending when the servers are taken down.

One such operation in Australia involved Queensland Police's Taskforce Argos which, in 2017, took down the servers for *Child's Play*, a CSAM forum operating on the darknet. This followed a year-long operation in which Queensland Police officers ran the website, gathering intelligence on the site users, which informed police operations to rescue children and arrest perpetrators in multiple countries. By the time the site was taken offline, it had attracted over a million site registrations, with 3,000–4,000 active users thought to be using the site (Knaus, 2017)[9]. New legislation in Australia has also made it possible for federal agencies (the Australian Federal Police and the Australian Criminal Intelligence Commission) to take over accounts of users for intelligence and evidence gathering, under the Surveillance Legislation Amendment (Identify and Disrupt) Bill 2021.

Another police operation was associated with the takedown of the *Welcome to Video* site on the darknet by US authorities in 2019. The operation included the Internal Revenue Service, Homeland Security and Immigration and Customs Enforcement, but was also a multijurisdictional approach involving law enforcement agencies from multiple countries. The servers for the website were in South Korea and the operation resulted in the seizure of approximately eight terabytes of CSAM videos (over 250,000 unique videos), reported to be one of the largest seizures of its kind (United States Department of Justice, 2019).

Using a similar methodology to that employed in the takedown of *Welcome to Video*, US law enforcement agencies, working closely with Dutch and German counterparts, seized and removed the *Dark Scandals* websites that had operated on both the darknet and open-net. *Dark Scandals* had made available over 2,000 videos of the most abhorrent content, including CSAM and rape of women. Users could purchase packages of content using Bitcoin, which would then be sent to them via email links. The operation also resulted in arrests of those responsible for the enterprise in both the USA and the Netherlands (United States Department of Justice, 2020).

In 2021, an operation by the German Federal Criminal Police resulted in the takedown of *Boystown*, a darknet site with over 400,000 registered users. The joint operation with police from the Netherlands, Sweden, Australia, the USA and Canada resulted in arrests in Germany and Paraguay (Europol, 2021a).

These examples demonstrate that CSAM sites operating on the darknet can be addressed through law enforcement activity. However, operations resulting in takedowns and arrests are, by their very nature, time-consuming and resource-intensive and law enforcement agencies will need to prioritise action towards the most serious cases. With finite operational resources, this limits the number of sites that can be removed via this method. However, operations of this kind, that often involve taking over and running the site as a method of gaining intelligence, have been considered ethically and legally controversial and are not permitted in many jurisdictions (Bleakley, 2019). Nevertheless, there is evidence to suggest that a concerted law enforcement effort can result in successful longer-term reductions in the availability of illicit material in a darknet environment. Broadhurst et al. (2021) demonstrated how a concerted law enforcement effort to take down and remove darknet sites that sold illicit fentanyl (a potent synthetic opioid) resulted in the eventual dispersal and reduction of the drug on the largest darknet marketplaces. However, this took multiple takedowns before the impact on the market began to be felt. Similar strategies may be required for CSAM on the darknet, before a significant reduction in the problem may be observed.

## Blocking content

As well as removing CSAM from servers and removing the servers on which CSAM is hosted, access to the sites can also be blocked. Like those other approaches this is intended to increase the effort associated with distributing CSAM and defeats / delays the ability to access such material. Blocking content should really be described in the next chapter, when discussing what can be done to stop the viewing of CSAM. However, in practice, it is so closely related to removing content that it makes sense to include it here as a measure to prevent distribution.

Blocking content is associated with preventing the distribution in the sense that those looking for CSAM will be unable to find it and that, in turn, means that it will not be downloaded and subsequently shared with others. Unlike search and destroy tactics, the content remains available on servers, just not visible to those seeking to find it.

Not so long ago, it was possible to use standard search engines to find CSAM. However, blocking on two levels is now standard practice. This includes blocking access to URLs that are known to carry CSAM and blocking the use of commonly used search terms to access such material.

### Blocking access to URLs

Where blocking access to URLs is concerned, authorities in some countries maintain lists of URLs found to contain CSAM (often based on reports received) that can be provided to organisations that produce web-filtering technology. Those filters may then be deployed as standard by ISPs centrally, or offered as a service by the ISPs to their customers, who can choose whether to deploy filtering. Clearly, voluntary use of filters can be problematic as those intent on searching for CSAM may turn off such filters and therefore still have access. Filtering systems may also be used by organisations that run their own networks, which stop users from accessing blocked material from that network. This is common in settings such as educational institutions, but is also often used by employers to filter the sites accessible to staff.

In the UK, the Internet Watch Foundation provides a URL list that is available to ISPs to use on a voluntary basis. This URL list is produced daily and consists of contemporary sites that have been found to hold CSAM. Once the

CSAM is removed from the URL, the site is removed from the list of blocked sites. Organisations that are subscribed to the Foundation's service update their list of blocked sites daily therefore allowing for accurate targeting of sites. In New Zealand, the Department of Internal Affairs has partnered with ECPAT to operate the Digital Child Exploitation Filtering System. This filtering system blocks sites known to host CSAM and is made available to ISPs to use on a voluntary basis[10]. Cleanfeed Canada performs a similar service, providing participating ISPs with lists of CSAM-related URLs outside of Canada to block[11]

However, there has been a general reluctance among most states to mandate the blocking of websites at the national level for fear of impeding on freedom of expression. In the European Union, Article 25 of Directive 2011/92/EU permits member states to block websites outside of members' territory if they contain or distribute CSAM, as long as the decision for doing so is transparent and that adequate safeguards are in place to ensure that any restrictions imposed by a state are necessary and proportionate[12]. In practice, however, voluntary agreements between regulators and ISPs would appear to be the preferred approach. There are, however, some notable exceptions where ISPs can be forced to block CSAM websites, such as in China and Saudi Arabia (ICMEC, 2018). In Canada, there have been recent proposals to introduce blocking orders that would compel ISPs to block access to certain kinds of content, including CSAM (Leavitt, 2021).

## Blocking CSAM search terms

Where blocking access through CSAM search terms is concerned, CSAM Content Producers, Content Distributers and Consumers have organically developed a language that is used to refer to different types of CSAM. This language is used in website content, URLs and metadata and therefore forms the basis of search terms used by CSAM Consumers. According to Steel (2015), common terms used by those seeking CSAM included, among others, 'ls models', 'nymphets', 'loli', 'pthc', 'hussyfan', 'teenies' and 'preteen nude'. Taylor and Quayle (2008) suggested that an effective intervention by search engines could be to refuse to provide search results when terms like this were submitted and this has now become a common practice. The Internet Watch Foundation maintains a database of over 450 words and phrases that are used by paedophiles to describe their preferences. These are distributed to the Foundation's clients (such as Apple, Amazon, Google, Facebook and Microsoft) who can then block the use of the terms in searches conducted with their applications (Burgess, 2020). The list of terms can also be used to monitor chat in social media and gaming platforms. This is, however, a constantly evolving language, with CSAM users constantly changing the commonly used terms to evade the search engine blocks, allowing them to discover new material.

There is evidence that search engines have been successful at restricting access to CSAM. In July 2013, Google and Microsoft announced that their search engines would take greater steps to block attempts to access CSAM via their platforms. According to Steel (2015) this led to an immediate reduction in CSAM searches.

Analysis of Google search queries in the 12 months following the announcement showed that searches using common CSAM terminology declined by 67 per cent, while searches for adult pornography remained stable. During the same period, searches of CSAM remained stable on another search engine that did not implement the changes (Yandex, a Russian search engine that was ranked fourth globally) (Steel, 2015)[13].

## The problem of encryption

Search and destroy and blocking strategies rely on knowing where the CSAM can be found in the ecosystem. Here, we are particularly focused on centralised servers with ISPs and ESPs providing capable guardianship that results in CSAM being identified, removed or blocked. But what if capable guardians can't see what is being stored on their servers?

As noted in chapter 3, Dance and Keller (2020) found that some cloud services owned by companies such as Amazon, Apple[14] and Microsoft did not routinely scan for CSAM. This is made more difficult by the expectation that files will be encrypted to ensure privacy is maintained. This is particularly a concern where end-to-end encryption is used to transfer and store files. With encrypted file storage on the cloud, a copy of the encryption key will sit with the host service, meaning that they could unlock the files if they wished to access them (Zhang, 2018). With end-to-end encryption, the key stays with the user who transmits or stores the data and means that, even if the hosting service wished to, it could not read the files.

Many of the commonly used instant messaging services (such as WhatsApp, Signal, Viber, Wickr and Telegram) use end-to-end encryption, meaning that CSAM can be distributed without being seen by others (e.g. law enforcement agencies) who may attempt to intercept the messages. With (at the time of writing) Facebook soon expected to move to end-to-end encryption for its instant messaging functions on Facebook Messenger and Instagram Direct, there are fears that this could make CSAM distribution easier and more likely than is currently the case (Hughes, 2021; PA Media, 2021). Following Apple's announcement that it planned to scan files for known CSAM prior to encrypting, WhatsApp confirmed that it would not be following a similar approach, instead relying on users to report CSAM content (Kan, 2021). Indeed, prior to this debacle, in March 2021, a news report in the *Guardian* included a statement from Facebook, claiming that its WhatsApp instant messaging app banned around 250,000 accounts each month for sharing CSAM (Grant, 2021). These detections are likely to result from WhatsApp users reporting receiving CSAM from other users, rather than from automated scanning of messages.

## Summing up the evidence on approaches that reduce the distribution of CSAM

Preventing the distribution of CSAM is, to a significant degree, at the heart of solving the CSAM problem. Regardless of whether the material is produced and whether Consumers want to view it, if it could be stopped from reaching its end point then this might ultimately reduce the demand (recognising that the opportunity to obtain it has fuelled interest in it) and that in turn may reduce the supply.

As highlighted in chapter 5, the CSAM distribution problem is largely associated with online applications. This means there is hope for preventing the distribution of CSAM because the capability and resources needed to be successful lie in the hands of a relatively small number of ESPs and ISPs who host the objectionable material through such applications. This chapter has demonstrated that corporations are indeed taking an active role in identifying CSAM, although the willingness to search and destroy CSAM is arguably stronger for those ESPs with public reputations to maintain, where the presence of material that breaches community standards can seriously damage the reputation of the business and its bottom line.

Search and destroy techniques are therefore actively deployed by many of the large social media platforms. Applications such as PhotoDNA are commonly used to identify known CSAM, while material reported by other users, machine learning algorithms and human moderators scan their sites for new material. This is supported by third-party organisations that can receive complaints of CSAM and pass them on to the relevant ESP / ISP to remove from their site.

While search and destroy approaches are possible when an ESP / ISP is willing to remove CSAM, there will be cases in which CSAM remains on the servers of corporations that are either unwilling to actively remove material, or which lie outside the jurisdiction of those identifying the material. In these cases, platforms running search engines have blocked the use of terms that are known to be used by CSAM Consumers to locate material. There are also various filtering systems available that can be used by ISPs to block access to URLs known to contain CSAM, thereby preventing it from being shared.

This approach to identifying, removing and blocking CSAM can, however, be described as akin to a game of whack a mole. As fast as CSAM is removed, or search terms are hidden, the same material appears on other sites, or the search terms are altered to allow Consumers to once again find the material. CSAM files may also be subject of alterations, such as cropping, scaling, altering colours and embedding in other legitimate images / videos, and then made available once again online. These alterations may prevent automatic web crawlers from identifying previously confirmed CSAM (United Nations Office on Drugs and Crime, 2021b).

The fact that the amount of CSAM reported to NCMEC is growing is testament to the success of the system in finding, removing and blocking material, but it also suggests that the problem has yet to be solved.

Chapter 6 identified a series of contemporary problems that facilitated the distribution of CSAM including file storage sites, forums, social media sites, instant messaging, internet relay chat, computer games and the darknet. The approaches described in this chapter go some way to addressing CSAM distributed via file storage sites, social media sites, (unencrypted) instant messaging, (unencrypted) internet relay chat and computer games. These all rely on centralised systems with clear capable guardianship vested in the ESP providing the service. Success in preventing the distribution of CSAM will rely on the willingness of those ESPs to fulfil their guardianship role. The measures outlined here will probably be less effective in preventing the distribution of CSAM via forums, (encrypted) instant messaging, (encrypted) internet relay chat and the darknet. Most of these rely on encryption to share information, which makes it difficult for moderators to identify what is being shared and therefore to confirm whether CSAM is involved. Looking to the future, these represent the distribution challenges that are likely to be the focus of attention.

## What more could be done to reduce CSAM distribution?

While significant effort has been devoted to addressing CSAM distribution, there is potentially more to be done to reduce the problem created by online applications. The solutions can broadly be differentiated between technical and policy approaches. Technical solutions need to focus of developing tools that will identify CSAM as it emerges and the analysis of metadata to identify unusual patterns of use in encrypted applications. Policy solutions need to focus on increasing responsibility among ESPs / ISPs to take CSAM as seriously as they possibly can and to focus attention on the relatively small number of companies that account for a disproportionate amount of the harm.

### *Technical solutions*

### *Applications to identify new CSAM early in its distribution lifecycle*

Technical solutions to CSAM distribution continue to develop. While the identification of known material, using hash databases (such as PhotoDNA), is now common, it fails to deal with the issues of new material that is constantly being added to the internet and which currently requires a human operator to identify in the first instance, with the consequent risk of vicarious trauma that creates. New tools that can identify CSAM (differentiating it from adult pornography) are being developed, which could help to further reduce the extent to which human operatives have to view the material and reduce the potential for wider distribution through the early identification and removal of content. A survey of ESPs by We Protect Global Alliance (2021) found that around half of companies (56%) were using new image-based classifiers based on AI technology. However, fewer were using technologies such as video-based classifiers (30%) or classifiers in livestream contexts (22%). This offers the potential for significant growth in the use of these technologies in future.

### *Analysing metadata patterns*

Technical solutions are still needed to address the problems of livestreaming and the sharing of CSAM on encrypted messaging applications. In both cases, analysis of metadata may help to identify CSAM distribution, in the knowledge that CSAM distributors have different patterns of use of such applications, compared with the typical user (Burgess, 2021b). Ideally, this could be used to flag cases in real time to moderators who were able to turn off the end-to-end encryption and view the content of the livestreaming session. This could, of course, be done with the knowledge of the users (perhaps with a pop-up message to notify them) that their session had been flagged for viewing by a moderator, or was being recorded for checking later. This might lead to the session being ended, but that in itself would be a small success, ending the immediate victimisation of a child.

## Designing out CSAM

As designers of systems and services used by billions of people globally, more could be done to ensure they are designed with the safety of users as a paramount concern, rather than as an afterthought. In the rush to bring new products to market, designers are often focused primarily on the user experience and not the bad things that result from using their products. In fact, we can liken the way the internet currently functions to the way that the automotive industry operated in the 1960s (Newman, 2004). Cars were designed with comfort and style in mind, but took little responsibility for the safety or security of their users. An accident was likely to end in serious injury or fatality. Cars were also more likely to be broken into or stolen outright. It should be noted that both safety and security only improved following concerted government attention, but the point is that change was possible thanks to design changes that incrementally improved the circumstances for users (Newman, 2004).

There are positive signs that designing out CSAM could be possible. Approaches to *safety by design*, as advocated by the e-Safety Commissioner in Australia, offer tools for conceptualising and planning the development of applications that take account of safety concerns from the outset, rather than ignoring or retrofitting solutions later. Although early in their adoption, they show positive signs of being able to make a difference to how systems are designed[15].

## Policy solutions

Chapter 11 returns to look in more detail at what could be done to address CSAM from a policy perspective. Here, two further thoughts are offered. There is a need to reconsider where responsibility for CSAM distribution lies and there is a need to pay closer attention to the concentration of distribution.

## Increase responsibility for CSAM

Section 230 of the Communication Decency Act (1996) in the USA provides immunity to ESPs / ISPs registered in that jurisdiction (as many are) from civil action for the content posted by third parties on their sites. However, they can remove obscene material in good faith without being considered responsible for that material. Amendments made by Congress under the Allow States and Victims to Fight Online Sex Trafficking Act (FOSTA) and the Stop Enabling Sex Traffickers Act (SESTA) in 2018 effectively removed the immunity in cases of sex trafficking. This made ESPs / ISPs liable in cases where their platforms were being used by third parties to sell sexual services, including those involving children. This shows reform is starting to happen.

There have been further attempts to erode the immunity of ESPs / ISPs at the US state level. In June 2021, the Texas Supreme Court upheld a ruling in which three plaintiffs, who were subject to sex trafficking, brought a case against Facebook for facilitating trafficking through its platform, thereby knowingly benefitting from the transaction. It was claimed in the case that Facebook had violated Chapter 98 of the Texas Civil Practice and Remedies Code, which makes a defendant who trafficks a person, or who knowingly benefits from the act, liable to the Victim / Survivor. Facebook maintained that under Section 230, it was immune from state action as it was covered under the Federal Act. At the time of writing, this was likely to be resolved in the federal Supreme Court (Golgowski, 2021).

In the meantime, in November 2020, proposed amendments to the Act included removing immunity when child sexual abuse material was involved, allowing for civil action to be taken by Victims / Survivors of child sexual abuse, presumably for failure to remove material that came to the attention of ESPs / ISPs[16]. So, this means that ESPs / ISPs may, in future, be vulnerable to legal action against them if they do not remove CSAM.

Then there is the requirement under Chapter 110, Title 18 of the US Criminal Code for ESPs / ISPs that are registered in the USA to provide reports of CSAM they discover to NCMEC as soon as reasonably possible. Although close, this is not quite the same as a notification and takedown regime, as the notification to an ESP / ISP is not court mandated, but rather will come via voluntary requests made by NGOs and law enforcement agencies. Nevertheless, it provides an expectation on the ESP / ISP that they will remove CSAM when they become aware of it.

At the time of writing, there were also proposals for amendments to Section 230 under the Earn It Act. This would see the formation of a National Commission On Online Child Sexual Exploitation Prevention, which would be responsible for producing and regularly updating guidance on best practice in dealing with online child sexual abuse, for use by ESPs. While supported by child protection experts, it has been heavily criticised by privacy advocates. The Act would remove the protections provided under Section 230 if they knowingly allow users to share CSAM. As this would include the use of end-to-end encryption to share CSAM, there are fears that ESPs would stop offering such security if it meant that protections provided under Section 230 could otherwise be lost (Marks, 2022).

So, while the climate and tolerance for CSAM is changing, the current circumstance for ESPs / ISPs registered in the USA is that they are permitted to remove CSAM from their platform in good faith without the risk of action being taken against them by the owners of that material and expected to proactively remove material associated with sex trafficking. Although not yet the case, they may in future be liable to Victims / Survivors of CSAM for failing to remove material associated with them and could lose federal protections if found to be facilitating CSAM distribution. In addition, they are expected to remove CSAM, within a reasonable period of time, when they become aware of it. So, as it stands, the regime is largely reactive at present. ESPs / ISPs are allowed to remove CSAM and should do so when they become aware.

These relatively light obligations can be contrasted with the somewhat more rigorous expectations that will be placed on ESPs / ISPs by the UK's Online Safety Bill, once it is enacted. The legislation will place an obligation on all ESPs / ISPs that offer user-to-user services (that is, those services that allow third-party users to make their content available to other users), or which provide search services, to UK users, regardless of where they are registered. They will be expected to proactively manage risk on an ongoing basis by conducting risk assessments associated with (among other things) the availability of illegal content (including CSAM) through their services, including conducting risk assessments prior to changes being made to the systems or services provided and prior to new services becoming available to UK users. In relation to illegal content found on their platforms, ESPs / ISPs will be expected to minimise its presence, minimise the length of time it is present, minimise the dissemination of such content and, when it becomes aware of the presence of illegal content, to swiftly take it down. There will also be an expectation on ESPs / ISPs to produce an annual transparency report that outlines the actions being taken to identify illegal content and to make sure it is removed. These regulations take a more proactive approach to managing the distribution of CSAM and could significantly change the way ESPs / ISPs view the content on their servers. If successfully implemented, this is an approach that might be replicated in other jurisdictions, resulting in less CSAM being distributed globally because of the positive response taken to its removal.

## Focusing attention on recidivist ESPs and ISPs

At various points through this book, attention has been drawn to the fact that CSAM, like other types of crime, is not evenly distributed. Some ESPs / ISPs are more likely to host CSAM than others and to be responsible for the same CSAM reappearing on their servers once it has been removed. In addition, some countries are more likely to host CSAM than others.

Given the concentration of CSAM in certain companies and certain countries, this could be the basis for introducing measures that target those concerned. This could include direct contact with the businesses, or engagement with major shareholders about the problem. In extreme cases, this could involve national blocks on certain ESPs / ISPs to prevent their servers being available in particular countries, thereby blocking opportunity for further distribution of CSAM in those places.

## Notes

1 As noted in chapter 5, peer-to-peer networks and websites are excluded from this list because the available evidence suggests that they are in decline. Nevertheless, some of the interventions that aim to address distribution of CSAM also address these two problems.

2 See paragraph 46 of Directive 2000/31/EC of the European Parliament and of the Council of 8 June 2000 on certain legal aspects of information society services, in particular electronic commerce, in the Internal Market ('Directive on electronic commerce') found at https://eur-lex.europa.eu/legal-content/EN/TXT/HTML/?uri=CELEX:32000L0031&from=EN

3 Found at www.microsoft.com/en-us/PhotoDNA.

4 Found at https://blog.google/technology/safety-security/our-efforts-fight-child-sexual-abuse-online/.

5 Found at https://safer.io/resources/video-hashing-challenges/.

6 Note that this process occurs outside of the encrypted environment and while still on the device. Presumably the files are impossible to identify once they have been encrypted.

7 One such company offering a commercial service of this kind is Identv, found at www.identv.com/content.html.

8 These figures are an underestimate of the true scale of recidivist media, as this analysis relies on exact matches of images (based on the same hash value). Yet, small changes to the image, imperceptible to the eye, can result in a different hash value, which would not be identified as recidivist media in this exercise.

9 During the police operation, they continued to make CSAM available to users and also provided 'new' material in a monthly newsletter to site users. This of course raises important ethical questions about the harm caused to victims by continuing to distribute CSAM. However, this needs to be weighed against the benefits that accrued from rescuing children from situations of abuse and in bringing offenders to justice.

10 Found at www.dia.govt.nz/Censorship-DCEFS.

11 Found at www.cybertip.ca/app/en/projects-cleanfeed.

12 Found at https://eur-lex.europa.eu/LexUriServ/LexUriServ.do?uri=OJ:L:2011:335:0001:0014:EN:PDF.

13 The changes introduced by Microsoft and Google in 2013 included pop-up messaging as well as blocking. However, pop-ups are discussed further in chapter 9 in relation to preventing the viewing of CSAM.

14 Although noting that Apple's August 2021 announcement that it will in future scan files for known CSAM (using PhotoDNA technology) on the device, prior to uploading to a cloud service, should address this previously identified shortcoming. However, it will not address new material (for which there is no current hash value in the PhotoDNA database) from being stored in an encrypted cloud service.

15 Found at www.esafety.gov.au/about-us/safety-by-design

16 Found at www.justice.gov/ag/department-justice-s-review-section-230-communications-decency-act-1996#:~:text=As%20part%20of%20its%20broader,of%20content%20in%20certain%20circumstances

## References

Apple (2021). Expanded protections for children. *Apple.* www.apple.com/child-safety/pdf/Expanded_Protections_for_Children_Technology_Summary.pdf

Bleakley, P. (2019). Watching the watchers: Taskforce Argos and the evidentiary issues involved with infiltrating Dark Web child exploitation networks. *The Police Journal* 92(3), 221–236. https://doi.org/10.1177/0032258X18801409

Broadhurst, R., Ball, M., Jiang, C. & Wang, J. (2021). *Impact of darknet market seizures on opioid availability*. Research Report 18. Australian Institute of Criminology. www.aic.gov.au/publications/rr/rr18

Burgess, M. (2020, 23 April). Researchers have finally cracked the secret paedophile code. *Wired*. www.wired.co.uk/article/child-sexual-abuse-keywords-iwf

Burgess, M. (2021b, 12 May). Police caught one of the web's most dangerous paedophiles. Then everything went dark. *Wired*. www.wired.co.uk/article/whatsapp-encryption-child-abuse

Canadian Centre for Child Protection (2021). *Project Arachnid: Online availability of child sexual abuse material*. Canadian Centre for Child Protection. https://protectchildren.ca/pdfs/C3P_ProjectArachnidReport_en.pdf

Dance, G.J.X. & Keller, M.H. (2020, 7 February). Tech companies detect a surge in online videos of child sexual abuse. *The New York Times*. www.nytimes.com/2020/02/07/us/online-child-sexual-abuse.html

Ekblom, P. & Hirschfield, A. (2014). Developing an alternative formulation of SCP principles – the Ds (11 and counting). *Crime Science* 3(2). https://doi.org/10.1186/s40163-014-0002-5

Europol (2021a, 3 May). *4 arrested in takedown of dark web child abuse platform with some half a million users*. [Press release]. Europol. www.europol.europa.eu/newsroom/news/4-arrested-in-takedown-of-dark-web-child-abuse-platform-some-half-million-users

Golgowski, N. (2021, 27 June). Texas Supreme Court rules Facebook can be held liable for sex trafficking. *Huffpost*. www.huffpost.com/entry/facebook-liable-sex-trafficking_n_60d881eae4b0dcd799a7f169

Grant, H. (2021, 2 March). 'It's an arms race': the tech teams trying to outpace paedophiles online. *The Guardian*. www.theguardian.com/global-development/2021/mar/02/its-an-arms-race-the-tech-teams-trying-to-outpace-paedophiles-online

Hughes, O. (2021, 5 May). Facebook: Don't expect full end-to-end encryption on Messenger until 2022 'at the earliest'. *TechRepublic*. www.techrepublic.com/article/facebook-dont-expect-full-end-to-end-encryption-on-messenger-until-2022-at-the-earliest/

ICMEC (2018). *Child Sexual Abuse Material: Model Legislation & Global Review*. International Centre for Missing & Exploited Children. www.icmec.org/wp-content/uploads/2018/12/CSAM-Model-Law-9th-Ed-FINAL-12-3-18.pdf

Independent Inquiry into Child Sexual Abuse (2020). *The internet: Investigation report*. www.iicsa.org.uk/publications/investigation/internet

INHOPE (2022). *Annual report 2021*. INHOPE https://bit.ly/3797mhd

Kan, M. (2021, 7 August). WhatsApp: Scanning iPhones for Child Sexual Abuse Images Is a Privacy Risk. *PC Magazine*. https://au.pcmag.com/mobile-phones/88693/whatsapp-scanning-iphones-for-child-sexual-abuse-images-is-a-privacy-risk

Knaus, C. (2017, 7 October). Australian police sting brings down paedophile forum on dark web. *The Guardian*. www.theguardian.com/society/2017/oct/07/australian-police-sting-brings-down-paedophile-forum-on-dark-web

Krishna, A. (2021). Internet.gov: Tech companies as government agents and the future of the fight against child sexual abuse. *California Law Review* 109, 1581–1635. https://doi.org/10.15779/Z38KW57J9B

Leavitt, K. (2021, 20 April). Should Canada block websites that post terrorist content and child porn? Ottawa is considering it. *Toronto Star*. www.thestar.com/politics/federal/2021/04/20/should-canada-block-websites-that-post-terrorist-content-and-child-porn-ottawa-is-considering-it.html

Marks, J. (2022, 23 February). Most cyber pros give thumbs down to the EARN IT Act. *The Washington Post*. www.washingtonpost.com/politics/2022/02/23/most-cyber-pros-give-thumbs-down-earn-it-act/

Martellozzo, E. & DeMarco, J. (2020). Exploring the removal of online child sexual abuse material in the UK: Processes and practice. *Crime Prevention and Community Safety* 22, 331–350. https://doi.org/10.1057/s41300-020-00099-2

Newman, G.R. (2004). Car safety and car security: An historical comparison. In M.G. Maxfield & R.V. Clarke (Eds.), *Understanding and preventing car theft* (pp.217–248). Crime Prevention Studies 17. Willan Publishing.

PA Media (2021, 19 April). Facebook encryption plans will hit fight against child abuse, warns Patel. *The Guardian*. www.theguardian.com/society/2021/apr/19/priti-patel-says-tech-companies-have-moral-duty-to-safeguard-children

Peters, J. (2021, 3 September). Apple delays controversial child protection features after privacy outcry. *The Verge*. www.theverge.com/2021/9/3/22655644/apple-delays-controversial-child-protection-features-csam-privacy

Roberts, S.T. (2017, 8 March). Social media's silent filter. *The Atlantic*. www.theatlantic.com/technology/archive/2017/03/commercial-content-moderation/518796/

Schulze, C., Dominik, H., Borth, D. & Dengel, A. (2014, April). Automatic Detection of CSA Media by Multi-modal Feature Fusion for Law Enforcement Support. In *ICMR '14: Proceedings of International Conference on Multimedia Retrieval* (pp.353–360). https://doi.org/10.1145/2578726.2578772

Steel, C.M.S. (2015). Web-based child pornography: The global impact of deterrence efforts and its consumption on mobile platforms. *Child Abuse and Neglect* 44, 150–158. http://dx.doi.org/10.1016/j.chiabu.2014.12.009

Taylor, M. & Quayle, E. (2008). Criminogenic qualities of the internet in the collection and distribution of abuse images of children. *Irish Journal of Psychology* 29(1–2), 119–130. https://doi:10.1080/03033910.2008.10446278

United Nations Office on Drugs and Crime (2021b). *UNODC Southeast Asia Pacific Written Submission to the Parliament of Australia Joint Committee on Law Enforcement*. Parliamentary Joint Committee on Law Enforcement Inquiry on Law enforcement capabilities in relation to child exploitation. Submission 7. www.aph.gov.au/DocumentStore.ashx?id=84dfa4c8-c020-4e07-8ccd-d09b153187a6&subId=712049

United States Department of Justice (2019, 16 October). *South Korean national and hundreds of others charged worldwide in the takedown of the largest darknet child pornography website, which was funded by Bitcoin*. [Press release]. www.justice.gov/opa/pr/south-korean-natio nal-and-hundreds-others-charged-worldwide-takedown-largest-darknet-child

United States Department of Justice (2020, 12 March). *Dutch national charged in takedown of obscene website selling over 2,000 'real rape' and child pornography videos, funded by cryptocurrency*. [Press release]. www.justice.gov/usao-dc/pr/dutch-national-charged-takedown-obsc ene-website-selling-over-2000-real-rape-and-child

We Protect Global Alliance (2021). *Global threat assessment 2021: Working together to end the sexual exploitation of children online*. We Protect Global Alliance. www.weprotect.org/glo bal-threat-assessment-21/#report

Zhang, H. (2018, 25 January). How secure is your data when it's stored in the cloud? *The Conversation*. theconversation.com/how-secure-is-your-data-when-its-stored-in-the-cloud-90000

# 10
## APPROACHES TO PREVENTING THE CONSUMPTION OF CSAM

## Introduction

Addressing the viewing of CSAM is a daunting task. The current situation is characterised by a seemingly endless source of CSAM online for those who wish to find it (notwithstanding the efforts already being taken to prevent its production and distribution). This supply of CSAM is meeting the demand of Consumers who number in their hundreds of thousands, if not millions, globally. This is a problem that will need to be addressed from multiple perspectives, just as with production and distribution. From the perspective of the 11 Ds of crime prevention discussed in chapter 7, there are multiple principles that could be applied to address the viewing of CSAM.

Defeat / delay tactics can be used to block access to the material that Consumers wish to obtain. This has largely been discussed already in the previous chapter from the supply perspective, when thinking about how to block the distribution of CSAM. This showed that blocking access to sites through manipulating search engine results and through simply turning off the ability to directly access a site at the ISP end can be very effective, although also recognising this is an ongoing activity as offending evolves to overcome the challenges posed by ESPs / ISPs. We will consider defeat / delay tactics as sufficiently addressed to skip over in this chapter.

In this chapter, greater attention will be paid to approaches that direct / deflect and discourage offenders, using pop-up messages, and through law enforcement approaches that aim to detect and detain offenders. This is also the arena in which the financial system becomes more relevant, offering opportunities to detect CSAM offenders through their financial transactions. It should also be noted that there are also opportunities to demotivate those who view CSAM from doing so and the potential for offender treatment will be discussed in this regard.

DOI: 10.4324/9781003327264-12

## Pop-up messaging to warn users

While pop-up messaging is often combined with blocking (as in the case of Microsoft's and Google's approach to blocking searches), this approach has been shown to be effective on its own too. Pop-up messages are messages that appear on a user's computer screen in response to action taken by the user. This will typically be in responses to clicking on a link to a URL, or using certain search terms that have been flagged to trigger the pop-up. This unexpected warning is intended to elicit concerns by the offender that they may be caught attempting to access CSAM (Edwards et al. 2021). From a situational crime prevention perspective, they may work by increasing an offender's perceived risk of detection (perhaps by reducing their sense of anonymity) and by potentially removing excuses that they were not aware they were about to click into a site containing CSAM (Taylor & Quayle, 2008; Edwards et al., 2021; Prichard et al., 2011). In the terms of Ekblom and Hirschfield (2014), this amounts to discouraging the offender from proceeding to view CSAM. These mechanisms by which pop-ups work may suggest that they are more likely to be successful with those early in their CSAM-offending career. Indeed, as noted by Taylor & Quayle (2008), one of the key features of the CSAM ecosystem is the ease with which a potential offender can become an actual offender by little more than clicking on a URL link. Therefore, pop-up messages might work with what Krone (2004) called *Browsers* – those that click on a link while browsing the internet, or click on a link in a spam email, and find they have downloaded CSAM and decide to keep it. Pop-ups may, to a lesser extent, work with *Trawlers*, who have wide sexual interests and experiment with a range of material, including CSAM. (Krone, 2004). However, pop-ups are likely to be less effective on more dedicated collectors of CSAM.

There have been two experiments that have demonstrated the effectiveness of pop-ups. These experiments have overcome the significant ethical constraints of undertaking research on this topic. Indeed, it would not be appropriate to undertake a study that involved actual CSAM or that lured people to break the law by accessing such material. The experiments described here have therefore skirted close to CSAM, without actually offering it, although the content is close enough to infer that the pop-ups would be effective if associated with CSAM.

The first experiment used a fake website dedicated to men's health and fitness (Prichard et al., 2021). This site was professionally designed and maintained to ensure it had credibility for the users. The site also had advertising embedded on some of its pages and this was mostly legitimate advertising, apart from one advert for just barely legal images and videos (as close to CSAM as the researchers could get). When a user clicked on this advert they were randomly allocated to one of five groups, either the control group or an experimental group. The four experimental groups included two that delivered messages associated with harm – 'Health professionals believe this material may lead users to become sexually aroused by children', or 'Health professionals believe the individuals shown may experience long-term feelings of *distress'*. The other two experimental groups delivered messages associated with law enforcement – *'Police may obtain IP addresses to track users'*, or *'Viewing this material may be illegal in some countries and lead to arrest'*. The control was taken straight to the landing page for the just barely legal site. The experimental groups were presented with a pop-up page that delivered the message relevant to their group. This pop-up page could only be closed by clicking 'exit' which would take the user back to the men's health and fitness site, or 'enter', which would take them to the just barely legal landing page. On reaching this landing page, users were presented with the options of entering the just barely legal site or exiting. Selecting 'enter' at this point would elicit a message indicating the site was not available, while exiting would take the user back to the original men's health and fitness site.

This randomised controlled experiment demonstrated the efficacy of pop-up messages. While 73 per cent of the control group clicked through to the just barely legal site, only 51 per cent of the group that received the *'Police may obtain IP addresses to track users'* message and only 48 per cent of those receiving the *'Viewing this material may be illegal in some countries and lead to arrest'* message did so. The differences between those receiving these law enforcement messages and the control group were statistically significant. In contrast the click-through rates of those that received the harm related messages were not statistically different to the control group. (Prichard et al., 2021).

The second experiment used the same men's health and fitness website to test the impact of still and animated pop-up messages (Prichard et al., 2022). This time, the website carried an advertisement for a site that allowed users to upload explicit images of their intimate partner (regardless of whether their partner was aware or not). The structure of the experiment followed that of the earlier one, with a control group and two experimental groups. Both experimental groups received the same message – *'It's a crime to share sexual images of people who look under 18. Visit esafety. gov.au to find out more'*. However, the one group received a static message, while the other received a nine-second animation. The results showed that both the experimental groups were statistically different from the control group. While 61 per cent of the control group clicked through to the site, only 43 per cent of those receiving the static message and 38 per cent of those receiving the animated message clicked through to the site. There was no statistical difference between the two experimental messages, suggesting that they were equally effective in preventing users from clicking through to the target site.

Taking the two experiments together, the findings would suggest that pop-messages that aim to increase the perceived risk of detection among consumers of CSAM (at least in relation to allied sites associated with just barely legal and uploading of explicit images) are likely to be effective in preventing users from proceeding to access the material in question. There would appear to be little benefit from using more sophisticated animated messages, rather than simpler static messages.

## Law enforcement detection of CSAM Consumers

Much of the activity undertaken to address the viewing of CSAM involves increasing the risk of detecting and detaining CSAM offenders. This can take several forms, including tracking the IP addresses of those that view CSAM and using the financial system to identify CSAM consumers.

### *Tracking the IP addresses of CSAM Consumers*

One approach that would appear to have been successful in using technology to increase the risk of detection has been the identification of IP addresses associated with users of peer-to-peer networks who have downloaded CSAM from such networks. The Child Protection System, operated by the Child Rescue Coalition in the USA is an automated web crawler that can track the IP addresses of users downloading files that have previously been flagged as CSAM. This is reported to be possible even when VPNs are used. The IP addresses can then be provided to law enforcement agencies to undertake investigations. The information generated by the Child Protection System typically provides enough probable cause to apply for a search warrant of the location associated with the IP address and can result in computer devices being seized for forensic examination. These often reveal collections of CSAM. However, the system does not guarantee that CSAM will be found, as it may be deleted or saved to encrypted devices that cannot be forensically examined (Solon, 2020). This approach is reported to have led to over 13,000 arrests around the world and rescued more than 3,000 children[1].

In some cases, law enforcement agencies are able to trick CSAM consumers into revealing their identity. In 2014, Queensland Police arrested the administrator of a darknet site – *The Love Zone* – and took control of the site in an undercover operation (another example of a takedown operation). As part of the operation, they sent a link to CSAM to targeted users. This link was configured in such a way that it took those that clicked on the link to a pathway outside of the darknet, thereby exposing the users' IP addresses, allowing users to be identified to the police (Cox, 2017).

Another example of tracking IP addresses for law enforcement purposes was use of Sweetie, an avatar of a 10-year-old Filipino girl that attracted CSAM Consumers from around the world, who requested livestreamed performances from her (see chapter 3). Terre des Hommes (2014), the NGO behind the operation, harvested the IP addresses of the CSAM Consumers and passed those details to law enforcement agencies to pursue. This led to the investigation of around 1,000 offenders from 71 countries (Broadhurst, 2019).

### *Using malware to track CSAM Consumers*

There have also been cases in which law enforcement agencies have taken over the servers of sites distributing CSAM and installed malware that would allow investigators to track down site users. During the police operation against *Playpen,* a site with more than 20,000 CSAM images and videos, the police used network investigation techniques to hack into the computers of CSAM Consumers, who had accessed the site on the darknet. This led to more than 900 arrests of the site's users, thanks to the ability to collect a range of identifying information, including the IP address of the computer, the media access control address and the computer username. However, the approach has been controversial, raising concerns over fourth amendment breaches in the USA, although these have mostly proven unfounded when tested in court (Broadhurst, 2019).

## *Using the financial system to identify CSAM Consumers*

As noted in chapter 2, the financial system is also relevant to the CSAM ecosystem, as a portion of the material that is shared and viewed online is monetised. One highly publicised case related to CSAM that was distributed by Landslide Productions (Wortley & Smallbone, 2012). Investigations by US law enforcement (Operation Avalanche) and UK authorities (Operation Ore) identified 250,000 subscribers to the websites operated by Landslide Productions. The investigations focused on tracing offenders through their credit card transactions. They reportedly resulted in over 2,600 prosecutions, although the case has also been criticised for the significant number of suicides of alleged perpetrators resulting from the law enforcement operations (Laville, 2009). There have also been reports that some of those prosecuted had in fact been the victims of identity crime (Palmer, 2009).

In the Philippines, police operations to address the livestreaming of child sexual abuse have resulted in facilitators of this crime being identified. Examination of their financial records (particularly through money service businesses) identified financial transactions from overseas consumers. Brown et al. (2020) discussed how financial transaction made to Filipino facilitators were traced back to 256 Australians, who had made over 2,700 payments over the course of several years. These individuals were then followed up by law enforcement agencies in Australia.

Aware of the risks of detection through the traditional financial system, there has been an increase in the use of cryptocurrencies to purchase CSAM-related services. Cryptocurrencies, which are typically purchased through online exchanges, allow financial transactions to be completed with a significant degree of anonymity. Although there will be a connection with the regulated financial system at the point when cryptocurrency is purchased through an online exchange, beyond that point, the traditional, centralised banking system maintains no record of transactions made via cryptocurrencies. However, there have been police operations that have targeted CSAM Distributors that have used cryptocurrencies. One such operation involved the take down of the *Welcome to Video* site, described earlier. This site used Bitcoin to monetise the distribution of CSAM. Each user was given a Bitcoin account to use when on the site[2]. Bitcoin was used to purchase credits that could be used to access CSAM on the site. Credits could also be earned by uploading new CSAM to the site. Using sophisticated software to analyse the patterns of Bitcoin transactions in the public ledger, it was possible to identify the exchanges commonly used to purchase the Bitcoin[3]. Those exchanges were requested to provide the details of the bank accounts used to make the transactions and this led back to the individual CSAM Consumers that were purchasing *Welcome to Video* credits. As a result of the law enforcement operation, 337 individuals from 38 countries were arrested (United States Department of Justice, 2019).

## Demotivating CSAM Consumers

The final approach to reducing CSAM consumption involves addressing the underlying motivations among Consumers. There are some long-standing programmes that work with CSAM Consumers that recognise they have a problem with CSAM. Here, we focus on secondary crime prevention (those that target people at risk of offending and undetected offenders) and tertiary crime prevention measures (those that target detected offenders).

### *Remote support through call centres and online chat*

Internationally, there are various call centre and online services that aim to help people with either problematic, sexual thoughts about children, or problematic behaviours including inappropriate touching of children and viewing of CSAM. These services include Stop It Now! (in the USA, the UK, Republic of Ireland, the Netherlands and Belgium), Safe to Talk (in New Zealand) and PrevenTell (in Sweden). These provide confidential, anonymous helplines for (inter alia) CSAM users to discuss their offending and to get advice about how to address their problems (Gannoni et al. forthcoming). There is some evidence to suggest these programmes are effective in mitigating risk factors and increasing protective factors in participants (Brown et al., 2014).

Evidence on the effectiveness of these programmes would appear to be mixed. For example, evaluations of Stop It Now! suggest that between 30 per cent and 80 per cent of CSAM offenders cease using CSAM as a result of the programme, and relatively high proportions of those completing the programme state it is helpful for increasing their motivation to change (Gannoni et al. forthcoming).

### *Online self-help*

Online self-help courses can also be found in Europe, the UK and the USA. Employing psychoeducation and CBT, these courses are generally aimed at individuals with problematic thoughts about children and aim to provide a framework and tools for helping to deal with such thoughts. These online courses are typically completed independently and are anonymous and confidential (Gannoni et al. forthcoming).

## Therapeutic treatment

Therapeutic treatment is often offered to both CSAM Consumers and contact child sexual abuse offenders without necessarily tailoring to the specific needs of the group. Therapeutic responses were discussed in relation to production of CSAM in chapter 8, although that was largely concerned with the more serious end of the CSAM offence spectrum, with the direct exploitation and abuse of children.

Where therapeutic treatment for the consumption of CSAM is concerned, Gannoni et al. (forthcoming) have identified numerous initiatives internationally that aim to reduce the motivation to view such material. These include programmes in Australia, Canada, Europe, New Zealand, the UK and the USA. These are sometimes standalone programs for CSAM offenders and sometimes part of a broader programme aimed at child sexual abuse offenders, although the level of intensity is generally lower for CSAM offenders. Indeed, Henshaw et al. (2020) have argued that the specific needs of CSAM offenders are typically different to contact offenders and their low risk of reoffending means that a lower dosage of intervention is warranted. Therapeutic programmes typically employ Risk–Needs–Responsivity principles and use cognitive behavioural treatment (see chapter 8).

Programmes that treat CSAM offenders as part of a wider child sexual abuse cohort have generally been found to be ineffective in reducing CSAM recidivism and, in some cases, have led to increased CSAM consumption (Beier et al., 2015). However, programmes specifically tailored to CSAM Consumers have shown more efficacy, although more robust evaluation is still required (Gillespie et al., 2018; Middleton et al., 2009).

## Support for family members

In addition to programmes that directly target CSAM Consumers, some programmes help to support non-offending partners and family members of CSAM Consumers, given the stress and stigma this type of offending can place on loved ones. These programmes can be found in Australia, Europe, the UK and the USA and offer confidential advice and support through online platforms and call centres.

## Summing up the evidence on approaches to reduce the consumption of CSAM

In thinking about how CSAM consumption can be addressed, it is important to recognise the connection between distribution and viewing. Many of the approaches that might be taken to address the viewing of CSAM are achieved by addressing its distribution and these are discussed in chapter 9. However, there is an important distinction. While measures aimed at reducing CSAM distribution are largely focused on how the ecosystem operates (especially in relation to the workings of online applications), measures aimed at reducing CSAM viewing are targeted on its *organisms*. More specifically, they are targeted at CSAM Consumers.

Three approaches may assist in changing the behaviour of CSAM Consumers. Firstly, pop-up warning messages, which appear when searching for CSAM, may help to increase the perceived risks associated with its consumption. There is emerging evidence that law enforcement-related messages may prevent some people from accessing CSAM online. However, it is likely that these will be most effective when targeting those early in their CSAM offending career, rather than more experienced collectors.

Secondly, a range of law enforcement approaches have been used to detect CSAM Consumers, resulting in criminal justice proceedings being undertaken against thousands of individuals globally. In some cases, these will result in prosecution and conviction. Where Consumers are also involved in production, it can also result in the rescue of abused children. However, law enforcement action of this kind is limited by the resources available to pursue such cases, which stands in contrast to the hundreds of thousands of CSAM Consumers that access such material annually. It also remains unclear whether law enforcement activity of the kind described in this chapter results in a general deterrent effect. Does it result in an increase in the perceived risk of detection that discourages people from accessing CSAM?

Thirdly, approaches to reducing the motivation among CSAM Consumers and potential Consumers are promising. Therapeutic interventions work best when delivered as CSAM-specific programmes, rather than when combined with other categories of sex offender. While they are not necessarily effective for all CSAM Consumers they do appear to result in CSAM abstinence for a significant proportion.

## What more could be done to reduce CSAM from being consumed?

Beyond the approaches described in this chapter, which are somewhat limited, based as they are on the actions of various *organisms* in the ecosystem (Consumers and law enforcement), any further impact on CSAM viewing is likely to require radical, large-scale change to the ecosystem. Anonymity remains a significant challenge. This has become a defining feature of many of the uses to which the internet is put in the 21st century. But perhaps we need to rethink how the opennet operates. Perhaps there is a need for a more transparent and open internet, based on registration and use of an online identity. This would mean that internet users could no longer operate anonymously in forums, or peer-to-peer networks, or use multiple identities on social media platforms. Neither would they be anonymous when searching for or viewing CSAM websites.

This raises a host of problems that are not easy to address. For example, how do we deal with the darknet, given it can't be unmade? How do we allow end-to-end encryption in some circumstances (such as for online banking), but not for other purposes (such as for private conversations or sharing files)? How do we then police the unregistered part of the internet? How do we ensure identities are not compromised (stolen, cloned or sold)? These problems and the many other technical issues that would follow a change of this kind may explain reluctance to move towards a less anonymous future. Some of these issues are discussed further, as priorities for action, in the next chapter.

## Notes

1 According to the website for the Child Rescue Coalition, found at https://childrescueco alition.org/
2 In fact, the site was found to have one million Bitcoin accounts available to users, although only a portion of these had been used.
3 This was achieved using Chainalysis Reactor. Further information can be found at https://go.chainalysis.com/rs/503-FAP-074/images/Welcome%20to%20Video%20Case%20St udy%20-%20FINAL.pdf

## References

Beier, K.M., Oezdemir, U.C., Schlinzig, E., Groll, A., Hupp, E. & Hellenschmidt, T. (2015). 'Just dreaming of them': The Berlin Project for Primary Prevention of Child Sexual Abuse by Juveniles (PPJ). *Child Abuse & Neglect* 52, 1–10. https://doi.org/10.1016/j.chi abu.2015.12.009

Broadhurst, R. (2019). Child Sex Abuse Images and Exploitation Materials. In R. Leukfeldt & T. Holt (Eds.), *The human factor of cybercrime.* Routledge. https://doi.org/10.4324/9780429460593-14

Brown, A., Jago, N., Kerr, J., McNaughton Nicholls, C., Paskell, C. & Webster, S. (2014). *A call to keep children safe from sexual abuse: A study of the use and effects of the Stop it Now! UK and Ireland Helpline.* NatCen Social Research. www.stopitnow.org.uk/wp-content/uploads/2020/01/stop_it_now_evaluation_uk_findings.pdf

Brown, R., Napier, S. & Smith, R.G. (2020). *Australians who view livestreaming of child sexual abuse: An analysis of financial transactions.* Trends and issues in crime and criminal justice 589. Australian Institute of Criminology. www.aic.gov.au/publications/tandi/tandi589

Cox, J. (2017, 7 April). Australian Dark Web Hacking Campaign Unmasked Hundreds Globally. *Vice.com.* www.vice.com/en/article/4xezgg/australian-dark-web-hacking-campaign-unmasked-hundreds-globally

Edwards, G., Christensen, L.S., Rayment-McHugh, S. & Jones, C. (2021). *Cyber strategies used to combat child sexual abuse material.* Trends & issues in crime and criminal justice 636. Australian Institute of Criminology. https://doi.org/10.52922/ti78313

Ekblom, P. & Hirschfield, A. (2014). Developing an alternative formulation of SCP principles – the Ds (11 and counting). *Crime Science* 3(2). https://doi.org/10.1186/s40163-014-0002-5

Gannoni, A., Voce, A., Napier, S. & Boxall, H. (forthcoming). *Preventing child sexual abuse material offending: An international review of initiatives.* Research Report. Australian Institute of Criminology.

Gillespie, S.M., Bailey, A., Squire, T., Carey, M.L., Eldridge, H.J. & Beech, A.R. (2018). An Evaluation of a Community-Based Psycho-Educational Program for Users of Child Sexual Exploitation Material. *Sexual Abuse* 30(2),169–191. https://doi.org/10.1177/1079063216639591

Henshaw M, Arnold, C., Darjee, R., Ogloff, J & Clough, J. (2020). *Enhancing evidence-based treatment of child sexual abuse material offenders: The development of the CEM-COPE Program.* Trends & issues in crime and criminal justice 607. Australian Institute of Criminology https://doi.org/10.52922/ti04787

Krone, T. (2004). *A Typology of Online Child Pornography Offending.* Trends and issues in crime and criminal justice 279. Australian Institute of Criminology. www.aic.gov.au/publicati ons/tandi/tandi279

Laville, S. (2009, 3 July). Legal challenge to web child abuse inquiry: Claim that hundreds were convicted through flawed credit card evidence. *The Guardian.* www.theguardian. com/uk/2009/jul/02/web-child-abuse-inquiry-challenge

Middleton, D., Mandeville-Norden, R. & Hayes, E. (2009). Does treatment work with internet sex offenders? Emerging findings from the Internet Sex Offender Treatment Programme (i-SOTP). *Journal of Sexual Aggression* 15(1), 5–19. https://doi.org/10.1080/ 13552600802673444

Palmer, A. (2009, 20 June). Has Operation Ore left a scar on British justice? Scores of men caught by Operation Ore may not be paedophiles, victims of identity theft. *The Telegraph.* www.telegraph.co.uk/comment/personal-view/5587354/Has-Operation-Ore-left-a-scar-on-British-justice.html

Prichard, J., Watters, P. & Spiranovic, C. (2011). Internet subcultures and pathways to the use of child pornography. *Computer Law & Security Review* 27(6), 585–600. https://doi.org/ 10.1016/j.clsr.2011.09.009

Prichard, J., Wortley, R., Watters, P., Spiranovic, C., Hunn, C. & Krone, T. (2021). Effects of automated messages on Internet users attempting to access 'barely legal' pornography. *Sexual Abuse* 34(1), 106–124.

Prichard, J., Scanlan, J., Spiranovic, C., Krone, T., Watters, P. & Wortley, R. (2022). *Warning messages to prevent the sharing of CSAM: Results of a randomised controlled experiment.* Trends and issues in crime and criminal justice 647. Australian Institute of Criminology. www. aic.gov.au/publications/tandi/tandi647

Solon, O. (2020, 17 July). Inside the surveillance software tracking child porn offenders across the globe. *NBC News.* www.nbcnews.com/tech/internet/inside-surveillance-software-tracking-child-porn-offenders-across-globe-n1234019

Taylor, M. & Quayle, E. (2008). Criminogenic qualities of the internet in the collection and distribution of abuse images of children. *Irish Journal of Psychology* 29(1–2), 119–130. https://doi:10.1080/03033910.2008.10446278

Terre des Hommes (2014). *Webcam child sex tourism: Becoming Sweetie: A novel approach to stopping the global rise of webcam child sex tourism.* Terre des Hommes. www.terredeshom mes.org/wp-content/uploads/2013/11/Webcam-child-sex-tourism-terre-des-hom mes-NL-nov-2013.pdf

United States Department of Justice (2019, 16 October). *South Korean national and hundreds of others charged worldwide in the takedown of the largest darknet child pornography website, which was funded by Bitcoin.* [Press release]. www.justice.gov/opa/pr/south-korean-natio nal-and-hundreds-others-charged-worldwide-takedown-largest-darknet-child

Wortley, R. & Smallbone, S. (2012). *Internet Child Pornography: Causes, Investigation and Prevention.* Praeger.

# 11
## CONCLUSIONS

### Addressing a complex problem

This book has demonstrated the complexity of the CSAM problem. In fact, it has demonstrated that this is not *a* problem but *many* problems, that are facilitated by an accommodating ecosystem that enables CSAM to flourish. The production of CSAM, encouraged by a demand for new material, largely sits outside of the ecosystem and is often produced as a consequence of child abuse in the physical world and is then captured and uploaded to the virtual ecosystem in the form of images and videos. Chapter 3 described a range of ways in which CSAM could be generated, ranging from strangers abducting or paying for access to children, to production by friends and family members. There are, however, also ways in which the ecosystem facilitates the production of more material. This is especially the case in relation to livestreaming of child sexual abuse which relies on an online infrastructure to monetise real-time abuse. Self-produced CSAM is also facilitated online through social media, chat and livestreaming functions that allow perpetrators to contact potential child victims and to persuade them to produce images.

Chapter 4 described the problems created by the online applications that facilitate the distribution of CSAM. Eight contemporary distribution problems were identified, each of which will demand tailored responses. These include the role of file storage sites, social media sites, instant messaging, livestreaming, forums, internet relay chat, computer game chat functions and the darknet. Chapter 5 described the various methods employed by CSAM Consumers to avoid detection, by using encryption and anonymity.

Each of these problems highlights the difficulty faced in eliminating CSAM and demonstrate that there is no simple, one-size-fits-all approach to solving CSAM. Instead, a series of solutions (both technical and behavioural) will be needed. While (at least in some cases) solutions should be possible, this will not be achieved

DOI: 10.4324/9781003327264-13

without considerable effort to shift some of the inertia that exists to changing the status quo. Not everyone with vested interests in the control and maintenance of the internet believes that child sexual abuse is of enough concern to eradicate it, at least when the potential consequences are taken into consideration. The experience of Apple in August 2021, when it proposed a new method to remove CSAM, is a case in point. As noted in chapter 9, the new approach would have required Apple to scan the user's phone at the point of uploading a file from an iPhone or iPad to an iCloud server. It was proposed that only previously identified CSAM would be searched for on the users' phone and any flagged files would be sent to a moderator to review. In the scheme of things, the change would have been relatively modest. The fact that only known CSAM would be targeted, when the very device that was being scanned had the potential to produce new material, limited the impact this technical solution would have, but it was nonetheless an important step in the right direction to eradicate, or at least limit, the spread of existing CSAM. In response, Apple received a torrent of criticism from privacy advocates who feared that this move would interfere with their right to share information confidentially. It was feared that this would be the thin end of the wedge, that the technology could be used to search for other types of data held on people's phones. Over 90 privacy interest groups wrote to Apple with their concerns, while an open letter that raised concerns about the move was signed by more than 9,000 prominent security and privacy experts (Burgess, 2021a). Within a month, Apple announced a delay to the implementation of this change while it worked out how to deal with the concerns raised. This is problematic because Apple does not routinely scan its iCloud file storage or image servers for CSAM, which means they can be used to distribute new and existing CSAM. The experience of Apple shows that change will not be easy.

## Priorities for action

Moving forward, there are CSAM problems that should be considered priorities for action and there are those that should not. In general, a focus on distribution is likely to be an effective approach to CSAM elimination because the capacity for change is concentrated on a relatively small number of capable guardians – the ESPs / ISPs that control the servers that make up much of the internet as we know it. So, something more needs to be done to galvanise action by this group.

Four other problems also need to be a priority for action. Firstly, end-to-end encryption facilitates the distribution of CSAM by making it impossible for third parties to verify what is being shared between two users and means that CSAM can be shared with impunity. Secondly, the problem (from a CSAM perspective) of online anonymity needs to be addressed as this undoubtedly breeds bad behaviour. This is the case in relation to use of social media to groom children into producing CSAM, where adult Content Producers are pretending to be children and befriending others online, who are subsequently encouraged into producing

CSAM. It is also relevant for those that consume CSAM online in the belief that they will not be identified. Thirdly, more needs to be done to assist the financial sector to identify transactions that are to purchase CSAM online. Fourthly, there is a fundamental need to address CSAM offending on the darknet, as this is a space that facilitates the most egregious forms of child sexual abuse. Without action, more offending on the darknet is likely to result from greater action to remove CSAM on the open-net, combined with greater availability of easy-to-use tools that require little technical skill to access the darknet.

Problems that deserve priority action are those that either relate to facilitators of CSAM, concentrations of CSAM or causes of considerable harm. Indeed, all of the five priorities discussed here are focused on addressing parts of the ecosystem that currently facilitate CSAM – such as the role of ESPs / ISPs, encryption, anonymity, the role of the financial sector and the darknet. These are not problems with CSAM, but problems in how to reduce its facilitation. There are, of course, many other specific problems that require attention and could equally be a focus of concern. Here, we can think of the role played by file storage sites for sharing material or livestreaming of child sexual abuse. These deserve attention, but starting with the five priorities will at least begin to address these problems.

There are some problems that should probably not be a priority for attention. This is not because these problems are unimportant, but because they are extremely difficult to solve, at least in the short term. For example, dealing with the production of CSAM would seem like an obvious starting point for eliminating CSAM. If it were not produced in the first place, then the problem would not exist. The issue, however, is that CSAM production is so diffuse and closely connected with physical child sexual abuse. Indeed, chapter 8 noted that there were more than 20 ways in which CSAM could be produced, each representing a challenge for CSAM prevention. Many countries have complex child protection systems to address problems of this kind. This can include mandatory reporting of child sexual abuse, law enforcement professionals trained to investigate child sexual abuse, a social care system that includes visits and reporting by social workers, out-of-home care for children removed from their families, court systems that facilitate child testimony, sex offender registries, sex offender treatment programmes and so forth. This system has evolved over many years to protect children, and is vitally important. Yet, CSAM production continues to grow and it is difficult to see how changes to this system could result in significant reductions in CSAM production, especially when there are likely to be so many alternative methods of production.

Targeting CSAM Consumers who view CSAM is equally difficult. While focusing on the individual Consumer is important from a justice and deterrence perspective, and may lead to children being rescued from abusive situations, it is costly for the criminal justice system. This can involve investigation to track IP addresses of individuals, identifying physical addresses and executing warrants to seize computer devices for forensic examination, followed by prosecution, all of which is time-consuming and resource-intensive for a system that is often under-resourced. With such a large population of CSAM Consumers, it is difficult to see how the current criminal justice system could reduce the extent of the problem without a very sizable increase in resources.

The following pages examine each of the five priorities, with a focus on how online applications can be changed to reduce the extent of CSAM distribution and, to a lesser extent, its production.

## Raising the stakes for ESPs / ISPs

ESPs and ISPs have a fundamental role to play in reducing CSAM because of the influence and control they have over the internet and, therefore, over the CSAM ecosystem. They are responsible for the code that is written to produce the services that sit on their servers and that are used by billions worldwide. This is fundamental for understanding why the solution for much of the CSAM problem must sit with ESPs and ISPs.

The crime that results from consumer products (both from them being used as tools of crime and also to create victims of crime) has been described as being like pollution. It is an unfortunate by-product of the manufacturing process (Farrell & Roman, 2006; Brown, 2013). In economic terms, it would be described as an externality in that it creates a negative cost to society that is experienced by third parties (victims of CSAM) that is not reflected in the price. This would suggest that the prices paid by advertisers to ESPs to market to their target audiences are undervalued. Viewed this way, ESPs and ISPs should be held responsible for the crime that results from use of their services. There are undoubtedly many arguments that can be put forward for why ESPs / ISPs should not be held responsible. These can include suggestions that a particular ESP creates more CSAM than others because of the popularity of its services, that the police should be responsible for tackling crime rather than a commercial company, that it would be uncompetitive for one company to invest resources in tackling CSAM if their competitors did not do the same. Similar arguments were made by motor vehicle manufacturers in the UK when the government threatened to mandate security requirements if manufacturers failed to improve security standards on their new vehicles, at a time when motor vehicle theft was at record levels.

The current CSAM prevention activities of ESPs and ISPs are patchy at best. There are numerous examples of their services being used to produce and distribute CSAM, whether that be grooming children to self-produce CSAM via social media, messaging and livestreaming applications, storage of CSAM on file storage sites, or the sharing of links to CSAM through online forums and groups and through messaging applications. So, what can be done to encourage them to take more action? Here, we can return to the hierarchy of interventions introduced in chapter 7 (Figure 7.2) and offer various suggestions for how greater leverage could be applied to achieve change.

Step one involves educating ESPs about their responsibility for CSAM in their online services. This is an activity that governments around the world have engaged in. It has involved reports by governments, NGOs and even the United Nations documenting the CSAM problem. Meetings are also held regularly by some of the larger ESPs and government officials to discuss how the problem might be addressed. So, there is no shortage of *educating* going on. In this context, governments have moved to step two, with straightforward informal requests being made to ESPs to deal with the CSAM issue. In 2020, this led the Five Eyes countries (Australia, Canada, New Zealand, the United Kingdom and the United States) to collaborate with the We Protect Global Alliance to launch the Voluntary Principles to Counter Online Child Sexual Exploitation and Abuse. Supported by the Technology Coalition, the Voluntary Principles set out the goals for eliminating online child sexual abuse[1]. These principles encompass the major challenges associated with the contemporary CSAM problem, including the need to remove CSAM from servers, online grooming, CSA livestreaming, availability of CSAM search terms, reporting material that is not illegal but is linked with CSAM, responding to a changing criminal landscape and the need for companies to work together to solve this problem. As such these principles are a powerful manifesto that provide a vision of what ESPs should be striving to achieve.

However, behind these principles there appears to be insufficient action by companies, beyond some (especially public-facing companies) searching for new and existing CSAM on their platforms and reporting it to NCMEC. Where the hierarchy of interventions is concerned, there has been little movement beyond step two, yet there is so much more that could be done to leverage action by ESPs.

Consider step five – collaborating with advertisers to demand that ESPs provide online services that are CSAM free. Many ESPs rely on advertising as a source of revenue, so focusing on ways in which income could be reduced might be a way to get ESP shareholders to take notice and demand action. In 2020, a group of Facebook shareholders attempted to raise concerns about the impact on CSAM of deploying end-to-end encryption on all of its messaging applications. However, the resolution was unsuccessful (Thomas, 2020). Nevertheless, it demonstrated that shareholders were taking a keen interest in the issue and were willing to raise their concerns at shareholder meetings. Reduced revenue because of a failure to take appropriate action to address the CSAM problem may provide the additional incentive required by ESPs to introduce the required changes.

This is, however, difficult territory for governments to traverse for fear of being seen to be anti-business or to be stifling competition. It could also lead to retaliatory action by an ESP when faced with unilateral action by a government. When the Australian government planned to introduce a new media code that would require social media platforms to agree payments to media companies for sharing news on their platforms, Google threatened to withdraw its search engine from the country (Lomas, 2021b). In February 2021, Facebook took matters a step further by turning off news provided by media outlets in Australia (Lomas, 2021a). This meant that Australian publishers were unable to post any content to Facebook and Facebook users in Australia were unable to view or share new content from Australia or internationally (Easton, 2021). Although short-lived, the debacle demonstrated the lengths to which ESPs might go to protect business and is a warning of the need to tread carefully when lobbying advertisers about their commercial decisions with ESPs.

Moving further up the intervention hierarchy, step eight suggests the creation of a new organisation to take responsibility for the problem. This could be a point of liaison between ESPs / ISPs and governments, law enforcement and NGOs seeking to effect change. This organisation could work with ESPs / ISPs to develop new approaches to tackling CSAM that could be shared with the tech sector, as well as keeping CSAM prevention on the radar of all ESPs / ISPs. This might also include more intensive support for start-up technology companies where safety by design may not be top of the agenda in the rush to bring a new product to market. However, it is recognised that this could be difficult because of the international nature of the internet, with any organisation that is created unlikely to have influence in all jurisdictions. Nevertheless, as a starting point, the Technology Coalition could provide the basis for an organisation of this kind. Launched in 2020, the Technology Coalition's Project Protect would appear to be a step forward. The project seeks to foster CSAM reduction by supporting research, sharing information and knowledge with members, supporting innovative technology to tackle the problem, providing a forum for collective dialogue between stakeholders and promoting transparency and accountability in reporting of CSAM[2]. Although needing to tread a careful line between its members' interests and the need to reduce CSAM, the organisation could be developed in ways that would create a stronger voice for change by all ESPs / ISPs.

An alternative vision of a new organisation could be a government agency whose remit is to encourage, incentivise and pressure ESPs / ISPs into acting to reduce CSAM. This would, however, typically be at a national, rather than international, level. In Australia, the e-Safety Commissioner provides a role of this kind by providing support and guidance to technology companies on designing applications that are safe, undertaking research and issuing takedown notices and lobbying for further change. However, internationally, government agencies like the e-Safety Commissioner are uncommon and a wider network of agencies of this kind could help to facilitate quicker change. One recent proposal has come from the European Commission, which has proposed a single organisation to deal with the prevention and detection of CSAM and to provide support for Victims / Survivors[3].

Step nine in the hierarchy involves supporting research and development efforts by ESPs to find solutions to the problem. Around the world, there are pockets of activity by universities, NGOs, companies and governments engaged in funding and undertaking research that explores ways of reducing CSAM. This could be better coordinated to avoid duplication and ensure that valuable research funding is focused on solving the most pressing CSAM problems. Here there could be a role for inter-governmental forums, such as the Five Eyes, ASEAN or the United Nations Office of Drugs and Crime to coordinate research activity, or to create a joint fund to support research, given the global nature of the problem.

There might also be ways of incentivising technology businesses to do more by providing tax incentives for investment in research and development that is devoted to CSAM prevention, or for making donations to universities or NGOs to conduct research of this kind.

This brings us to step eleven – providing tax incentives or subsidies to encourage ESPs / ISPs to take responsibility for the problem. This could work as both a carrot and a stick. Tax incentives might not only be offered for investment in research and development to find ways to reduce CSAM, but could be offered for adherence to standards, or evidence that a business has taken certain defined actions to identify, mitigate and report CSAM. The alternative approach could be to take a 'polluter pays' approach by associating taxation with the level of CSAM found on the servers of an ESP / ISP. However, this could disincentivise companies that actively search for CSAM if they had to pay more for reporting more material. An alternative approach would be to place a blanket levy on all ESPs / ISPs operating in a given jurisdiction, perhaps based on their customer base or on advertising revenue. Taxing advertising revenue offers an interesting option because, with CSAM acting as an economic externality, with the burden of costs falling on Victims / Survivors, the price of advertising is unlikely to reflect the true cost of providing the service. Taxation that prices-in the cost of CSAM could therefore be a way to address this market failure.

Revenue from CSAM-related taxation could then be hypothecated for investment in prevention and detection of CSAM and Victim / Survivor recovery. However, this potentially removes responsibility for addressing CSAM away from ESPs / ISPs, who might argue that they were already paying for CSAM reduction through taxation and so government should take responsibility for dealing with it. This approach might also disincentivise a technology company from operating in the jurisdiction concerned if the burden of taxation was considered too high.

Step twelve involves introducing legislation to regulate preventative action by ESPs / ISPs. It is one of the final steps in the hierarchy of government interventions because it represents one of the most punitive responses that can be taken by governments and is typically reserved for situations in which self-regulation or market mechanisms have failed to adequately protect a population.

## Self-regulation

Before discussing government regulation, it is worth exploring the case for self-regulation. The work of the Technology Coalition demonstrates that there is at least some appetite for self-regulation among those businesses that sign up and support the Coalition's work. The voluntary principles are a good case in point, offering a set of objectives for companies to seek to attain. However, while an important first step in acknowledging the problem, it will be interesting to see which companies agree to follow the voluntary principles and to document how they seek to meet these challenges, while recognising that efforts are already underway by some companies to address these issues. It is likely that those companies that publicly sign up to the voluntary principles will include those with an existing policy that favours social responsibility. The problem is that voluntary approaches will fail to take account of those that are least willing to act – especially those companies that operate in the internet ecosystem that do not garner publicity (especially ISPs who host content for others). Here it is worth thinking about the recidivist ESPs / ISPs that repeatedly allow CSAM to be stored on their servers. For example, the fact that both the Internet Watch Foundation and INHOPE find that a large proportion of the CSAM found in Europe can be traced back to just one country – the Netherlands – is evidence that a small number of corporations, located in favourable jurisdictions, are responsible for a disproportionate level of CSAM. Similarly, with a high rate of recidivist media on the servers of some ESPs, as found by the Canadian Centre for Child Protection, not all corporations can be expected to act in the public good all the time. Some will bend the rules and some will find places to operate where rule-bending is less risky.

So how might self-regulation by ESPs / ISPs result in favourable outcomes in terms of CSAM reduction? This would appear to be particularly problematic when thinking about how self-regulation could be applied in the fragmented, complex environment that constitutes the tech sector. One possibility would be to take a leaf from the Phoebus Cartel, which controlled the manufacture and sale of light bulbs between 1924 and 1939. During this time, Osram, Philips, General Electric and Associated Electrical Industries agreed the markets in which they would compete and the price they would charge for incandescent light bulbs. As part of this cartel, the member companies agreed that the light bulbs they produced should have a standard life of 1,000 hours. This was rigorously monitored by a company they formed to oversee the cartel – Phoebus, Inc. Industrial Company for the Development of Lighting – which fined member companies for selling light bulbs that significantly deviated from the agreed 1,000 hours standard. Now, this story is not included to suggest that the tech sector should form itself into a cartel, nor to control prices or markets. However, it does demonstrate that companies were able to mutually penalise each other for failing to uphold standards. While it is accepted that this was only possible because of the clear economic self-interest to accrue from membership (unfettered access to markets), it also demonstrates that companies can self-regulate and hold each other to account if there is a clear economic imperative.

From a CSAM reduction perspective, the voluntary principles could be adhered to through mutual obligation and regulated by means of fines agreed within the industry. This could be entered into on the basis of good corporate citizenship, or the basis of some other gain that would accrue from signing up, although admittedly, it is difficult to conceive what that might be. There is also the risk of unintended negative consequences. Corporations may find ways to minimise the number of instances of CSAM that could be identified by third parties on their sites. Indeed, in the current climate in which there is a movement towards end-to-end encryption for messaging applications, such a move would benefit the host platform as one would not be able to identify CSAM being shared and therefore the platform could not be fined for hosting the material. Any regime of self-regulation would need to be designed in such a way to avoid these negative unintended consequences.

## Government regulation

Around the world, the case is being made for stronger government regulation of ESPs / ISPs. While relatively minor regulatory changes are being proposed in the USA that will make it easier for civil action to be taken by Victims / Survivors of online sex trafficking, the UK's online harms bill proposes to place greater obligations on ESPs / ISPs to conduct regular risk assessments, including when changes are made to their systems and to manage the risk associated with CSAM. They will also be required to produce annual transparency reports that outline how they identify and deal with CSAM on their systems. The European Union is also currently proposing new regulation that would require ESPs / ISPs to scan for CSAM on their systems and to report CSAM that they find to a central authority, although noting that these changes will need to be compatible with Europe's General Data Protection Regulations.

These proposed regulatory changes largely leave it to ESPs / ISPs to work out how they comply with the regulations, which will probably lead to a variety of different responses, with varying degrees of effort and efficacy applied. An alternative regulatory approach might be to introduce a framework of standards, testing and inspection that would be applied to all services that are made available in a given jurisdiction to ensure that they are child-safe. This could be like the safety standards applied in building codes that require materials to withstand certain forces as specified in the safety standards[4]. Developers of systems could be required to produce designs that met child-safe standards that could then be tested by a third-party accreditation body to ensure they complied with the standards[5]. Once accredited, an ESP / ISP could launch their service in a jurisdiction. Major changes to systems would also require updated accreditation. This would undoubtedly be an additional cost to business that would probably be reflected in the prices charged. However, this needs to be weighed against the savings in child victimisation that one would expect to result from the change.

The e-Safety Commissioner in Australia has developed a set of Safety by Design principles that could be used as the basis for safety standard. These principles include the requirement for service provider responsibility, so that the burden of safety does not fall solely on the user; the requirement for user empowerment and autonomy to ensure the dignity of users is maintained; and the requirement for transparency and accountability, which are hallmarks of a robust approach to safety. Supporting these three principles is a set of 18 steps that could be taken by ESPs / ISPs to demonstrate a commitment to the principles[6]. These could be developed into a set of standards that are expected to be achieved to receive accreditation, although it is important to note that this is not the stated intent of the principles / steps established by the e-Safety Commissioner, with a voluntary approach being preferred. In contrast, a report by the UK Joint Committee on the Draft Online Safety Bill (2021) proposed that a requirement for ESPs to follow safety by design principles should be included in the new legislation, supported by a mandatory safety by design code of practice.

A regulatory approach would need a system of penalties to ensure ESPs / ISPs complied with requirements. This could range from fines for failure to adequately comply, through to removal of a license to operate in the jurisdiction. This could be achieved, for example, by blocking a site at the national level, or removing the right to use a locally issued domain name (less effective when an overseas domain name is used).

## Ending end-to-end encryption

End-to-end encryption offers a means by which CSAM can proliferate. It enables users to communicate via messaging or livestreaming without the ability for others to see what is being shared. It also allows files to be transferred between devices or between users without the ability to detect what is in those files. Ending the use of end-to-end encryption would eliminate one method by which CSAM perpetrators could operate with impunity.

There are, of course, legitimate reasons for using this level of encryption. For example, one would expect data relating to financial transactions and banking and health records to be transmitted with the highest level of security as disclosure could result in significant data breaches and potential crime consequences (fraud and identity crime). However, beyond a relatively small group of use cases, there is a good argument that end-to-end encryption may be an over-engineered option. Other forms of encryption may be sufficient for transmitting data most of us use on a daily basis, relying on the server sending data to encrypt it, although accepting that this can be viewed by the sender and so is not entirely secure[7]. Use of end-to-end encryption is therefore a choice we make, although that choice is often made, by default, by the ESP.

Consideration therefore needs to be given to limiting the proliferation of end-to-end encryption in new online services and encouraging ESPs to reduce its use. Here, the hierarchy of interventions in Figure 7.2 may again offer a means of escalating pressure on ESPs to a point where change is made, with regulation preserved as a final step if all else fails.

In the meantime, there is a need to reduce the negative impacts of end-to-end encryption by developing and refining new methods to detect the distribution of encrypted CSAM. As previously noted, analysis of metadata can provide an indication of distinctive patterns of distribution that act as a signature for CSAM distribution. This could be used to seek out accounts for further investigation (internally by ESPs, or externally by law enforcement agencies), or could (more controversially) be used automatically to flag, suspend or terminate accounts that exhibit patterns determined to be CSAM distribution. Other technical solutions might involve introducing checks at the point of encryption (as suggested by Apple in 2021) or decryption. Ideally, this would be a universal approach to scanning at the point of encryption, although in the meantime it might be exploited by law enforcement agencies that might seek to compromise devices that are thought to be distributing CSAM.

Any proposal to wind back end-to-end encryption will inevitably lead to criticism by powerful online stakeholders that have called for greater privacy online, rather than less. There are legitimate concerns with how one's data may be misused online which calls for stronger rather than weaker encryption. These include the potential for data theft, resulting from being hacked (Endeley, 2018), through to political activism against authoritarian regimes that may seek to limit dissent (Barbosa & Milan, 2019). As a result, there will always be a trade-off between privacy and child protection in any discussion on maintaining end-to-end encryption in its current form.

The European Electronics Communications Code, introduced in December 2020, brought in strict rules that limited the ability of ESPs to intercept or examine the content of communications on their platforms. This related to all communications and not just those that were encrypted. As a result, ESPs were restricted in their ability to scan routinely for CSAM as that would involve examining the communications that the Code protected. This resulted in a 53 per cent reduction in CSAM reported by ESPs in the European Union (Woollacott, 2021). In response, the European Commission issued a three-year exemption to allow ESPs to continue to scan for CSAM while it worked through the implications for the Code and more generally for the EU's General Data Protection Regulations. This is just one example of privacy concerns conflicting with child safety and conflicts between these two competing interests are unlikely to be resolved entirely. It will be a task for societies to determine the appropriate balance between the two, although this would best be left to national and international governmental bodies to decide, rather than vested interests operating in the wider internet ecosystem.

## Reducing anonymity

Besides encryption, anonymity is a key facilitator of online CSAM perpetration. A variety of tools can be used to disguise the online identity of an individual, from using a pseudonym for a username through to remailers, VPNs and TOR. Anonymity gives perpetrators assurance that they will not be identified when they upload, distribute or consume CSAM and therefore will not be caught by authorities in the real world. Anonymity gives adults the ability to take on the persona of a child to find, befriend, groom and coerce children into self-creating CSAM. Anonymity gives perpetrators the confidence to share their darkest fantasies with like-minded others in chatrooms and forums.

While anonymity-creating tools will continue to exist into the future, more can be done by ESPs and ISPs to reduce this problem. Control of the platforms used by billions of people and which are used to share millions of CSAM images gives these companies the opportunity to play the role of capable guardians, increasing the effort and risk associated with CSAM perpetration on their platforms. A starting point would be to require proof of identity from users signing up to use a new service. As noted earlier, there are various methods of age verification and this can be extended to identity verification, with third-party providers offering a range of methods to verify identity in a secure, confidential way.

This would likely displace CSAM distribution and consumption away from centrally moderated platforms and towards places where anonymity remains possible, such as through peer-to-peer networking and through TOR. This strategy could have many benefits. It would remove CSAM from places frequented by the general population thereby preventing distress for those that accidentally come across it (although noting that this should already be difficult), but more importantly it would remove excuses for those that might stray into this area by searching for more extreme sexual content. If they were to do so they could be identified and this could act as a deterrent to searching for such material. Pushing CSAM into more anonymous spaces would also likely result in an overall net reduction in the number of CSAM Consumers because of the increased effort that would be required to go looking for such content. Some (especially those just browsing or exploring new interests) may just be dissuaded by a lack of know-how, or a lack of intent to invest the time needed to find material anonymously. Another benefit is that it could help to concentrate offending into a smaller number of sites that would make it easier for law enforcement to investigate using tools that remove anonymity. Over time, efforts could then focus on reducing the sites where true anonymity is possible.

### *Following the money*

While a minority of CSAM is distributed through sites that operate behind paywalls or involves livestreaming in return for payment, it is likely that this involves some of the more serious cases of child sexual abuse and warrants special attention. There is the potential to identify Consumers of monetised CSAM through the financial system. Much of this is through conventional payment channels involving interbank transfers and debit / credit card payments, but there is also a shift towards decentralised cryptocurrencies where transactions are not scrutinised and payments can be made with some degree of anonymity. However, as has been described at various points in this book, law enforcement operations are able to track individuals using both conventional payments and cryptocurrencies (although noting the latter may be more difficult).

So, the case for following the money is proven. It can lead to detection and prosecution of CSAM Producers, Distributors and Consumers. Law enforcement agencies can use financial intelligence to build a case against individuals involved in the worst kind of online child sexual abuse. The task then, is to work out how financial institutions can work more effectively with law enforcement agencies to identify CSAM perpetrators from the many millions of legitimate financial transactions that occur daily. There are two separate pieces of the jigsaw that need to be brought together. On the one hand, police will have information (from intelligence and criminal investigations) on individuals that have been linked with CSAM. However, this information cannot simply be handed over to financial institutions to run against their databases. On the other hand, financial institutions will have information on all the financial transactions these individuals make. While information is often provided (through court orders) on a case-by-case basis to help with an investigation, this takes no account of most cases where CSAM perpetrators have never come to the attention of the police and have no criminal record (Brown et al., 2020). Here there is a real opportunity for change. Statistical modelling (especially machine learning) techniques offer an opportunity to identify CSAM perpetrators in financial transactions. As a starting point, Cubitt et al. (2021) demonstrated that it was possible to identify the most harmful offenders based on financial transactions, although this was based on a dataset consisting only of perpetrators. The next step would be to train a model on financial transactions where the dataset consisted of both perpetrators and non-perpetrators, which would allow the model to identify the factors that were most important in predicting which financial transactions were made by potential CSAM perpetrators and which were not. This, however, requires law enforcement agencies to provide financial institutions with the details of known perpetrators in the first instance, which faces potential cultural, legal and ethical considerations that have yet to be resolved.

In time then, it may be possible for banks and even money service businesses to identify financial transactions that have a very high probability of being made to purchase CSAM. The next question is how can this be used? Would it be possible to block transactions on this suspicion, inform banks that are recipients of transactions that these are suspicious transactions, or even suspend the accounts of those making transactions? And, on the basis of a statistical model (where there will always be a probability of false positives, even if the model can reduce these to a small fraction of those targeted), would it be appropriate to provide this information to law enforcement agencies, who might undertake reputation-damaging investigations against innocent people? These are important issues that need to be resolved if following the money is to prove a successful strategy for not only detecting, but also preventing CSAM distribution and consumption in future.

Financial Intelligence Units (FIUs), such as those belonging to the Egmont Group, will no doubt play an important role in these developments in future. These FIUs, typically consisting of governmental (administrative and regulatory) and law enforcement agencies, cooperate on international requests for information and conduct joint initiatives / operations to address crime issues. Online child sexual abuse has been a priority for the Egmont Group's Information Exchange Working Group, which analysed transactions made by CSAM perpetrators to produce profiles of their characteristics (Egmont Group, 2020). These profiles can identify common patterns of financial transactions that can indicate CSAM production, distribution and consumption. This can include (among others) low-value fund transfers to a person in a jurisdiction of concern outside of normal business hours; purchases from vendors selling online privacy and anonymity products; payments to online file hosting sites; payments to peer-to-peer fund transfer sites; purchases from adult entertainment sites and dating platforms; transactions to reload prepaid credit cards etc. (Gibraltar Financial Intelligence Unit, n.d.). Such profiles are then used to block and report suspicious transactions (Western Union, 2021).

Beyond FIUs, there have also been efforts to build the capacity of the financial sector to tackle CSAM. Since 2009, ICMEC has been convening the Asia–Pacific Financial Coalition Against Child Sexual Exploitation, providing an important platform for banks and other financial companies in the region to share information on the nature of the problem and new initiatives to address it[8]. Recognising the importance of financial transactions in preventing and detecting CSAM, ECPAT Indonesia has recently worked with financial institutions to improve understanding and build capacity to better identify and block transactions that may be CSAM related[9]. This provides an indication of what might be possible in future, especially if combined with other forms of non-financial data[10].

This approach may in time push CSAM perpetrators to use decentralised cryptocurrencies to trade in CSAM in even greater numbers than they are already. This is not necessarily a negative consequence of improved surveillance in the regulated financial sector as it increases the general levels of risk of detection and effort associated with offending. This means there is still likely to be a net reduction in financial transactions associated with CSAM. As we have seen, sophisticated tools that can analyse blockchain transactions are increasingly becoming available for law enforcement investigation and this means that the migration towards cryptocurrencies does not give perpetrators impunity. This is, however, an area in which technology will continue to evolve and new anonymous financial products will emerge that make it difficult for law enforcement to identify by whom the transactions have been made. This will be an ongoing co-evolutionary arms race that will need resources devoted to new methods of detection, to combat new and emerging decentralised financial products.

## Dealing with the darknet

The fifth and final priority for action is dealing with the proliferation of CSAM content on the darknet. As the open-net ecosystem for CSAM production, distribution and consumption contracts, we will continue to see growth in the darknet. Yet, methods of preventing CSAM proliferation on the darknet are difficult to implement because of the anonymous way in which sites are run. One can't simply issue takedown notices to sites operating on the darknet.

Dealing with the darknet should therefore be a task for law enforcement, with the support of the private sector and NGOs in developing tools that can be used to aid detection. This is also justified on the basis that this is where the most egregious child sexual abuse material will be found, so focusing law enforcement efforts on this space is likely to result in the prosecution of the most serious perpetrators and the rescue of children in the most need of help. Historically, there have been successes in tackling CSAM darknet sites such as *Love Zone*, *PlayPen*, *Child's Play*, *Welcome to Video* and *Boystown* – all of which have been taken down as a result of law enforcement action. This also needs to be viewed as part of a long-term strategy, with success only likely to follow from successive detections (Broadhurst et al., 2021).

Policing the darknet will, however, require improvements in training of law enforcement officers, increased investigatory resources and improved information sharing between agencies, in the recognition that darknet operations are often multijurisdictional (Goodison et al., 2019). While there are well-established specialist units that investigate CSAM on the darknet, the growing scale of the problem highlights the need to boost these units with additional resources and, if necessary, new powers that allow them to investigate these crimes in as frictionless a way as possible. There may be a need to further address the legal ambiguities associated with international operations with, for example, covert operations possible in some jurisdictions and not others, leading to questions over the extent to which intelligence and evidence generated in one jurisdiction can be used in another (Bleakley, 2019). Consideration also needs to be paid to ensuring the psychological well-being of those tasked with investigating CSAM on the darknet (Burruss et al., 2017). This needs to ensure that the regular exposure to the most abhorrent sexual abuse material does not create long-term harm for those trying to investigate it.

## Concluding remarks

The task of this book was to explore how changes could be made to the internet to eliminate child sexual abuse material. By applying a crime science approach, that carefully unpacked the CSAM problem, it became apparent that this is, in fact, a set of inter-related problems, each of which demand their own response to bring about an overall reduction in CSAM. While a difficult task, it is clear that significant inroads could be made to reducing CSAM if attention was focused on addressing five key priorities – encouraging ESPs / ISPs to act, ending end-to-end encryption, addressing anonymity, following the money and dealing with the darknet.

However, without a considerable, concerted effort to change the current circumstances, it is difficult to see how this problem will be resolved, given the global growth in CSAM. Yet, the answers lie in the actions of a relatively small number of corporations to make changes that will make a difference to the lives of thousands of children. History is replete with examples of crime being designed out of systems, services and products, whether it be the design of a bank safe, chip and PIN security on a credit card, remote deactivation of stolen mobile phones or vehicle electronic immobilisation. Better design can eliminate crime problems. And better design by ESPs, combined with improved investigation, will go a considerable way to addressing the production, distribution and consumption of CSAM.

## Notes

1 Found at www.justice.gov/opa/press-release/file/1256061/download
2 Found at www.technologycoalition.org/annualreport/
3 Found at https://ec.europa.eu/info/law/better-regulation/have-your-say/initiatives/ 12726-Fighting-child-sexual-abuse-detection-removal-and-reporting-of-illegal-content-online_en

4 Admittedly, the Grenfell Towers disaster in London is an example of how building codes can fail, but that will probably turn out to be a failure in how the standards were implemented, rather than a failure of the standards themselves.
5 There are different types of testing that could be undertaken. For example, in the UK, Thatcham Security Certification involves a vehicle's security being bench-tested to make sure it includes the standards specified by Thatcham Research, an organisation that accredits automotive safety and security standards. Further details can be found at www. thatcham.org/

An alternative approach is employed by Sold Secure, which awards security products with a gold, silver or bronze designation, based on the length of time and tools required to overcome the security, rather than on their adherence to set standards. Further details can be found at www.soldsecure.com/
6 The e-Safety Commissioner's Safety by Design principles and steps to achieving the principles can be found at www.esafety.gov.au/industry/safety-by-design/principles-and-background
7 See, for example, IBM's explanation on this issue. Found at www.ibm.com/topics/end-to-end-encryption
8 Found at www.icmec.org/apfc-asia-pacific-financial-coalition-against-child-sexual-exploitation/
9 Found at https://ecpatindonesia.org/berita/catatan-akhir-tahun-2020-ecpat-indonesia/
10 The Egmont Group (2020) suggest the potential for greater results if financial transaction data is combined with data held by organisations like the Child Rescue Coalition, which typically seeks to identify IP addresses associated with CSAM perpetrators sharing material through peer-to-peer networks.

# References

Barbosa, S. & Milan, S. (2019). Do Not Harm in Private Chat Apps: Ethical Issues for Research on and with WhatsApp. *Papers in Communication and Culture* 14(1), 49–65. https://doi.org/10.16997/wpcc.313

Bleakley, P. (2019). Watching the watchers: Taskforce Argos and the evidentiary issues involved with infiltrating Dark Web child exploitation networks. *The Police Journal* 92(3), 221–236. https://doi.org/10.1177/0032258X18801409

Broadhurst, R., Ball, M., Jiang, C. & Wang, J. (2021). *Impact of darknet market seizures on opioid availability.* Research Report 18. Australian Institute of Criminology. www.aic.gov.au/publications/rr/rr18

Brown, R. (2013). *Regulating crime prevention design into consumer products: Learning the lessons from electronic vehicle immobilisation.* Trends & issues in crime and criminal justice 453. Australian Institute of Criminology. www.aic.gov.au/sites/default/files/2020-05/tandi 453.pdf

Brown, R., Napier, S. & Smith, R.G. (2020). *Australians who view livestreaming of child sexual abuse: An analysis of financial transactions.* Trends and issues in crime and criminal justice 589. Australian Institute of Criminology. www.aic.gov.au/publications/tandi/tandi589

Burgess, M. (2021a, 8 September). How Apple can fix its child sexual abuse problem. *Wired.* www.wired.co.uk/article/apple-photo-scanning-csam

Burruss, B.W., Holt, T.J. & Wall-Parker, A. (2017). The hazards of investigating internet crimes against children: Digital evidence handlers' experiences with vicarious trauma and coping behaviors. *American Journal of Criminal Justice* 43, 433–447. https://doi.org/10.1007/s12 103-017-9417-3

Cubitt, T., Napier, S. & Brown, R. (2021). *Predicting prolific live streaming of child sexual abuse.* Trends & issues in crime and criminal justice, 634. Australian Institute of Criminology. https://doi.org/10.52922/ti78320

Easton, W. (2021, 17 February). Changes to sharing and viewing news on Facebook in Australia. *Facebook.* https://about.fb.com/news/2021/02/changes-to-sharing-and-viewing-news-on-facebook-in-australia/

Egmont Group (2020). *Combatting online child sexual abuse and exploitation through financial intelligence.* Information Exchange Working Group. https://egmontgroup.org/sites/default/files/filedepot/20200901_CSAE%20Public%20Bulletin.pdf

Endeley, R. (2018). End-to-End Encryption in Messaging Services and National Security—Case of WhatsApp Messenger. *Journal of Information Security* 9, 95–99. https://doi.org/10.4236/jis.2018.91008

Farrell, G. & Roman, J. (2006). Crime as pollution: Proposal for market-based incentives to reduce crime externalities. In M.R. Stephens & K. Moss (Eds.), *Crime reduction and the law* (pp.135–155). Routledge.

Gibraltar Financial Intelligence Unit (n.d.) *Combating online child sexual abuse & exploitation.* HM Government of Gibraltar. www.gfiu.gov.gi/uploads/docs/publications/Online%20CSAE%20Guidance%20Notes%20v1.0.pdf

Goodison, S.E., Woods, D., Barnum, J.D., Kemerer, A.R. & Jackson, B.A. (2019). *Identifying law enforcement needs for conducting criminal investigations involving evidence on the dark web.* RAND Corporation. www.rand.org/pubs/research_reports/RR2704.html

Lomas, N. (2021a, 19 February). Facebook applies overly broad content block in flex against Australia's planned news reuse law. *Techcrunch.com.* https://techcrunch.com/2021/02/18/facebook-applies-overly-broad-content-block-in-flex-against-australias-planned-news-reuse-law/

Lomas, N. (2021b, 23 January). Google threatens to close its search engine in Australia as it lobbies against digital news code. *Techcrunch.com.* https://techcrunch.com/2021/01/22/google-threatens-to-close-its-search-engine-in-australia-as-it-lobbies-against-digital-news-code/

Thomas, Z. (2020, 27 May). Facebook shareholders try to block encryption plan. *BBC News.* www.bbc.com/news/technology-52779897

Western Union (2021). *Western Union's modern slavery and human trafficking statement for 2020.* Western Union. www.westernunion.com/content/dam/wu/pdf/2020_Modern_Slavery_Statement-Final(70544.2).pdf

Woollacott, E. (2021, 7 July). EU passes emergency law allowing tech companies to screen messages for child abuse. *Forbes.* www.forbes.com/sites/emmawoollacott/2021/07/07/eu-passes-emergency-law-allowing-tech-companies-to-screen-messages-for-child-abuse/?sh=783078a21e2c

# INDEX

*Note*: Page numbers in **bold** indicate tables; those in *italics* indicate figures.

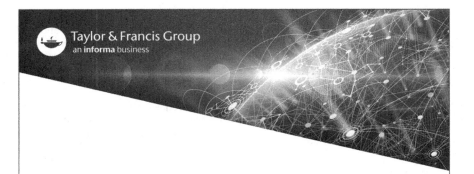

Printed in the United States
by Baker & Taylor Publisher Services